Transforming Fellowship

19 Brain Skills That Build Joyful Community

Chris M. Coursey

Shepherd's House Inc.
P.O. Box 2376
East Peoria, IL 61611

www.lifemodelworks.org

Transforming Fellowship
19 Brain Skills That Build Joyful Community

By: Chris M. Coursey

A shortened version of this material was released as an e-book through Life Model Works in 2015 called *The Lifeboat In Your Brain*.

ISBN 978-1-935629-21-4

Printed by:
Shepherd's House Inc.
P.O. Box 2376
East Peoria, IL 61611
www.lifemodelworks.org

Cover design by Nancy L. Haskins

Contents

Preface

My mother used to drag my siblings and me out of bed every Sunday morning to attend church. The first step was turning on the bedroom lights. If that didn't work she turned off my fan. When that failed she pulled off my covers while singing, "Up and at 'em! Time to get up. Rise and shine!"

Going to church felt like a chore. I much preferred to stay home with Dad and watch television but Mom would have none of that. Mom worked hard to get us up and out the door be it rain, snow, or ice – we were going. In spite of Mom's best efforts we inevitably arrived late. Some of my earliest memories include the feeling that I was preparing to attend church because God was there. I needed to put on my best Sunday clothes, comb my hair and brush my teeth because I was going to hear God's Word in God's house and this was a big deal!

We arrived as hymns and organ sounds filled the church. Soon the pastor would preach his fiery message and ask for an "Amen" at just the right times. He sweated profusely while preaching and paced the aisle, but I admired him for his enthusiasm. I learned about God through these sermons and a much-needed foundation was established that I would later fall back on in my early 20's. People at church donned a smile and by all appearances everyone seemed happy. Deep down I knew I wasn't happy, but for some reason I didn't think I was allowed to say that in God's house.

My parents married at a young age, Mom was 17 and Dad was 19. Soon after the first year of marriage my sister was born and my brother and I followed. Dad was a tough, hard-working factory worker at the big tractor company in town. By the time I was 6 years old Dad's job was gone because the workers went on strike. With no income we lost our house and relied on food stamps to get by. We then suffered another painful setback when my grandfather, Dad's father, died unexpectedly from a heart attack. Conflict at home and Dad's drinking soon took a toll on the family joy levels. In a most redemptive way these turbulent times would set the course for my ministry pursuits later in life. As we will soon explore in Skill 18, one of the five levels of pain the brain knows, the pain of loss is the hardest level of pain to process. These difficult moments rocked my family's world. We were overwhelmed and hurting. We eventually moved in with Grandma Shirley. Like most young parents, Mom and Dad were doing their best to make ends meet, but they were not fully equipped to raise young children and deal with mounting pressures of work and family. We were missing something, and I wondered where God was in all of this.

In some ways going to church was a refreshing outlet for Mom who enjoyed singing the hymns and hearing about the God who saves. Like most people, Mom was going to church looking for real answers to real problems. My impression during those early years was that the church community felt helpless to fully engage and enter in to my family's struggles. Once the service ended people discussed the message and the weather, but no one knew how to help my grieving family. By all accounts their intentions were good and their faith was strong, but something was missing. As I grew older Dad eventually put down the bottle, but I would later pick it up. My drinking turned into a vain attempt to substitute what was painfully absent in my life. This book represents the treasure I found after years of asking God for help and praying for answers to what had been missing in me, my family and my world. I believe this book offers solutions to what is missing in many churches today, churches filled with people struggling with pain and problems. I also feel this book can restore some credibility to the Western church so we raise up mature, joyful believers who keep relationships bigger than problems.

Thanks to neuroscience, scripture and the work of Dr. Jim Wilder I now have answers. In case you are wondering, I eventually quit drinking but it took two DUI convictions within the same year to do it. I fell on the foundation I mentioned earlier and became a pastor. I started working as a pastoral counselor with the goal of equipping people. When I met Dr. Jim Wilder in 1997 I learned about the Life Model and listened to Dr. Jim introduce how God designed us for joyful relationships. A light bulb went on when I heard the word joy. I then heard about emotional maturity and how people need other people from all stages of life within the context of a multigenerational community in order to fully develop and blossom. The light bulb shone even brighter when I discovered that I and everyone I knew could live with the awareness of God's interactive presence during the good and bad times of life. Immanuel, *God with Us*, is the experience where a relational God interacts with His children through His Spirit. This discovery became a game-changer for me. Little did I know that four years later I would be working with Dr. Jim to design training and write books together about these exciting topics. The icing on the cake would be a training package called *THRIVE Training* where we train people in the nineteen relational brain skills that, for the most part, our brain would have learned during the first three years of life. Sadly, most of us learn only a few of these skills, so we need some remedial work in order to strengthen and pass on what we learn to our loved ones.

Research in neuroscience was clear that a mother could download and pass on these skills to her infant, but a big question remained. Can adults train and pass on these essential brain skills to other adults? We could not find a single person or organization that was doing this, but we would soon discover for ourselves a resounding YES; people can – and should learn and practice these skills together within the context of a high joy environment. We call these skills "relational brain skills," but we also like "gentle protector" skills because the skills help us express our gentle protector qualities so we stay tender to weaknesses in ourselves and other people. When we have solid relational brain skills we become a good shepherd within our family and community. When the skills are missing "predator" and "possum" qualities surface so we either pounce on weaknesses or we hide our weaknesses. Pouncing or hiding drains joy levels in a most harmful way. My friends Jim, Ed, Shelia and I wrote a book about this called *Joy Starts Here: The Transformation Zone*.

The book you are holding in your hand is an introduction to the nineteen skills learned at *THRIVE Training* as well as through *Connexus*, a wonderful training package for communities. Gentle protector skills are what allow us to *relationally express the life of Christ* within the context of our families, communities, churches, schools and the world.

While working on this book I encountered a certain tension because the nineteen skills are experiential and relational. We learn new skills from interactive practice with people. Writing about the skills when our brain is designed to *experience* the skills is much like trying to describe the splendor of a beautiful sunset to someone who has never seen a sunset in their lifetime. While I can tell how magnificent and breathtaking a sunset is to watch and do my best to describe the panorama, at the end of the day there is simply nothing like seeing a dazzling, colorful sunset for yourself. Words fail to fully capture the moment. I found this to be true while writing this book because you, the reader, must ultimately try to taste the skills for yourself. To solve this dilemma I give you a "taster" - each chapter contains an *Action Step* to provide you with a small activity to think about and practice the skill. Following this is a *Next Step* to give you additional resources to go deeper into the skills. Finally, an *Application Step* is added to demonstrate the skill in a person's life. The stories I use are taken from a training context and any identifying information has been altered by changing names and combining stories so the details do not reflect any one person. Each skill section begins with a reflection on God's heart. Here is my best attempt to interact with Immanuel about what He sees valuable in each skill. I trust some of these are my thoughts and some are God's thoughts. I hope you enjoy this addition.

I credit Dr. Jim Wilder from Life Model Works and the research of Dr. Allan Schore (UCLA), Dr. Daniel Siegel (UCLA), Dr. Bessel van der Kolk (Boston University Medical School) and the many colleagues, friends and family members who have been a part of creating this learning community with me. I am grateful for Jo Getzinger and Cheryl Knight who invested and believed in me, Kitty Wilder for supporting me and Dr. Jim Wilder for his presence and hand in the preparation of this manuscript. Thank you Jen Hopp for reviewing my work. Many hands and minds have helped further this process along. I am especially grateful for my wife Jen who has been an integral part of this entire journey. I couldn't have done this without you, my love!

Imagine a world where people are glad to be together, quickly recover from upsets, keep relationships bigger than problems, recognize overwhelm and see each other as God sees them. May you be encouraged as you discover answers and solutions to what is missing in your world.

May the God of peace, who through the blood of the eternal covenant brought back from the dead our Lord Jesus, that great Shepherd of the sheep, equip you with everything good for doing his will, and may he work in us what is pleasing to him, through Jesus Christ, to whom be glory for ever and ever. Amen. Hebrews 13:20-21 (NIV)

Introduction

Relational Skills That Produce Sustainable Transformation

My 93-year old grandmother lives with my family. Grandma Knight, as my sons call her, has an amazing long-term memory and she enjoys sharing stories from her life. One of the stories Grandma frequently recounts comes from the days of the Great Depression when there was little work, little food and little money - and a lot of distress. Even though Grandma's family didn't have much, Grandma's mother, my great-grandmother, would make extra food to share with hungry neighbors and families in her neighborhood. "A little would go a long way during those days" Grandma tells us. Grandma also talks about her father who was blessed to have a job through those hard times. Each week Great-Grandpa Berg would give up days of work so his brothers could work his job and make a little extra money for their families. People needed help so families pooled their resources together to make ends meet and share what they had. This pooling of resources is what the Greek word *koinonia* means. Koinonia, mentioned some 20 times in scripture, refers to *fellowship, joint participation, sharing in common, a collection* and *communion.*[1] While fellowship sounds nice it does not reflect the richness that koinonia represents. When we think of pooled resources we may think of money but rarely do we think of relational capacity that is shared in harmonious community. God created us to rely on one another so much so that our character, identity and the vast gold mine of our relational skills comes from pooled resources within the emotional/mental/physical/spiritual storehouses of our families and communities. In one of the longest studies on human development ever done, Harvard researchers confirm the need for community by showing that deep, intimate, personal relationships are the key to a happy life.[2] As parts of one body each of us holds the elements needed for true transformation to take place but rarely do we pool together our relational resources. We now live in a time where relational resources are diminishing at a most alarming rate. There is no better time than the present to increase our relational capacity.

We are part of something bigger than ourselves. Until we can combine our efforts and exchange our strengths we remain stuck, stunted and stagnant - all to varying degrees. It is time we start a transformation, and we cannot achieve it without each member of the body working together guided by *chesed*[3], the Hebrew word translated as mercy, lovingkindness, steadfast love, compassion and goodness, which we will talk about shortly. Chesed in loving communities leads to transformation and is the result of personal and corporate transformation. I believe it will take personal and corporate transformation to restore some relevance and credibility to the Church, particularly the Western Church, which has lost credibility over the last 50 years. Now we turn our sights to the brain for a moment.

The Brain

The human brain is a magnificent three-pound work of art that directs everything we say, think and do. It weighs less than 2% of our

1 http://www.gotquestions.org/koinonia.html

2 https://www.washingtonpost.com/news/inspired-life/wp/2016/03/02/harvard-researchers-discovered-the-one-thing-everyone-needs-for-happier-healthier-lives/?wpisrc=nl_az_most

3 Chesed is also spelled hesed.

body weight and uses one-fifth of our body's energy. In all its grandeur the brain dictates our decisions, runs our relationships, and produces the unique blend of our personal preferences. The brain tells us what to eat, when to go to bed and what to post online. At this very moment your brain is busily working to keep you alive and interpret the letters on this page. Isn't that impressive?

When properly trained, the brain is a God-given instrument that sustains our relationships, improves our marriages, furthers our friendships and creates joyful churches that change the world. Our brain works best when we have people who are genuinely glad to be with us. When joy and pooled resources merge we can learn a select set of relational skills that equip us to effectively respond to the onslaught of shifting, moment-by-moment circumstances in the most efficient manner.

As I mentioned in the preface, Dr. Jim Wilder and I identified nineteen brain skills that must be learned for optimal relational, personal, emotional, spiritual and mental health across the lifespan. In an ideal world we acquire most of these skills by the time we finish our third year of life.[4] When the nineteen skills are not fully mastered, we feel inadequate. We cope with life in a rigid, painful, stunted sort of way. We sense something is missing. We reactively respond to people and circumstances. We make decisions out of fear and, deep down, believe there must be more out there, just beyond our reach. We feel comfortably numb or we relentlessly pursue activities to make us feel better, calmer and more secure. Relationships are confusing or, worse, abrasive. Who we are on the inside does not match our outside appearances. Simply, we are lost and end up feeling like an empty shell of who we wanted to be. At some point along the way we lost our momentum and our relational capacity started slipping. Some of us have given up hope so we live a resigned life given over to the belief that our current conditions are as good as they are going to get. We live each day getting by. We wonder how long we can hold our breath until heaven. We may call this normal, but there is hope of a new normal filled with transformation into the likeness of the Good

4 The "seeds" of the skills should be planted that will grow throughout life with practice.

Shepherd who goes about His Father's business in the most gentle, compassionate, life-giving way possible.

With some focused effort and training, we can be transformed into a confident, emotionally intelligent person who engages the world with efficiency, style and grace. Young or old, we can learn every one of the nineteen skills mentioned in this book. Whether a tune-up or renovation is needed, there is no better time to begin. After a personal relationship with Jesus Christ, relational brain skills may be the best investment you and I can make in our lifetime.

The process of learning these nineteen skills requires human interaction, practice and time. We start by focusing on the easier skills such as joy and quiet before we dive into the harder skills such as pain mastery and interactive quiet. We find people in our pocket of pooled resources who are strong where we are weak and weak where we are strong. When learned, the nineteen skills keep us connected so that problems do not ruin our relationships. We remain curious during conflicts and flexible during distress. We regulate our emotions so we continue to interact with people in creative, meaningful ways. We tell stories that express our values and convey our character so listeners feel seen and inspired. When learned, the package of nineteen skills form a resiliency within us so we endure under stress and suffer well when feeling pain. With each interaction, our relationships become the canvas to paint a relational masterpiece.

My Missing Skills On The Airplane

I remember the time I missed an opportunity to make a difference in the life of a young man who was sitting across from me on an airplane. While engrossed in a book I noticed a young teenager watching me. He was probably 14 or 15 years old. I had the sense he was curiously looking up to me as teenagers can do with young adults. I then felt the strong urge to speak to him about Jesus, but I fearfully resisted. The urge grew louder and louder. I spent the rest of my trip arguing in my head. "But Lord, he is sitting there with his parents. What am I going to say? How will he and his family respond?"

My doubts, fears and unbelief kept me from speaking. Soon the plane landed and we walked opposite directions in the terminal. I looked back and wondered if I should chase him down. At this moment I remembered a passage in the Bible where God told the prophet Ezekiel about the cost of being a watchman and the responsibilities that go with this important role. I cringed thinking about the consequences of a watchman who fails to blow the trumpet as a warning signal. I felt ashamed and guilty after this missed opportunity to share God's joy, but it revealed something important about my character that needed attention.

After some prayer I knew something was still missing in me. In this case I needed to learn how to quiet my fear, Skill 11, and have the courage to stay relational, speak up, and share my heart, Skill 12. Ironically, in this situation I could clearly sense Immanuel's guidance in that moment using Skill 13, *but I failed to relationally reflect God's heart.* Two simple skills could have made a critical difference and turned this situation into something meaningful and beautiful. I asked Immanuel for more opportunities to speak up and to have the courage to love my brothers and sisters as I loved Him. I even prayed for the skills to thrive. To this day I pray for the young man I never met.

Missing Skills In The Airport

Apparently, God heard my request for more opportunities because opportunities came rolling in to practice my new skills and share how Immanuel changed my life. One particular episode stands out from the rest. After working on Skills 11 and 12, I was traveling once again when I met a man in an airport, and this time it wasn't me who was missing the skills. Things were going badly for this fellow and his escalating emotions were scaring bystanders. Here was a person drowning in his overwhelm; he needed help. I share this story in the book, *Joy Starts Here: The Transformation Zone.*

> *We were standing in line to board an airplane when the announcement was made that our plane was full. Because this was the last flight, I knew we faced an overnight stay. One passenger in line suddenly lost it. In a rage he threw his bags and spewed profanities. His raging voice echoed in the terminal. Passengers scattered. This guy was no longer in relational mode. As I made my way over to the ticket desk, he walked*

around the terminal screaming at anyone in a uniform. I could see his red face and intense emotions were scaring people. By this time his eyes were bulging and he was sweating profusely. As he neared the ticket desk, I felt compelled to reach out to him. I knew this man was drowning. He needed some serious help returning to joy, so I took a deep breath and walked up to him. For a moment I wondered if he would knock me out.

"You are really having a bad day, aren't you?" I asked affirmingly. "You are __ __ right I am having a bad day!" he fired back. We locked eyes for a few moments then I said, "Well, I am a pastor, a follower of Jesus and I would be honored if I could pray with you." I was pleasantly relieved when he muttered, "Ok, yeah, sure." Standing in the middle of the terminal we bowed our heads. I put my hand on his shoulder, and we took a moment of quiet (Skill 2). Then, I invited Immanuel to share our distress and bring some vision (Skill 13).

I noticed tears running down his face. "You see," he explained, "I have been traveling for medical help because I was recently diagnosed with serious cancer. This flight cancellation takes away precious, limited time with my wife and daughters." For a few moments we shared sadness then he said, "Wait! I have to do something." He retraced his steps and apologized to every single airline employee he offended. After several minutes he returned. "I have been feeling like I need to get right with God," he told me. "I wonder if this whole ordeal is God speaking?" A sparkle of joy appeared in his eyes as his face muscles relaxed.

The next morning I saw him boarding the flight with a smile and a brand new Bible under his arm.

By God's grace and because I had been practicing the nineteen skills, I was able to stay anchored long enough to toss him a life preserver. He needed help in the form of a trained brain who could stay connected with him in the midst of intense emotions. His brain's emotional control center required another person, a mirror, to show him the way to Skill 2, *Simple Quiet*. Skill 2 allows us to take a moment and catch our breath. To some degree, all of us are taking in water. Some of us have grown accustomed to sloshing in the water. Some of us are ready to bask on the beaches of joyful change. Which are you?

In an ideal world every one of us would already have the nineteen skills because our environment was full of people who used the skills. Sadly, this doesn't happen, but we don't have to wait to experience lasting change. This book casts the vision for a life rich in relationship skills where people express the heart Jesus gave them[5] and quickly recover when things go wrong. This kind of a resilient character is expressed relationally in a person who excels at loving others. At the end of the day, your silver and gold will perish[6] but how well you love and how well you express your love is what creates your lasting legacy.

Joy

Speaking of character, relational joy is the fundamental ingredient in the formation and expression of personal character. Our character is molded through ongoing interactions with people who are weak and people who are strong. We share life together. We receive from individuals who have the nineteen relational brain skills and give to those who are missing or weak in the skills. Joy is the foundation where we learn new brain skills and joy is also the bedrock to strengthen existing skills. Joy not only transforms us and our relationships but also puts a smile on our faces when we see or even remember someone we enjoy. This smile is the self-addressed stamp of approval that says, "I am glad to see you!"

Neurologically, joy means we are the sparkle in another person's eyes, be it my mother, father, brother, sister, friend, coworker, barber or bank teller. Recipients of our joy feel valued. With practice and experience, joy becomes the wind in our relational sails. Learning a new brain skill starts with joy.

Those of us who have learned the nineteen skills as children do not remember how we gained the skills. With no language or stories to remind us, we end up using the skills because each skill is available at our disposal - much like a habit or a reflex. We don't think about it; we simply do it. For this reason we may misunderstand why other people do not respond or recover like we would in a given situation.

---

5 *The Life Model: Living From The Heart Jesus Gave You* book by James G. Frieson, et. al. Shepherd's House, Inc. 2000.

6 James 5:3

"Why don't they quit fretting?" we wonder. "Just stop getting angry!" If only people followed our advice. We do not realize there is more to the iceberg that people keep crashing into, and this trouble is the result of missing relational brain skills more than their lack of motivation or will power. We easily neglect the role that relational brain skills play in how a person thinks, feels, responds, lives and loves, but research continues to show that people must learn relational brain skills that allow them to be gentle protectors instead of predators who attack or possums who play dead.

Thanks to brain plasticity, experience reorganizes neural pathways in the brain so we can learn new skills. Experience, particularly joyful interactions with people who already have the skills, allow us to master new skills. Just think of someone you know who handles upset in a way that inspires you. What about a person who loses their cool at the drop of a hat? For too long the nineteen skills have flown under the radar. There was no language, much less a training structure in place, to learn new skills. At Life Model Works we now have the language. We have the training structure. All we need is you.

The next two chapters provide history and context for the nineteen skills, so let's review the reasons why there is not enough transformation in our lives and why relational skills are so hard to identify.

Chapter One

Not Enough Transformation In Our Lives

The Life Model behind this book developed out of dissatisfaction with the amount of transformation that Christians, counselors and ministers were actually achieving in their lives and work. Even those who had breakthroughs and mountain-top moments found it hard to hold on to their gains. In addition, it seems everyone had a different idea of the cause and conflicting plans for a solution. Wave after wave of promising programs for healing, deliverance, renewal, accountability, education, recovery, prayer, Bible study and spiritual gifts have swept the world. While each program has had spectacular success stories, an honest appraisal would notice that in most cases there is little evidence of transformation five years later and significant numbers of participants have failed to experience or retain gains. Way too frequently, the leaders of the movement and their careers have ended in personal character failure, burnout or failure to work well with their teams. Transformations have not matched the anticipated results. Why?

You are not likely to be interested in this book unless you are dissatisfied to some degree with the level of success you have had changing your own character or helping others make and sustain changes in theirs. Our conclusion after thirty years of study is not the answer most people expect. In fact, since it is not the answer most people expect, this is also the reason why so many great programs have had disappointing results trying to address the causes people do expect. If you want the usual answers, you are reading the wrong book. At the same time, when the answer is different than what we have always believed, our first response is usually, "That isn't really important." Twenty-five years of telling people about the solution has proven this true. The solution is not more healing, deliverance, faith, Bible study, therapy, recovery groups, education, diet, drugs, spiritual gifts, worship or even better choices. Programs built on these solutions will help many people who are lacking one or more of these elements, but none are the path to lasting transformation. Perhaps this upsets you, but, for those who have tried all the above, this book will be fresh air. Take a deep breath!

This book will present the evidence that a lack of relational skill has stopped all the transformations we wanted from getting very far. We will see how we reached this conclusion from observation, scripture and science as well as why most discipleship, evangelism, church growth, spiritual formation, group building, counseling and ministry models have failed to significantly improve relational skills and thereby foster sustainable transformation. Models that set out to solve problems often end by inadvertently making problem-solving more important than relationships. *It is not the lack of faith, knowledge, commitment or accountability that is slowing us down as much as how often we become non-relational.*

The conclusion of 30 years of study that forms the basis for this book says that just like learning to read Hebrew fluently, sing well or play an instrument, developing a godly character that holds up under pressure and "suffers well" requires *training* in nineteen specific skills that retrain the way our brain sees the world and responds to people.

These relational skills are needed to hold on to healing and deliverance so we can practice what we study in scripture as gentle protectors instead of predators. We must learn to leave our lion ways behind us and eat straw before we can lie down with the lambs.

Relational brain skills are all relational in nature because at our core we have relational identities. Character is an expression of how we see ourselves in relationship to others. If training relational brain skills were a matter of sharing information, we would not need relationships to learn them. I will explain in detail how relational skills are learned and passed on to other people. This is the core of discipleship and fellowship. However, before we go into the details, here is the conclusion of the matter. Relational skills that build godly character can only be transmitted in the presence of chesed, also known as "sticky love." Without chesed, the love that sticks us together, there is no lasting transformation. With some chesed, there is some transformation potential.

Chesed without relational skills is a brutal and heartbreaking story of people who clearly care but cannot stop hurting one another. Relational skills without chesed are manipulative and even cruel. Education, authority, spiritual gifts, wealth, health, intelligence – none of these provide chesed or relational skills. No amount of chesed provides relational skills although without chesed we cannot learn these skills.

Chesed is the kind of strong attachment to others that no matter what they do or how many times they do it we still want to be with them. We might call it love, but attachment is more like swallowing a fishhook than what we usually think of as "love." Chesed binds us together, and God is described as chesed 253 times in the Old Testament. In the New Testament the word "agape" is used to translate chesed. 1 Corinthians 13 is a good description of the sticky love known as chesed. It would be good to read that passage again today.

Life Before And After Relational Training

Like most people who become interested in the Life Model, Amy and Gary were disappointed with the amount of transformation they had experienced in their Christian life. Even though they had dedicated their lives to God, attended spiritual retreats, participated in small groups and church and even tried some counseling for their marriage, Amy and Gary had the haunting feeling that something was missing. Everything changed once they learned about relational skills. Soon they started to practice the skills together as a family. Amy learned to quiet and rest while Gary's joy levels increased so he felt confident and peaceful instead of anxious. The new skills provided an anchor for Amy and Gary to feel grounded, hopeful, even joyful for the first time since they could remember. Some of their friends noticed the difference asking, "You seem different in a good way. What are you doing?"

Every spiritual improvement and self-help book in the world can point to someone they helped. What makes this story different? Let us examine what happened to Amy and Gary to answer the important questions their story raises.

What Are Relational Skills?

Relational skills are a set of abilities that help us coordinate our lives, understanding, motivation, timing, moods, values, attitudes and actions with whatever is going on in the hearts and minds around us. More than simple rules of engagement or maps to the world of people, relational skills let us know at a glance far more than we can usually put into words about what is going on in someone else. Relational skills help us know when to keep quiet and when to speak up. Relational skills provide empathy that keeps us all from acting like sociopaths. Relational skills make us feel loved, special, understood, and properly corrected, and they help us recover when something goes wrong. Relational skills provide our motivation through understanding how we stand with others in the world. People who have relational skills "get it" while those who do not "don't seem to have a clue." Ultimately, relational skills are about accuracy of perception. The best relational skills allow us to see and treat ourselves and others as God sees and treats us. We use the same relational skills with God as we do with people; therefore, John can say, "Whoever claims to love God yet hates a brother or sister is a liar. For whoever does not love their brother and sister, whom they have seen, cannot love God, whom they have not seen" (1 John 4:20 NIV).

Why Do Relational Skills Use The Brain?

Pastor Brent spends most of his life in ministry. One of his greatest passions is seeing people encounter the Living God, a value his church emphasizes for true spiritual growth. Lately, Pastor Brent feels tired and frustrated because many in his congregation who experience God's presence and joy still struggle with harmful addictions, broken marriages, depression, and a host of problems that hinder their growth. Pastor Brent sees some people experience lasting change after their "God-encounters" while others flounder and stay stuck. When a friend recently handed Pastor Brent the book *Joy Starts Here*[7], he discovered the missing piece for his congregation. Those who made progress had some level of relational skills while others do not. Now that Pastor Brent understands the problem he can bring the solution.

Since none of us remember how we learned our relational skills, it seems to most of us that people simply "have them." Christians, in particular, believe that a whole new personality comes from salvation and from our spirit being – and so it does. However, many people further expect that this change in the spirit requires nothing in our brain to change. If you have ever had the chance to watch good Christians develop Alzheimer's or suffer certain strokes or brain injuries, you are aware that as the brain is damaged some important parts of character, self-control, understanding of others and moral behavior can disappear as the brain gets worse. For example, the leader of a major healing ministry had a stroke and from that point on he could not be allowed near women due to his crude responses and actions. Food had to be kept in a locked area because he ate everything he could reach. He lied, cheated and stole whatever he could because the part of his brain that did relationships was dead. Though many people with gifts of healing prayed for him, he did not change.

I once had an amusing loss of character while recovering from anesthesia. On the way home from a medical procedure my wife Jen drove by a donut shop and I insisted she buy a dozen donuts - all for me! I wanted to eat them all without sharing a single one with my beloved wife. My moral compass was asleep in my groggy brain and

---

7 *Joy Starts Here: The Transformation Zone* by E. James Wilder, Ed Khouri, Chris Coursey and Shelia Sutton. Shepherd's House, Inc. 2013.

she was especially relieved when my brain woke up later in the day. Relational skills not only need a working brain, but one that is also properly trained. Let's have a look at training.

Why Do Relational Skills Need To Be Learned?

Nora couldn't wait to have children. Ever since she was young she longed to have a family. Once Nora and her husband had children something unexpected happened to her. Nora became overwhelmed by the constant demands placed on her. On the verge of being incapacitated by her big feelings, she turned to friends, parenting books and classes at church for guidance and support. While inspiring, these resources brought little lasting relief. Exhausted and desperate, she prayed for help. One day Nora's sister told her about a marriage retreat called *Joy Rekindled*[8] that was coming to her city the following weekend. With the help of her family and community, Nora and her husband attended the training, and it changed her life. The couple practiced several skills including quieting, overwhelm recognition, joy and interacting with Immanuel. These were just a few skills she and her husband were missing, which explained her distress. Here was the turning point she was praying for, and within a short time joy, peace and calm restored her to her relational, grounded self.

Consider a baby. Does a baby have a good range of social skills when he or she is born? Does she demonstrate good understanding of her mother's need for sleep? Does he control his reactions in reasonable ways? Will she learn bad habits from others around her as she grows? Will he be sweet and kind to everyone if only we put a Bible in the crib? Does the way we train a child affect the way they will go?

Let's keep going a step farther. If a child hears everyone around him using poor grammar, will the child suddenly have proper grammar when he or she becomes a Christian? If people are illiterate, can they suddenly read with understanding in their own language or the Greek and Hebrew of the original Bible texts? Of course not. Why then would we expect that the learned patterns that govern our relationships would change without learning anything new?

---

8 *Joy Rekindled*® Marriage Weekends are designed by Chris and Jen Coursey.

Experience tells us (simply by observing long-term Christians) that many have not seen much change. We have lived with this lack of transformation ourselves. But there is a reason why we do not consciously know how we learned the relational skills we have. This same reason explains why knowing what we are supposed to do or feel or how we should react does not simply make everything right. The reason is found in the brain and how it learns.

Fast track – slow track

While we strongly rely on our conscious thoughts, the actual regions of the brain that control character run faster than conscious awareness, words or focused attention. These different speeds of brain processing put conscious thought, will and choices on the slow track while our reactions, perceptions and relational skills run on the fast track. Because the speed of relational skills and interactions is always too fast for us to consciously observe, we tend to think these responses are "automatic" although this is not true. What is true is that what we learn in the slow track does not transfer to the fast track. Therefore, our good ideas like "I will love my enemies" do not become our first response the next time we are attacked. We react first with our relational skills, or the lack thereof, and only later do we try to compensate and override the fast track. We will examine this carefully in the next chapter.

Born predator – learned gentle protector

Everyone is born with a disadvantage in terms of relational skills. While good relational skills are always chesed and protective, all of us are born wired as predators. To babies, the world and everyone in it is theirs to eat. Everything goes in the mouth. This predator wiring never goes away and cannot be disabled. It is possible, though, to learn protector skills that become stronger than the predator wiring. This is part of lions learning to eat straw like the ox so it is safe to be near lambs. With practice and skill training we can learn to tame our predatory cravings. As we will soon see, developing the relational, gentle protector skills only happens in the presence of chesed.

How Are Relational Skills Learned?

Elliot ran a successful company he started years ago from the ground up. Elliot's employees liked working for him with the exception of one issue. Elliot never learned how to feel, manage and return to joy from shame, which cost him both customers and friendships. Elliot lost his cool whenever there was a conflict or criticism of his leadership style. One day Elliot's pastor shared this observation over coffee, and after some heart to heart discussion, Elliot realized his friend was right and there was work to do - in him! Over time, with focused practice and training, Elliot began to learn this missing skill and use it in his life. Skill 11, *Return to Joy*, equipped him to keep relationships bigger than problems during moments he felt ashamed or criticized. Returning to joy transformed him in an entirely new way, and the results were deeply satisfying for Elliot, his workers and his customers.

Relational skill acquisition forms the core of brain development for the first two years of life. Most of these skills are copied from whoever the baby bonds with first, provided that the baby can interact with that person directly for enough time. This phase is the acquisition phase. Once acquired, children and adults go through a very long practice phase that grows relational skills to useful levels in times of difficulty and strong emotions. However, people only practice with the skills they have acquired. If you trained from someone who lacked some of the skills, you will also lack the same skills but have no idea what it is you do not know. Finally, we have to develop the motivation to use the skills we have and this proves to be the hardest of all skill-related elements to develop. Lack of motivation also proves to be a large factor blocking the rather difficult process of acquiring missing skills later in life, yet supplementing weak and missing relational skills is the path to deep transformation. Let us consider these topics one at a time.

Acquisition requirements

Relational brain skills are only acquired face-to-face in a trusting relationship with someone who is glad to be with us. Relational skill acquisition requires a high-joy relationship and environment. In the presence of this secure bond with someone we admire, we will actually allow our brain to become like them and copy how they live. We duplicate part of their identity as our own. We become one of their people or "tribe" and they become a sort of parent to us. This process runs faster than conscious thought, so once it starts we lose direct conscious control or choice over what it will do. This process is a mutual mind[9] fast-track highway and not a one-way street. To allow someone this deeply into our souls and minds means that both identities will emerge distinctly changed. A bond will form and deepen. In the absence of chesed, cult-like, deformed, sexual, dysfunctional and controlling relationships will become VERY strong and even dangerous.

With proper relationships both God and others can be the source of missing relational skills in the acquisition phase. We will examine why God is essential to correct acquisition later. First, we must say that even when God is the source of new skills, those skills will do us no good without practice, and practice is almost entirely with other humans.

Practice requirements

Once we acquire a new relational skill a great deal of practice is required. Practice does not require bonded relationships. Practice does not require someone who possesses the skills we have not mastered. Practice is best done with our peers. Most discipleship, small group, counseling, recovery, marriage and self-help groups are built on practice models – as though people already know what they should do and only need to practice. Coaching, encouraging, accountability, healing and deliverance are used to remove the blockages and encourage the practice. Practice requires the least relational commitment and investment of any element of relational skill development.

Motivation requirements

Motivation development is the most relationally intensive element in developing relational skills. We can learn skills that we never use in

9 Mutual mind refers to a shared mental/emotional state between two people that synchronizes brain activity and chemistry. We weep and rejoice together because of a shared mutual mind state.

real life because we are not motivated to be kind, love our enemies, forgive those who hurt us, endure hardships patiently and return good for evil. It is not that we have no capacity to be kind – we just do not want to be. Consequently, most development and transformation programs are like the joke about how many psychologists it takes to change a light bulb? Only one, but the light bulb must be motivated. Our best programs only work with people who arrive already motivated. They fail when motivation runs out, and then they must wait for people to hit rock bottom to be motivated again. Particularly when it comes to learning new relational skills that we do not have, large numbers of people are not motivated, and they see no need for the training they so desperately need. However, motivation transfer requires a huge relational investment compared to all the other elements of relational skill development, and it is a rare person or program that even considers this degree of investment in others. In fact, without high levels of chesed, no one would. With the absence of a full range of relational skills, chesed will produce little more than a huge sticky mess. Here is another profound reason why God must be an active part of all restoration – not only does God provide the guidance, but God can model missing skills and then provide part of the extended relational involvement needed to create motivation. Neither God alone or people alone will work.

Why Are Relational Skills Disappearing?

Ahmed is a successful entrepreneur who struggles with a short attention span. During meetings his colleagues expect him to be distracted so they quickly tell him what they want him to know before he "wanders off" in his own world of busyness and distraction. For years Ahmed has tried to change himself using a variety of techniques, medicine and programs, but it wasn't until he learned Skill 2 - *Simple Quiet*, that everything changed. After learning and practicing Skill 2, Ahmed's friends and colleagues noticed the remarkable change in him and asked about it: "You are so different now and calm! What did you do?"

Since every aspect of developing relational skill competence requires interaction with people, the three central questions are 1)How much time do we spend interacting directly with people? 2)Are we exposed face-to-face with people who have more relational skills than we have? 3)Does our joy levels stay high long enough to develop motivation to use the skills we are learning? The nine hours or so[10] most Americans spend watching or interacting with digital screens proves to be a direct block to relational skill development. No relational skills are used during media time. Mobility and city life mean that we spend most of our people-time far from older generations of our family and most of the time with people we have known for less than a year or two where levels of trust are too low for real relationship skills development. War, AIDS, displaced people and drug use have further shattered the social fabric. The resulting lack of social skills is becoming the new norm. For more details on this, read Chapter 10 of *Joy Starts Here.*[11]

Lemurs are disappearing

Well-designed documentaries help us understand why the lemurs of Madagascar are disappearing and the extensive efforts that must be made to restore a habitat with enough bio-diversity to prevent their extinction. As our pool (koinonia) of relational skill holders age and die in the old-folks homes and villages, the number of children with depression, attention deficits, autistic spectrum disorders and behavioral problems that grow into gangsters, addicts, inmates, divorced and gender uncertain adults is on the rise. Transformed lives are increasingly rare and people surge toward whatever seems powerful – whether that is spiritual or sensual. More power seems to be the solution to everything, and it is if you want to be the chief predator. "That was powerful" is now considered the best thing to say about a drink or a worship service. We need to restore missing relational skills just as the lemurs need their home back.

Identity transmission in fear/trauma versus a gentle protector

The whole cluster of our relational skills becomes our identity. We become what we see and how we treat other humans. We become

10 http://www.news.com.au/lifestyle/health/medibank-survey-adults-spend-nine-hours-a-day-in-front-of-screen/story-fneuzlbd-1226879144378

11 *Joy Starts Here: The Transformation Zone* by E. James Wilder, Ed Khouri, Chris Coursey and Shelia Sutton. Shepherd's House, Inc. 2013, Pages 201-229.

predators and prey or we become gentle protectors with our lambs. When this process of developing and transmitting relational skills is powered with fear or hate instead of chesed, the amount of relational investment needed to create motivation is much, much lower. We can become like the people we hate without them so much as spending a day with us personally. These are predatory skills or a perversion of protector skills used to con others and lure them into striking range. Dangerous leaders use their skills to instill fear in order to manipulate and control others. Corruption breeds corruption. Chesed, on the other hand, comes with a deep commitment to share the sufferings of others, including any suffering that we might create for them.

Should Christians Do Something About Restoring Relational Skills?

Jim Wilder sat on the stoop, his 12-year old mind filled with despair. The previous weekend he had been at youth camp and on the final night he made a commitment to fully serve God with his life. Now, less than one week later, he had lost his temper with his younger brother. This was not the commitment he had made so earnestly at camp. It seemed increasingly obvious that he would never be able to please God or keep his commitments. Most children, like Jim, would like to experience more transformation in their lives but have never seen anyone make the kinds of changes they long to experience. Instead they revert to the only game in town – being like their peers. Little did Jim know that he was on the path to discovering what brought deep and lasting transformation. He could not have understood at that time that his failure to manage his anger and love his brother at the same time represented a relational skill that was missing in his entire family and most of the community around him. In time, Jim became part of the team that set out to find what produced deep and lasting transformations, design ways to implement answers, and introduce solutions into the normal life of every church.

Our goal

Rather than doing what we have always done only longer and harder, the team developing the Life Model wanted to look at everything that was working, should work but didn't, worked for a while but didn't last, lasted but ended up badly, gave partial results, and shouldn't work but did; then they wanted to build a model that would explain why. The model needed to match God's creation, God's word, and God's people's experience, and it could not be limited to one culture or methods that were only created recently in human history. This model should explain why some people needed treatment and medication, and why some developed disorders, but it should also explain how to raise families, run churches and restore cultures after devastation regardless of their culture, race or language. The result of applying this model should be lasting transformations that could be passed from one generation to the next and result in a spontaneous spread of good news we call evangelism. Recovery is incomplete until it ends in evangelism.

Rather than collecting a pile of things that seem to work or making a theory to explain the effect we are watching (which usually sounds like science or theology but in some rather biased ways), the team set out to create a working model and from there develop working solutions based on the model so that they could be tested to see if they really worked. If the model worked, then the solutions would be the simplest solutions possible and therefore the easiest to spread.

An idealized model

There are many ways to build models. Most are statistical. Do you want a model of a middle-aged man? Then measure and test a large cluster of middle-aged men and take the average and find the range of variation and you have an answer. But suppose we do not want to create average people. Suppose instead that we want to transform people into profoundly better than average. This calls for an idealized model where the objective is to find the ideal development and then work to create that ideal. An ideal model of a human at every age and stage of life would be a sort of "life model" for our development.

The Christian ideal

Christians believe that at least three models of ideal human life have lived on earth. The first two lasted such a short time that little can be learned about them that is helpful now.[12] The third was the "Second Adam - Jesus." Through this Second Adam many lives have come to be examples of transformation and new life. Although the Second Adam only lived on earth until his mid-thirties, due to his continuing presence as Immanuel (God with us) we are offered both an example and guidance for all of life. Consequently, our idealized model of life and transformation should match precisely with both God's creation and the example and teachings of Jesus. We are from beginning to end relational beings designed for fully relational lives with God and others. Therein lie the two greatest commandments and the central principles of the good news in this new creation and Kingdom. If we live according to the new identity Jesus creates in our hearts, we will transform into the best expression of our identities at each age and stage of life. You could call that Living From the Heart Jesus Gave You.[13]

Iniquities and the self

Growing a new identity is like any kind of new growth. We need weeds cleared from our lives. Gardening is not simply clearing weeds, though. We need new things planted in our lives – plants and life that were not there before. We need cultivation over time and, due to many reasons, we still do not grow properly so we need trimming and shaping. We are inevitably deformed and scripture uses the term "iniquities" to speak of our deformities.[14] As humans we try as hard as possible to justify, normalize or hide our deformities and this creates, directly or indirectly, a much less relational identity for us all as we consider our deformities as our great weaknesses. However, transformation requires us to bring our weaknesses (iniquities) into the light of our relational world and let them be transformed or we will neither change deeply nor sustain our changes over time.

---

12 Adam and Eve

13 *The Life Model: Living From The Heart Jesus Gave You* book by James G. Frieson, et. al. Shepherd's House, Inc. 2000.

14 Listen to JIMTalks audio lessons Volume 30 for more.

Enough transformation this time

If the effort is too high and the change too small, we will stop trying. Without much transformation of our own we are not about to invite someone else to bring their problems into our churches, lives and relationships. We will certainly not want to tell others what we believe lest they say, "Then why do you still do this?" or "Why don't you then do that?" Those who find themselves drawn to the Life Model almost universally arrived here because they have not experienced enough transformation doing every good thing they have learned to do up to this point.

Self-propagation

If the means of transformation are clearly seen, the necessary elements are made as simple as possible, and our participation yields results that repay the effort, then transformation should spread on its own. Everything about the Gospel suggests that it should spread on its own in a most contagious way with the wind of God's Spirit behind the move. Our goal is to reach this level of contagion with each of the relational skills in this book. We are not there yet.

Normal part of the church

How then will transformation spread to the world? Will we require everyone to have a Western education and be led by professors and doctors? Not only is this not practical, but it would not work. Since, as we will examine in the next chapter, relational skills only spread through relationships and grow properly in the presence of chesed, then there is only one existing distribution system – the Christian church. The answer will not be to make the global church more like the church in the West so they can have the same results we get in the West when it comes to transformation. Our solution must fit the normal life of every follower of Jesus.

Restoration of communities with weak and strong together

Any profound transformation will only happen when the weak and the strong are together. When we speak of the weak and the strong all kinds of fears come to people's minds about being weak as practically every human society despises, abuses and exploits (if not enslaves and kills) the weak. People who want to be gracious by being politically correct object to our calling anyone "weak." Yet 1 Thessalonians 5:14 speaks very clearly about the weak and how the strong are to help them.[15] Weak and strong are Kingdom terms and part of Kingdom reality.

From a brain perspective, the weak are those who are missing some or many relational skills and consequently, no matter how hard they try, they lower the joy around themselves rather than raise it.[16] We normally avoid "those people" rather than help them. But to be perfectly clear about the weak and the strong we need to make one further observation: when we lack necessary relational skills we continue to think and act like predators and prey rather than good shepherds with lambs.

Let me drive this home for a moment. The weak still act like predators. The weaker yet act like prey, or as we called them in *Joy Starts Here*, like possums.[17] Being weak means being low on joy as well as the skills to create joyful people around oneself. Therefore, many of the weak are running for president, buying weapons, leading gangs, climbing to the top of corporate ladders, making and hoarding money, dressing well, eating the best organic food, sporting "six-pack abs" and looking "hot," leading churches, running schools and making loans. They are the last to know that they are the weak because they can, and often do, help themselves to whatever they want. They readily let others know what they think but keep their best ideas to themselves. These are the lords of the earth and the weak, for they are at best predators who would be seen as benevolent and even great philanthropists to the causes they prefer. We barely need to add that all who fear these predators are as weak as them because no one has escaped the predator system that rules the human mind in the absence of the gentle protector set of relational skills. The result of mixing the

15 "And we urge you, brothers, warn those who are idle, encourage the timid, help the weak, be patient with everyone" (1 Thessalonians 5:14, NIV).

16 The only exception is a baby and we expect him/her to be weak. In spite of weaknesses, babies are a source of joy and delight.

17 *Joy Starts Here: The Transformation Zone* by E. James Wilder, Ed Khouri, Chris Coursey and Shelia Sutton. Shepherd's House, Inc. 2013.

predators and prey together is a massive exploitation, manipulation and even rape of the prey even when revolution and revenge flip the food chain.

And what of the strong? The strong are easily despised because whenever they have the chance to exploit a weakness and "win" they fail to do so. The great apostle Paul called it, "being poor we make many rich[18]" and the writer of Hebrews said that the strong are often naked, hungry, roaming the world without a home and living in caves.[19] The strong are those with sores that will not heal but have the gift of healing to help others. The strong suffer well and do not become predators when attacked. Job passed through such a phase and prayed for his weak friends who thought of themselves as strong and Job as weak. There is always some way to disqualify the strong from leadership and participation when viewed through a predator's eyes. When seen through Kingdom eyes (or what the writers of *Joyful Journey*[20] call *i*Sight – meaning we see like Immanuel would see) what at first appears to be a slain lamb proves to be the Lion of Judah.[21] In fact, you will find that this skill of seeing with Kingdom eyes is what we call relational Skill 13, *Heartsight: See what God sees.*

The Western church has lived and practiced as though pure doctrine and proper values produce transformation. The evidence is in with less than persuasive results. Do we find mountains of gentle protectors, relational skills, transformed lives and high-joy Kingdom life in the halls of those who have kept the best doctrinal purity and spoken loudest about the evils in society? It is to just such a church, the one in Ephesus, Jesus said in essence, "Your doctrine and your values are excellent. You work very hard. But you have lost your chesed. Unless you quickly see things in a new way and regain your chesed, I will pull your lamp."[22]

Transformations happen where chesed is high, the weak and strong (in Kingdom terms) are together so the leopard can lie down with the

18 2 Corinthians 6:10
19 Hebrews 11:32-40
20 *Joyful Journey: Listening to Immanuel* book by E. James Wilder, Anna Kang, John and Sungshim Loppnow.
21 Revelation 5
22 Revelation 2:1-7

kid and they do not hurt or destroy in all the Holy Mountain.[23] Oh, but you say, "There are no relational skills mentioned in those verses." Yet, when we become disciples (learners) and make disciples (learners) in a high-chesed environment, relational skills are exactly what we will learn. Profound transformations will follow. Are you ready?

23 Isaiah 11:6

Chapter Two

Why Relational Skills Have Been So Hard To Identify

Why 19 Skills (Rather Than 3 Or 27)

As the brain science behind relational skills began to become clearer, our Life Model team was developing and testing ways to train and strengthen the skills. No exercises had ever been invented for this purpose and, while the science and the sequences were clear, no one had broken the learning sequence into discrete skills. My wife, Jen, one of the developers, was a teacher by training and determined to count the specific skills. When we were finished listing the number of skills we needed to train it came to 19. Some of the later skills require and include earlier skills but we have numbered them separately because they need to be learned separately.

How Our 19 Skills Were Identified And Developed

It is safe to say that the Life Model team was not looking for relational brain skills when the Life Model was first developed. They were looking for ways to reduce the fights between different professionals, professionals and Christians, and between Christians about how to help people transform. Deliverance, addiction treatments, trauma recovery, behavioral and drug-based approaches were but a few of the dissenting parties. Certainly the principles used for parenting were widely different from those used for treatment or church life. However, all these different groups were hoping for some degree of transformation and, more often than not, disappointed by the amount of change being achieved.

Comparing people who made and sustained transformation and those who did not

Back when the Shepherd's House counseling center was operating in southern California, referrals from about 200 churches created a convergence of people with severe issues. In time, a few patterns emerged. People with emotional issues were remarkably immature emotionally in spite of numerous strengths, artistic abilities and often considerable intelligence. It also emerged that a large number of those with struggles had suffered abuse. The earlier in life the abuse started, the more pervasive the lack of maturity they exhibited. It was as though abuse and trauma stopped the development of maturity in key areas of life at the point of impact. With a bit of experience the team could often predict the age of abuse by the characteristic pattern of immaturity that followed. Of course, the solution seemed to be one of resolving the trauma. However, once the trauma resolved and the person was no longer in pain they did not suddenly become mature. In fact, they started growing from where they had left off. At this point growing more maturity required the same kind of training and resources they would have needed when they were young and at the right age to learn. With a little help they seemed to mature at a rate of about one month of recovery for every year they were behind in maturity - except that some didn't. Try as they might, they could not make gains or sustain the small gains they did make. We needed to know why.

A couple of years of observations yielded a major clue. Those who were making progress with maturity, keeping their gains and making profound transformations were part of a "spiritual/social" family that functioned like a replacement for their biological family. Most of these replacement families were found in their local church. Those who were not transforming could not find or sustain a "church family." It appeared that the spiritual family was supplying something. It was not clear what that something might be, but it appeared to include some love, acceptance and support. We were learning the importance of a chesed community for deep and lasting transformation.

Some reflections made it clear that people needed to receive something from their families and in the absence of that "something" they were more stuck and unable to transform their lives because of the trauma they received. It was also clear that the something they needed could be provided by a community if they could find one. Once this something was added, deep transformations could be seen. It was also clear that while therapists were doing well at resolving traumas, therapists were unable to effectively provide the missing something.

What they didn't teach in graduate school

In the 1970's it was often said in graduate schools that therapists were born not trained. The solution, at the time, was to admit more students than were expected to graduate. Through the process of training exercises that required empathy and emotional skills, the poor candidates could be weeded out the first year and those who had the special "something" could continue on to graduate. What could not be measured or trained in potential graduate students would prove to be the same something that produces profound transformations – a set of relational brain skills that form the basic package needed for a fully functioning personality. There is a set of skills the brain must learn in order to fully participate in a chesed community as a gentle protector. Without all the 19 needed elements, personalities continue to collapse back into old patterns no matter how hard they try.

The Science

The Life Model team had developed much of the maturity and healing elements of the model before discovering any of the science. Because we were building an idealized model, there was no need to measure where people were on an average to discover where they would be ideally. Until we discovered the science, exactly what people needed from their families and communities remained a mystery as did how these essential ingredients for deep transformation were transmitted.

Damasio and testing the right hemisphere

Dr. Antonio Damasio began studying case histories of people with brain damage that had fundamentally transformed their identities – for the worse. He studied people who had good relationships and values and after brain damage lost all sense of the values that had defined their character. From this research, Dr. Damasio determined that damage to the executive center in the right brain or the connections in and out (effectively isolating that center) were responsible for the changes. However, he also discovered that the psychological and neurological tests available in the 1980's could not evaluate the right hemisphere functions. He needed to develop a whole new set of tests to even check this essentially non-verbal and non-mechanical part of the brain. As tests were developed it became clear that what we call character was strongly impacted by what these right-brain systems learned and was lost when they were damaged. Once damaged in this critical region, people reverted to predatory behavior with others.

Here is an outline of the nonverbal right hemisphere. We will look at each of the four main levels later in this book.

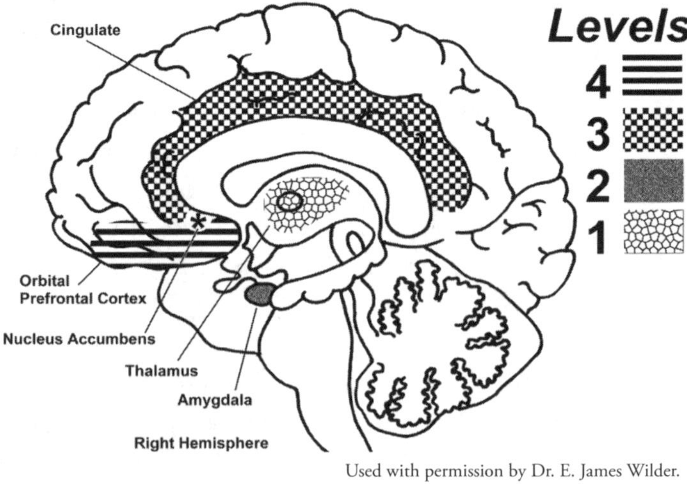

Used with permission by Dr. E. James Wilder.

The decade of the brain

The 1990s were known as the decade of the brain because for the first time, brain scans were available to study the brain while it was still alive. Until then almost everything we knew about the brain came from dead brains. You can imagine that knowing what it did before it died might help us understand how it works. As Damasio was discovering how the right brain functioned compared with damaged brains, he was soon able to discover from living brains that the personality region in the right brain that controlled character and values also controlled emotions and relationships. In fact, here (Level 4 in the brain graph on the previous page) was the place where our working identity was assembled and run. Changes to this physical part of the brain produced profound changes both temporary and permanent in identity. In addition, this was the dominant section of the whole brain. Whatever determined our identity also controlled our options before choices could even be made.

We will be careful to say that while the brain cannot be shown to be the source of our identities, it can certainly be demonstrated to provide the limits of our working identities. That is, we may feel in our heart that we are people of faith but, subject to the limitations of our identity center, may find ourselves responding out of fear and worry in spite of our determination not to live that way. Only people who have no experience watching those with damaged brains will doubt the truth of this assertion.

Schore and his theory

As he emerged from over 17 years in the libraries studying research journals, Dr. Allan Schore from UCLA brought a structure to the sciences in the area of identity development. Starting with the developmental reality that the identity centers involved in the expression of character are not yet present at birth and develop extensively in the first year and a half of life, Schore was able to add the other half of the picture we had learned from brains that are damaged. It turns out that identity and character develops in attachment relationships formed with people who are glad to be with us. This experience of joy with someone stimulates the growth of the identity center that then copies the older and stronger brain. If the brain being copied has a full set of relational skills, then the younger brain gets a complete set. If the older brain is missing skills, then these skills are omitted in the copying process. In essence, the brain comes wired with a duplicator but not with the skills that need to be duplicated. Relational skills are learned relationally in the presence of joy – assuming the older brain has the skill and if there is enough face-to-face interaction to run the duplicator.

The duplication process runs only in the presence of joy where it creates a mutual-mind state. Mutual mind, mentioned in Chapter 1, is the sharing of minds and this mutual mind state operates and changes faster than conscious thought so we can never consciously grasp exactly what it is doing by direct observation. We have called this brain processor the "fast-track" and it is here in the fast-track that profound transformations take place - or fail. Trying to achieve transformations through the slower brain process of conscious thought is doomed to fail. The relational identity that is the core of who we are must be updated at the speed of joy as we learn to become skilled operators of a fully working relational identity.

Here is the answer to what that "something" was that people who transformed deeply were receiving from a loving (chesed) community of more mature (gentle protector) Christians. Here was the answer for how they learned. Here was the answer to what people needed for lasting transformations. The people who we observed failing to maintain their gains and needing years of support in therapy showed the predator/prey style of thinking about relationships and could not find a community with enough chesed and gentle protector skills to teach them how to become a gentle protector.

While this new science showed us how we learned to be ourselves as the people God created us to be, *science could not supply the answer to what kind of people we should be* – except to confirm that our two essential identity components were 1) relational and 2) joyful. As we began examining the scriptures we discovered that God had no problem telling us what kind of people we should be and that the three essentials were 1) joyful, 2) peaceful and 3) relational (in a chesed way) with both God and others. It was as though the God of scripture was the designer of the brain found by science.

Looking below consciousness rather than above

Ever since Freud, psychology had been looking below consciousness for the answers to what steered our lives and choices. While looking below consciousness, science was diverted from looking above consciousness for a faster, stronger and more powerful mind system. Once Schore was able to identify the fast and powerful identity system that is formed by and devoted to creating our identities as individuals and groups, the door was open for science to advise how we might best learn or retrain the system. However, while there was evidence that retraining was possible, no one had ever used this new science to develop a training method. There were several reasons why it seemed risky to try.

Professional "Catch 22"

Professional counseling is to be guided by "informed consent" from the participant. This means you are told ahead of time what will be done and you agree with understanding to the process and results. However, the fast-track system of the brain produces transformations we do not understand until after they have happened and faster than we can consciously watch. In addition, it copies one brain onto another "as is" not "as desired." It sounds a bit risky to ask someone to receive a permanent copy of my brain in the way I would give one to my children - in return for my hourly fee.

A second problem for professionals is that the mutual mind state used to duplicate and train relational skills is a two-sided process. It copies both ways depending on who happens to be the stronger brain. Sure, the therapist may think they are stronger and better, but if this proves to be untrue in some part of the identity center, then the process runs the other direction. But, because the process must run on joy and chesed love, it is necessary for the therapist to love the client and the other way around as well.

Professional detachment is seen as the basis for objective care. The moment a therapist begins developing a personal, intimate, loving attachment to the client, some big red flags begin to appear. Yet, the relational brain skills are designed to create a permanent bond along with an identity change for both participants. We become each other's people for life. Professional ethics all but prohibit this kind of relationship because it is much more powerful than any conscious choices or informed consent. In addition, deep bonds will always guide our judgement and not the other way around.

Finally, these changes are not reversible and there is no professional ethical basis for deciding if the change is good. Who is willing to say Dr. X should be allowed to charge for duplicating him or herself in the brains of others and creating people who will love him or her for life? We may do this with our children but licensing people to do so with the public is not professional.

Christians have a solution to shared values and consent to change our personality in ways we do not understand that forms permanent relationships for life and beyond. Christians are not only allowed to form communities but expected to develop chesed groups of gentle protectors. Christians are instructed to chesed their enemies and teach others not to be devils and predators – fully knowing that we once were such ourselves. We are expected to learn and teach the skills our brain must master to fully participate in a chesed community as gentle protectors. The reason most people develop an interest in the Life Model is that they know in their hearts that this is the heritage of Christians but it has not been their experience with Christians thus far in life. Everything was about to change.

How We Were Ahead Of The Curve And Have Stayed There

As I have said, much of the Life Model was complete before the science came along. The mystery of what that "something" spiritual families provided was so complete that no one thought to look into relational skills and brain development for answers. Indeed, when a brochure about Dr. Schore's lectures crossed Jim Wilder's desk in the late 1990's he did not recognize either the speaker or the topic. What he recognized was a strong sense that someone from staff attend the lecture, but he could not give a reason. So, an intern with no excuse was sent for the weekend and came back with a series of tapes where Dr. Schore read from the text of his books that were published five years later in 2003. The intern said, "Here is the brain science that matches everything we have written in the Life Model down to the ages when it happens." The team, led by Dr. Wilder, began to unpack and translate in easier terms what was in those lectures five years before the books were published. Next came the process of testing the theory in real life.

How it had never been tested aside from parents and babies

While Schore explained very carefully how mothers and babies learned relational skills when babies were 9 months old, such training had never been tried with adults who had missed significant parts of the skill set as infants. The tragedy of 9/11 happened which rocked the world. This is where I come in to the story.

The experiment (Jen and I develop THRIVE Training)

Attending conferences around the country was very popular until planes rained out of the sky to the shock and horror of the Western world. Immediately following the tragedy, attendance at conferences steeply dropped. Travel now required a compelling reason and one of the few reasons counselors would travel was to learn about the neurology and spiritual healing elements of the Life Model. Jim Wilder was tired of talking about the model because talking went into the slow track of the brain and trained no one to actually do the things that could bring about transformation. Teaching needed to give way to training, but how would that training work? No one had tried this kind of training before. Because I lived and worked in a therapeutic community I agreed to help develop and test exercises that could be used in a sort of conference format to train others – if it worked. We agreed that if we could get 25 people to travel after 9/11 by a certain date we would hold the first such training and call it *THRIVE*. On the day of the deadline we had 23 people registered; then the phone rang and two more people signed up just in time. We now had the green light to move forward with our first *THRIVE Training*.

We decided to start work with the closest thing to a mother/child pair and try training adults who already had a permanent bonded relationship with each other. While there were a number of unknown factors in our plan, what we did have was the science, motivation and the format to train people to learn new skills and strengthen existing skills. The first few days were filled with excitement. It was obvious something deep and profound was happening. Attendees confirmed our observations by saying, "If I would have known *THRIVE* was going to be like this, I would have brought more people!"

We learned a lot from this first event. One of the major lessons we gleaned was the significance of emotional capacity. While building joy was fun for people, even healing, another factor was at work. Jim and I had combined what were actually three separate training tracks into one track - which overwhelmed people and proved to be too much for one week. Trying to drink from a firehose doesn't work very well. We needed to slow down the pace to match the capacity of the attendees. Without realizing it, we were doing three things that needed to be separated: 1) increase emotional capacity with joy and rest, 2) return to joy from negative emotions and 3) learn solutions for the five kinds of pain the brain knows.

We adjusted our sights and made changes to the training flow. We now have three separate but interconnected training tracks that focus on each of these goals: Track One trains joy, Track Two trains return to joy skills and Track Three trains solutions for pain. We learn basic skills early in the training process then we shift to the more demanding skills later on. These tracks focus on the top three essentials of our identity: I am relational, I see with my heart and I am a source of life. We created an optimal training environment by using a variety of exercises and alternating activities in order to train new skills and strengthen existing skills.[24] Along the way we also shift the focus from learning skills to propagating the skills. In other words, we do not simply give people fish to consume; we want to equip people to both learn how to catch fish then train other people how to catch fish within their communities. Skill acquisition and skill propagation are two essential elements in the *THRIVE Training* package.

Adding another important element brought even more clarity. My wife, Jen, carefully numbered the actual skills we were training and, as mentioned before, we discovered nineteen in all. In these

24 Research shows we can learn new skills much faster, in some cases twice as fast, by modifying and altering the learning routine. http://www.hopkinsmedicine.org/news/media/releases/want_to_learn_a_new_skill_faster_change_up_your_practice_sessions

early years we included teaching as part of the day, but to optimize the training format we later removed the teaching to focus entirely on experiential, hands-on training. We now have all the theory and teaching available on the *THRIVE Lectures* DVD's with online courses to apply the theory in what we call the *THRIVE-at-Home* package.

Victoria attended one of the early *THRIVE Training* events and after practicing joy with her friend she quickly felt the difference a little joy can make. As a wife, mother, grandmother and full-time counselor for couples and families, Victoria's life was changed by practicing the nineteen skills she learned at *THRIVE Training*. Victoria says, "My life, marriage, family and ministry are profoundly transformed by what I gained from learning the gentle protector skills. I feel my heart and character becoming more like Jesus every day!"

Connexus and THRIVE: True Identity developed from the bonded pairs starting place

Now that we demonstrated how relational brain skill training could be done with bonded pairs, *THRIVE Training* was used to launch the next level of difficulty – training adults who do not have a permanent bonded relationship. Obviously, the difficulty is higher and the severity of the missing skills can be larger as well. Jim Wilder began developing this program called *Connexus* with Ed Khouri which is now transforming people, groups and communities around the world in remarkable ways.

As we continued to seek ways to make it easier to start training we then developed *THRIVE: True Identity* as a "starter track" at *THRIVE* where anyone can attend without the bonded partner requirement. *THRIVE: True Identity* provides a foundation of basic brain skills to help people "normalize" their lives and relationships using joy and peace as motivators instead of fear or pain. *THRIVE: True Identity* focuses on seven parts of our identity: I create belonging, I eat, I rest, I pray, I give, I play and, last but not least, I am thankful. We now have shorter versions of *THRIVE: True Identity* so churches and groups can host a weekend for people to jumpstart their joy.

Joy Rekindled and 30 Days of Joy for Busy Married Couples

Jen and I started hearing from couples who were eager to attend *THRIVE Training* but were unable to get away for a week because of young children at home. As we looked around at many of the couples we knew, most not only had young children but all of them lived busy, overwhelming lives. It was becoming clear that training programs were needed for couples who could not take a week off to attend *THRIVE*, our premiere training. We also recognized our friends could use the joyful brain skills in their marriages and families, but they lacked the ability to get away. Seeing this growing need, we decided to pull and modify some of the exercises from *THRIVE Training* that had deeply impacted our marriage; then we created new exercises and put them into a shorter format and called it *Joy Rekindled*. This marriage weekend has become one of the easiest ways to introduce joyful transformation into the lives of couples and families.

Keira and Leo attended a *Joy Rekindled* marriage retreat, and after a weekend of joy exercises they noticed a deep connection between each other and with God. "It was like our hearts were on fire!" Keira writes. "For the first time in our married life we not only had a language to better understand each other but we now had actual skills to stay connected during the ups and downs of our relationship. We feel hopeful and energized for a deeper intimacy with each other." Keira and Leo practiced basic skills that were missing in their busy lives.

Many people did not need to acquire the relational skills so much as they needed to practice these skills until they were masterful enough to use them in their marriages when emotions ran high. Jen and I looked over the exercise format in *Joy Rekindled*, and then we developed a book called *30 Days of Joy for Busy Married Couples* which includes a variety of fun, simple, engaging exercises for couples to increase their joy levels and strengthen existing skills. While the book is written for couples to practice joy 15 minutes a day for thirty days, couples can practice on their own timeline. These are a few of our attempts to make relational skill training more accessible.

Transformations

Oliver and Audrey were successful realtors with busy lives. Over time the pair noticed they were feeling crispy in their marriage and tired in their work. After years of counseling, reading books and attending seminars, someone told them about *THRIVE Training*, and after doing some research, they felt like this was worth a try.

After practicing gentle protector skills at *THRIVE Training* they quickly noticed a soothing calmness begin to replace their busy, chaotic thoughts. Learning new skills that had been missing bolstered their relationship. They were more patient and kind to one another. They were beginning to become gentle protectors defined by chesed. Oliver and Audrey's transformation not only profoundly changed them but, it also inspired their friends and colleagues who would ask, "What's gotten into you two?" after spending a few moments with them. "You love birds have changed!"

Once Oliver and Audrey knew what was missing in their lives they could strategically remove the blockages to transformation - and this is one of the nineteen skills.

Making It Safe

In a professional model of transformation the people at the center would be the properly trained, educated, licensed and healthy role models with tested slow-track conscious mastery of the field. They would be the most qualified and have the most resources. In a professional religious model, those at the center would be the most gifted, anointed, appointed and established clergy. However, if the brain's built-in fast track duplicator that creates identity is to be involved, these qualifications are of little use. The duplicator is looking for a high-joy person who feeds him or her and is consistently peacefully, relationally engaged in times of trials and distress. If God planned to use this high-speed identity duplicator, God would have insisted on a chesed community with people at the center who were older, had demonstrated unusual success raising peaceful children, had sustaining relationships with their spouse, earned a reputation for good relationships in the community, did not allow anger to disrupt their relationships and were not very attracted to alcohol for pseudo-joy.

God would have given such people the job of feeding others and creating high-joy meals where God's presence was easily perceived and comforting to people in their times of suffering and loss. Here would be the solution to using the fast-track duplicator to replace missing gentle protector brain skills.

But there remained an additional problem for God. Since no single person would have all the skills, people would need to meet regularly as a group. In that group they would need to humbly and easily admit their failings and allow God's presence to actively illuminate the true character they were to exhibit. Indeed, it is as though God would need to live a human life and demonstrate a complete personality and then actively guide every generation to experience that model in a community where everyone was learning to grow this character as well. The only safe guidance would be God's model in an active presence with God's people. Then, those who experienced this model while practicing and encouraging it in others would be transformed. People would need to see beyond the predators and prey they saw around them no matter how many times people relapsed and return to the restoration task of training the "children of God" to emerge from the relationally defective selves around them as they learned the relational skills and identity of a chesed life. The center for all guidance would come through those who experienced the active presence of God in daily life – this is also a learned skill.

Guidance

Christians who are accustomed to receiving all their guidance from slow-track, conscious thought are understandably nervous about letting God into their fast-track control system where they cannot consciously keep up and monitor God's actions. The main objection is that allowing God to actively engage our minds is either 1) a charismatic gift or 2) the writing of a new scripture text. As the Life Model team struggled with these issues, Dr. Dallas Willard came to our aid.

Dallas was married to Jane, the long-time assistant director of Shepherd's House where the Life Model was first developed. Dr. Willard wrote a book called *In Search of Guidance,* and later retitled it *Hearing God*, to carefully show, from Biblical sources and Church history, that God guides our thoughts in active ways today. Knowing God's voice and being guided by God's Spirit are the inheritance of God's people. Rather than fearing God's guidance we should seek it and expect it to fully fit with God's word, God's character and God's actions in the past. Dallas also declared the Life Model to be the best model he had seen for bringing Christ to the center of counseling and restoring the disintegrated community fabric within Christian churches.[25] We have called the process of relationally interacting with God the *Immanuel Lifestyle*. Learning to live this way with a human brain requires specific brain skill training. Here we have added to the list of brain skills proposed by Schore and science by believing that the brain must not only be trained to relate well to other people, but it must also be trained to relate well to God. For some of us this reality may not sound very spiritual, but the process of being a mature human as well as interacting with Immanuel is a relational, formative one where the sheep know the Shepherd's voice because something relationally happens for the sheep to *personally* recognize the Shepherd's voice.[26]

Maturity, education and Immanuel

Our conclusions about guidance of transformation are, to quote from what Dallas Willard told the Life Model staff, that "the main requirement in the care of souls is that we should love them." In a chesed community it is not education or title that qualifies leaders but maturity and an active awareness of God's presence as a guide. Maturity is nothing other than a full working set of the relational skills that create and are created by chesed life in God's presence.

---

25 *The Life Model: Living From The Heart Jesus Gave You* book by James G. Frieson, et. al. Shepherd's House, Inc. 2000.

26 John 10:27. To know is the Greek word, Ginosko, NT 1097. Ginosko is a personal, relational process that signifies "to take in knowledge, to come to know, recognize, understand," or "to understand completely." It is not merely the transmission of information rather an experience of knowing that comes through relational connection and interaction. The woman in Mark 5 with the issue of blood "felt (Ginosko) in her body that she was healed of the affliction" after touching Jesus' garment.

Making It Useful

Applying an idealized model to a real-life community requires us to re-vision and retrain ourselves to a much more relational life than is the norm in Western culture. It is to identify with a far different tribe than is customary in tribal cultures. It is to transcend ordinary life in a very different way than Asian cultures. The Bible uses the Greek word koinonia that is often translated fellowship to speak of the way that followers of Christ share resources and suffering. Koinonia can be viewed as a pooling together of each member's capacity to be Christ-like. The koinonia of pooled relational resources helps each individual be more like Christ. Let us consider how these relational skills that bring a mature and chesed life affect us as leaders, workers, families, communities and followers of Jesus.

Leadership

RARE leaders[27] keep relationships bigger than problems and minimize relational casualties. Leaders with relational skills inspire their followers, excel at calming big emotions and maintain unity in their teams by remembering who they are when upset and overwhelmed. Mature leaders raise mature followers through the process of nurturing and valuing relational skills. Leaders can only give what they have otherwise they function out of fear and stunt the growth in those they serve. Good leaders understand their limitations and aim to be their best with what they have to work with at any given time in themselves and with other people. Prioritizing joyful relational skills means embracing and emphasizing personal growth as a value for successful leadership development. Research shows effective leaders are joyful, relational and creative rather than fear-based, problem-focused and rigid. This means their relational brain is both trained and working well. Having good information, a good education and captivating charisma does not automatically create a great leader. Relational leaders who possess emotional and relational intelligence and lead by example create a lasting legacy.

---

27 RARE is an acronym Dr. Jim Wilder and Dr. Marcus Warner use in the *RARE Leadership* book that focuses on 4 essential brain skills for leaders: **R**emain Relational, **A**ct like Yourself, **R**eturn to joy and **E**ndure hardships well.

Business applications

We do not normally think of the importance of having a joyful identity and relational competency as keys to success in the world, especially the world of business, but whether you run a corporation, answer phones, manage an office, work in sales or negotiate trade talks, having relational skills builds trust, increases efficiency and develops emotional intelligence. Knowing when to rest, when to stop and how to return to joy are just three crucial skills that significantly improve how well people succeed in the business world. Without these skills we simply do not build trust nor do we stay focused on what's important: people. The lack of these skills erodes trust, and can you imagine doing business with someone you don't trust or who doesn't trust you? As a wise man once said, "A good name is more desirable than great riches; to be esteemed is better than silver or gold."[28] Our name should reflect our character and relational skills bring peace, joy and stability to our work.

Family

Whether its parenting or marriage, learning joyful brain skills starts with our families. When we lack the necessary skills to stay relationally connected we become disorganized, disconnected, depressed and distressed. By far, parenting is one of the hardest jobs in the world and if you question this reality just ask a parent! Similar to leadership, parents can only give what they have otherwise they stunt the growth of their children. Parents rely on the skills they have learned and used throughout their lives to guide their children. Here is a more demanding environment where we must use every ounce of our relational skills and plenty of sacrificial giving during moments of fatigue, sickness and stress. While this is demanding, the blessings are much richer and rewarding because families provide the ideal format to acquire, strengthen and propagate relational skills.

While marriage is no easy task either, marriages blossom when joy levels are sustained and they crumble when joy fades. Marriages stay intact with relational skills to navigate hardship and keep relationships bigger than problems. Relational skills are the hidden ingredients that form the foundation our families rely on to stay connected

---

28 Proverbs 22:1, NIV

and joyful. Families are in the best possible position to introduce, practice and spread the skills that change lives.

Rebuilding communities and lives

Relational skills restore communities where violence, neglect and pain have all but destroyed joy levels. As people learn new skills they begin to practice and propagate these skills to others. While families are the ideal environment to learn new skills, communities become the delivery system to spread the skills. Here we remedially learn the skills our families could not pass on. We strengthen and pass on the skills to others. Relational skills are the result of chesed people who are growing and developing into the people God created them to be.[29]

As we begin to reflect back to one another how God sees us, our communities become anchored in hope. People discover who they are designed to be because it is mirrored back to them by other people who have the skills. Forgiveness flows from seeing one another as God sees, which dramatically transforms our communities into lush gardens of chesed where people blossom. Any lasting change to rebuild communities must include the purposeful acquisition of relational brain skills so that possums and predators transform into protectors in some of the most remarkable ways. We are talking about character change and identity transformation that changes generations.

Recovery

We are as good as our ability to manage what we feel; therefore, successful recovery must help people manage and quiet their big feelings. Joy-based relational skills equip people with the tools to build relationships, retrain the brain and build emotional capacity to process pain. Without these skills people stay stuck, revert to old patterns of dealing with pain and simply become overwhelmed with no idea how to stay their relational selves and suffer well. Relational skills provide the needed momentum to develop an interactive relationship with Immanuel who is always with us, Skill 13. People learn solutions for the five kinds of pain the brain knows, Skill 18, which saves time

---

29 Learn more in the *Belonging* module of *Connexus* developed by Ed Khouri and Dr. Jim Wilder.

and effort simply because we avoid using solutions that no longer work. We receive and give life and effectively restore our joyful identities to become gentle protectors.

Evangelism

The result of all healing and maturity is evangelism. Having once been transformed to a full and joyful life it is beyond imagination to consider keeping this good news from others. Evangelism is nothing other than spreading the good news of what has so transformed our lives for the better. Telling people what we believe is of relatively little value or power compared to the radiance of profoundly transformed lives. Most people do not evangelize because they have no good news to share. They are not much transformed, so they have very little to tell others. Most counseling and healing ministries stop when the pain is gone but before the joyful chesed life is fully achieved. While pain relief has its value, a radiant and relational self even during pain and trials is of far greater value.

What If Joy And Skills Mattered?

What would our churches, schools, youth programs, soup kitchens and counseling offices look like if we believed that joy (being glad to be together) was fundamental to deep transformation? We don't mean "gathering to feel good." Serving free pizza and beer would gather huge numbers of people together to feel good. No, we mean that "your being here with me brings me joy in a personal way" is fundamental to deep transformation. If we find ourselves thinking such a plan is idealistic, silly or impossible, then we lack the skills to experience or teach others how it is done. In this case we can predict that deep transformation has eluded us - until now.

If you don't remember seeing relational skills in the Bible we need to examine the word koinonia (fellowship) more closely under the conditions of a chesed community. Koinonia is *the process of sharing resources between comrades* but the comrades in koinonia fellowship are really bonded to each other forever (chesed). This bond is much longer than "till death do us part" and more transforming of who we are together. In 1 Corinthians 1:8-10 Paul says that it is the koinonia with Christ that will make us blameless when Christ returns and help us maintain unity with each other - free from divisions. We will have a perfectly unified mind. Koinonia (fellowship) between God's people who stick together creates perfect relationships. These relationships start out with conflict as Paul points out in the following verses but somehow in the koinonia we learn better relationships – we acquire the skills.

Paul points to the fellowship (koinonia) of meeting each other's needs.[30] Our areas of service and ministry are established through koinonia[31] and Paul's own area of ministry was making everyone understand this mysterious fellowship.[32]

The grace of God and knowing God's chesed love comes from koinonia with the Holy Spirit.[33] In fact, Paul goes on to say that even our sense of compassion for other people is created by koinonia so that without koinonia there is no comfort in our lives.[34] This means that koinonia is also the fellowship of shared suffering.[35] Under these powerful conditions of shared grace, love (chesed) and suffering we learn to share the same outlook and responses as God and all of God's people if we share (koinonia) what we have learned of God's character in our lives together.

John takes the koinonia *sharing of learned character* one step farther when he makes fellowship the sign that we have been forgiven for our sins.

> "But if we walk in the light, as he is in the light, we have koinonia with one another, and the blood of Jesus Christ his Son, purifies us from all sin" (1 John 1:7, NIV).

Now that we have seen that the principles, practices and conditions for learning the relational brain skills that produce Christ-like character are in the center of the Gospel message we now turn our attention to the mechanics of how this learning happens. My hope in this book

30 2 Corinthians 8:4
31 Galatians 2:9
32 Ephesians 3:9
33 2 Corinthians 13:14
34 Philippians 2:1
35 Philippians 3:10

is that by understanding the mechanics of learning the relational skills that form character we will save our concept of fellowship. Transforming fellowship is not found in coffee, donuts, comparing cell phones, admiring dresses and chatting about the weather after church – let us explore how real transformation works.

Chapter Three
Brain Skill 1 - Share Joy
Facial expressions and voice tones amplify,
"We're glad to be together!"

After taking a moment to ask God, "Why does this skill matter to You?" I found myself thinking,

> "Joy is the mark of My people. Joy is fundamental for the unity of My people and much like a bee to a flower, joy is the fragrance that draws My children to the Father's heart, for I am a God who is glad to be with My people. When My people have joy they taste my presence and share My character with the world."

These thoughts inspire me, and I hope they inspire you. Let's talk more about relational joy. Think about a time someone was glad to be with you. Their face lit up. Their body language, voice tone and words all conveyed, "Hey, I am SO glad you are here!" You feel seen and cherished. This jubilant response made you feel special. Your heart rate increases. Your pupils dilate. Your face lights up. You feel loved.

Relational joy grows into an emotional state as it is shared with people who express warm delight to be together. Joy is contagious and spreads when it is shared and expressed with at least one other person. A wonderful blend of nonverbal signals allow joy to grow with each glance. Joy increases with every shared smile of the eyes. Joy creates a most remarkable chemical cocktail that simply feels euphoric. Joy excites us and motivates us to interact and stay connected.

Technically, this nonverbal dance of warm voice tones, bright eye smiles and attuned body signals is described as right-hemisphere-to-right-hemisphere communication that amplifies our most desired positive emotional state. Relational joy is best conveyed face-to-face but voice tone comes in a close second.

We develop a strong bond with people who light up to see us. Skill 1 makes life, church, marriage, business and everything else better. Joy gives lovers the fuel to endure, friends the strength to persevere and families the ability to recover. Ideally we return to joy from every unpleasant state the brain knows. We will discuss negative emotions in more detail with Skills 11 and 12.

We have become so accustomed to breathing we rarely think much about it until smog, second-hand smoke or congestion from a cold interrupts us. We do not spend much time thinking about joy either until something happens. Either our joy levels drastically sink or we experience joy in such a profound way that the feelings are exhilarating, like when we marry or welcome a child to our family. Thanks to the neurotransmitter dopamine, messages are sent through cells to the brain telling us we need to breathe. Dopamine plays a key role for starting and sustaining joy as well. Relational joy empowers, motivates and fuels us. We feel a reward when we share joy just as we enjoy eating a favorite meal. In fact, the brain's reward circuitry releases dopamine when we eat food, do aerobic exercise, have sex and give charitably to other people.[36] Joy is foundational to life and should always lead to rest. After we catch our breath it is time for serotonin to recharge us for more joy.

If joy levels sink, we are compelled to seek comfort from the same mechanisms that propel us to inhale after holding our breath. When

36 The nucleus accumbens and the dorsal striatum.

our joy levels drop to dangerous levels we turn to BEEPS. BEEPS is an acronym my friend Ed Khouri came up with for his *Connexus* curriculum that builds joy for communities. BEEPS stand for Behaviors, Experiences, Events, People and Substances that hijack the joy mechanism of the brain. BEEPS artificially regulate our feelings. Pseudo-joy always leaves us empty.

We become overwhelmed and weak when joy levels sink due to loss, pain and the absence of a familiar face to share our smiles. We feel depleted when our joy is met with anger, disgust or silence. Sinking joy consumes and destroys our marriages. Families substitute joy with activities, sports, movies, television, computers, busyness and endless distractions. When churches lose joy people focus on rules and become rigid and irrelevant. At this point people become numbers to fill pews or problems to solve. Parents with low joy focus on correcting behavior instead of enjoying their children. Cultures around the globe associate joy with sex, shame, fear and skepticism because people know something about joy is powerful. It does not take long to remember times in life when our joy was dashed due to rejection or ridicule. These moments hurt because we are wired for joyful connection. Without Skill 1 we risk passing on the very patterns we despise.

As we remember, create, express and share joy, this positive state comes to define our personality. "Why are you so happy?" people wonder. While joy is not happiness, people notice the joy glow. The fun does not stop here. Joy has counterpart we will soon look at called Skill 2, *Simple Quiet.*

How Skill 1 Is Normally Acquired, Practiced And Propagated

We learn Skill 1 from people who are glad to be with us, specifically mom, dad, grandparents, aunts, uncles and friendly faces in our churches and communities. With consistency this glad-to-be-with-you response becomes internalized as our normal state and we are highly motivated to return to Skill 1 anytime we notice our joy has disappeared. We strengthen Skill 1 with practice from our peers. Bonds of friendships develop with our peers who are glad to see us and we light up to see them as well. When we are young, joy becomes the foundation for our identity, later on for our friendships, and after puberty, joy will dictate the quality of our group identity as well as motivate us to find a mate. As joy levels increase so does our ability to share joy at each stage of life. We spread Skill 1 with the addition of every new relationship we encounter and we start joy in the places with the people where we notice joy levels are low or missing - one smile at a time.

How Skill 1 Is Remedially Acquired, Practiced And Propagated

Let's examine how transforming fellowship/koinonia can restore the missing *Share Joy* skill. It is no accident the blessing of all blessings, the priestly blessing God gave Aaron the priest to recite over Israel says,

> "The Lord bless you and keep you. The Lord make His face to shine on you and be gracious to you. The Lord lift up His countenance upon you and give you peace" (Numbers 6:24-26, NIV).

Here we see God's face and countenance as the source of joy and blessing over His people. Jesus would have used the priestly blessing throughout His ministry, especially in Luke 24:51 when He ascends to heaven while lifting up His hands and blessing His flock. Joy is reciprocal, and it is after this parting gift that the disciples shift into worship then return to Jerusalem *with great joy*.[37]

In the Bible, to have God's face is to have life, joy and blessing while the absence of God's face is equated with death, abandonment and rejection. It is no accident that the face is where joy starts and stops. When needed, babies who have mommy's face and gaze feel euphoric joy while the absence of mommy's face and gaze feels much like a certain death.[38] With forty-three muscles, the face is an ideal platform to convey our love and express our delight toward one another. Joyful glances grow into high-energy smiles before we look away to rest with Skill 2. We see a similar transaction when Jesus tells the disciples to keep His commands and remain in His love,

> "I have told you this so that my joy may be in you and that your joy may be complete" (John 15:11, NIV).

37 Luke 24:52

38 Dr. Allan Schore

Joy is the relational/emotional/mental/spiritual transaction that both reflects our love and is a reflection of God's love. Fellowship/koinonia within our chesed communities is where *Share Joy* changes lives and restores relationships.

While Skill 1 is first learned in our natural families, a quick glance at the world tells us this is not always the case. We learn Skill 1 within the pool of resources our chesed communities offer. Here we spend much time sharing glad-to-be-together moments. Skill 1 blossoms in this garden of face-to-face interactions within the limits of our emotional/relational capacity. This means we practice Skill 1 according to our ability and availability. The need for a joy makeover is one reason Dr. Jim Wilder and I developed *THRIVE Training*. Each training track includes a variety of exercises to train pairs to build and amplify joy. By the time attendees reach Track Three they are well-versed in acquiring, practicing and propagating Skill 1. Ed Khouri and Dr. Jim Wilder created *Connexus* to train communities to use and transfer Skill 1. The Action and Next Steps below start your remedial practice.

Skill 1 - Action Step

In the next 24 hours convey genuine joy to people you know and trust. Use your face and voice to say, "I'm glad to see you!" Also, think about some special joy moments you've had then notice how these moments felt for you.

Skill 1 - Next Step

You can start building joy with the book, *Joy Starts Here: The Transformation Zone*, with a few friends. Begin the group by taking the online *JOYQ Assessment* and measure your progress of growing joy.

Read how joy grows maturity with *The Complete Guide to Living With Men* book by Dr. E. James Wilder. Learn how joy impacts leaders and organizations with the *RARE Leadership: 4 Uncommon Habits For Increasing Trust, Joy and Engagement In The People You Lead* book by Warner and Wilder. If you are married, attend a *Joy Rekindled* marriage retreat or use the *30 Days of Joy for Busy Married Couples* exercise book to jumpstart your joy.

Learn more about the theology and brain science behind joy by listening to the brilliant *Jesus In Mind: Talks on Kingdom Life* audio lessons, particularly Volume 3 in the series. Watch the *THRIVE Lectures* and participate in the *THRIVE-at-Home* online curriculum. If you are a serious student determined to start and spread joy, attend *THRIVE Training* or bring joy to your church and community using the *Connexus* program. Learn more at joystartshere.com.

Conclusion

Skill 1 is the natural result of a chesed community where people love the Lord their God with all their heart and they love one another as God does. Skill 1 not only flows from pockets of chesed but it also develops chesed communities because you can't help but love the people who light up to see you. People want to be where Skill 1 is prevalent and any group of people who value and use Skill 1 can change the world. In this context joy grows when it is shared so the wealth of koinonia in our communities provide the opportunities to start, sustain and propagate Skill 1 in some of the most practical and profound ways possible. Deep transformations always includes Skill 1. Conversely, Skill 1 leads to deep transformation in our identity and our character because joy gives us strength. The Good News of the Gospel is that we have a God whose face lights up to see us and He beckons us to draw near. Skill 1 can warm the coldest of hearts and cool the hottest heads.

When I have Skill 1: I frequently look for opportunities to be glad to be with people. I value relationships and amplify good things as much as I can.

When Skill 1 is missing or underdeveloped: Joy is fleeting. I feel overwhelmed by life. My tendency is to focus on pain.

Skill 1 Application Step - *Gene's Joy*

My friend Gene was a successful salesman who was driven to succeed and be the best in everything. After learning about Skill 1, Gene noticed he was a few quarts low on relational joy and he compensated for his joy deficit by spending much time working long hours and disconnecting by watching TV or surfing the web. Gene decided it was time to join a small group at his church. Gene heard about an available discipleship group who was looking for new members to join, so he signed up and gave it a try.

After a few weeks Gene decided it was time to share what he was learning about joy. After some discussion the group found creative ways to build joy together using Life Model Works exercises and fellowship meals. The group took turns having someone find a creative way to build joy during each small group meeting. It did not take long for Gene to notice a shift in his life and priorities. Gene stayed successful at work but he was now working less overtime and pursuing more relational connections with friends and community. Gene even surprised his coworkers by being glad to be with them on a regular basis. Skill 1 was the beginning of something good for Gene.

Chapter Four
Brain Skill 2 - Soothe Myself
Simple Quiet:
Quieting (shalom) after both joyful and upsetting emotions is the strongest predictor of life-long mental health.

After taking a moment to ask God, "Why does this skill matter to You?" I found myself thinking,

> "One of the gifts I give My children is the gift of rest. I remember you are weak and you grow weary. I invite you to rest with Me. I created you to need and enjoy rest. I long to see My children enter My rest. Even your breathing will tell you when you need to calm and quiet yourself. Breathe, My child."

Can you identify a time in your life when you were wrought with worry and dread? Intrusive thoughts robbed your peace. Maybe you felt misunderstood, even wrongly accused. Possibly you were concerned about paying the bills or worried about health issues. Your shallow breathing and tense body gripped you. You wondered if this riptide would ever end. When Skill 2 is missing we do not effectively quiet our thoughts and body. We wonder where the "off" button is to our emotions and mind. The absence of rest feels exhausting.

Relationships require a rhythm of joy and rest. We rest then cycle back to joy. We build joy then return to rest. This moment by moment interaction leaves us satisfied and refreshed. Short moments of rest provide the strength and stamina for more joy. We see this pattern in infants who reflexively look away from faces and break eye contact once they reach a peak of joy. Then, after a short breather, they quickly return for more face to face joy. The connect/disconnect dance continues. Would you let the baby rest if she looked away during an interaction with you?

When interactions are synchronized and attuned, energy levels mutually climb and drop with each glance and averted gaze. Much like a conductor leading an orchestra, a trained brain knows these patterns and follows them so the fun feels natural. We come to expect joy and rest as "how we do relationships." The absence of rest overwhelms us, and it does not take long to feel depressed and depleted.

Alternating joy with rest prevents health casualties. In one study just eight weeks of a relaxation program helped participants cut their use of clinical services by 43%.[39] This eight-week course consisted of weekly meetings for a total of 3 hours focusing on relaxation through meditation, yoga and stress-reduction exercises including resiliency-building through social support, cognitive skills training and positive psychology. They estimated this cut health costs anywhere from $640-$25,000 per patient each year. That's a lot of dough. People were quieting and feeling shalom, and it makes a big difference.

Just think about a time you enjoyed a tasty meal with a friend. You enjoy each moment as you synchronize your breathing, eating, tasting and swallowing with your speaking and laughing. Much like your good meal, Skill 2 is a primary commodity that keeps relationships and interactions balanced. Skill 2 releases serotonin on an "as needed" basis to recharge your relational battery. Serotonin leaves you feeling content and peaceful. As a sunrise leads to a sunset, Skill 2 follows Skill 1 to soothe your body and calm your mind. Joy and quiet are complimentary, we need both to keep our interactions mutually satisfying.

39 http://time.com/4071897/stress-relief-healthcare-costs/

Memories, language, talent, muscle and skills that are not used will atrophy. When it comes to relational skills, every generation can only transmit what they learn and use. As skills drop out, generations will spread undesirable traits such as abuse, pain, addictions and distortions. Regardless of intention and determination, we cannot give what we do not have. Skill 2 starts to diminish when families and communities do not allow or have not learned to rest. Without Skill 2 we overwork, burn out, feel depressed, become lost in our devices, avoid states of quiet and push ourselves until something gives. In one recent study that looked at graduate and undergraduate students, nearly half (48.1%) were considered internet addicts who experienced withdrawal symptoms if they did not stay connected with their devices while 40.7% were considered to be potential internet addicts.[40] Many with problematic internet use said their families also overuse the internet. While this study was done on a small group of people, it does show that when Skill 2 is missing we stay overly busy and preoccupied. We even pass on our destructive patterns and call it normal.[41]

As in the internet study, Skill 2 can be difficult to identify because replacement patterns are socially acceptable. We replace quiet and rest with BEEPS in the form of busyness, work, sex, music, internet, television and sugar. When this happens our world busily consists of the things we do, the items we buy, the people we know, the cars we drive, the places we work or the brand of clothes we wear. Synthetically calming our emotions and ignoring rest signals creates strain and dysregulates the brain. BEEPS replace the natural ebb and flow families rely on to keep interactions manageable and meaningful.

According to Dr. Allan Schore, respected researcher in neuropsychology from UCLA, the inability to down-regulate emotions to rest and up-regulate positive emotions to joy lead to the largest risk of developing a mental illness in a lifetime. How well can I calm down? How well do I start and share joy? These two ingredients alone make up a large factor of what our mental health looks like as we age. A myriad of personality and behavioral disorders - from depression,

---

40 http://qz.com/619035/a-new-study-says-half-of-us-students-could-be-internet-addicts/

41 See JIMTalks Volume 30 by Dr. Jim Wilder for more on this concept.

anxiety, attention deficit/hyperactivity disorder, phobias, addictions, sleep problems and more - can spring up when we have not learned to use the brakes or properly press the accelerator of our nervous systems. At the end of the day we must learn to regulate and quiet what we feel. We recognize some work is needed for Skill 2 when we fear slowing down, resist rest states, frequently feel bored or surrender to an urge to disconnect in non-relational ways.

How Skill 2 Is Normally Acquired, Practiced And Propagated

Like all of the nineteen skills, Skill 2 is relationally transmitted, and the learning process starts with our families. From the moment we are born, quiet together moments with mom will calm, soothe and form a lasting bond. We feel safe and secure when Skill 2 is used. When we have Skill 2, we can't help but use it because it has now become a crucial ingredient in the fabric of our character. We crave quiet moments and feel "off" when we haven't rested. Our example shows others how to quiet and calm down, and people who lack Skill 2 feel drawn, even inspired by our ability to stay peaceful and "grounded" during intense emotions and overwhelm. We remember to breathe, and over time we look for opportunities to spread Skill 2 to the people we notice are "running high" and lacking peace. We invite them to take a break, catch their breath and rest.

How Skill 2 Is Remedially Acquired, Practiced And Propagated

Let's examine how transforming fellowship/koinonia can restore the missing *Soothe Myself* skill. Families and communities who rest together create safety and bring refreshment to all members. God so values rest that He rests at the end of the creation narrative early in Genesis as an example for us to follow. Scripture tells us about this "pause" in activity,

> "It will be a sign between me and the Israelites forever, for in six days the Lord made the heavens and the earth, and on the seventh day he abstained from work and rested" (Exodus 31:17, NIV).

I like the New King James Version where it says at the end of verse 17, "He rested and was refreshed." The Sabbath rest is a sign God's people are to wear, much like a wedding ring, to show we are set apart. Rest itself should not feel like work rather rest refreshes and restores us. Honoring the Sabbath rest is one of the most mentioned commandments in all of Scripture and it is also number four of the Ten Commandments where God requires people and animals to rest one day each week.[42]

God not only wants His people to rest, He commanded His people to give the land rest one out of every seven years and during the year of Jubilee year the land must rest two years.[43] Remarkably, God provides for His people when they honor Him with rest by giving an increase in provision on the sixth day before the Sabbath and the sixth year before the land rests. For good measure God throws in a blessing of protection for observance,

> "Then the land will yield its fruit, and you will eat your fill and live there in safety" (Leviticus 25:19, NIV).

How can God make it any easier for His children to rest? We know that giving the land a year off restores vital nutrients and minerals in the soil and similarly, rest restores our relational capacity to persevere.

In addition to the gift of rest we have in the Sabbath, we see the importance of rest in the life of the bold prophet Elijah who, at one point, becomes intensely afraid of the wicked queen Jezebel who threatens his life. The prophet flees and, after much running, sits down under a broom tree, prays for his death and collapses. Now this is some serious fear! An angel wakes the prophet from his nap where he drinks and eats before falling asleep once again. The angel wakes Elijah a second time saying, "Get up and eat, for the journey is too much for you" (1 Kings 19:7b, NIV). Eventually God meets with Elijah and shows the prophet he is not alone. Rest is the reminder that the journey is too much for us and we have limitations that require us to pause from interacting. Rest means, "I need a breather." Fellowship should always lead to refreshing pauses and moments to rest while we stay in relationship.

42 Exodus 20, Deuteronomy 5. Note, this is the third commandment in Roman Catholicism and Lutheranism.

43 Jubilee comes every fifty years so the land rests on the 49th and 50th year. Leviticus 25:8+.

When we haven't learned Skill 2 we need to spend time with people who are good at quieting and resting. We may recognize these individuals as people who are "content" and "at peace" with themselves and the world around them. Their example helps, but we need some good old fashion personal practice. We may be pleasantly surprised to discover that rest and quiet feel enjoyable, even restorative. Small steps of quieting create a positive change that extends into our relationships.

With a friend we can practice quieting for short periods of time by breathing deeply from our belly. This type of breathing allows the diaphragm muscle in the lower ribs to expand so that our deep breaths allow more oxygen to enter our bloodstream thus going to our brain, which calms us down. We then discuss what we notice after taking small moments of quiet. Over time we increase the length of our quiet practice and notice Skill 2 begins to replace previously learned behaviors that were counterfeiting a genuine need for rest. Racing thoughts start to slow down, impulsive responses are managed and cravings are tamed. To varying degrees, relaxation techniques, silent retreats, the sabbath and mindfulness exercises are some of the ways culture embraces Skill 2. At *THRIVE Training* Skill 2 exercises are woven throughout each day where we practice calming our minds and our bodies.

Quiet and rest is a gift we give other people. As we demonstrate this skill we become better equipped at recognizing the need for rest. We allow others the freedom to rest with a break in eye contact, a breather during moments of overwhelm or a time-out when tension levels increase. Sometimes we have to plan rest into our busy lives and when we do, rest is one of the most productive skills we can practice at home, school, church and work. Research shows that rest increases worker productivity and efficiency. One Cornell University study, for example, showed that workers receiving alerts for a break were 13% more accurate in their work than coworkers who were not reminded to take breaks.[44] The highest work performers are those who rest and take breaks rather than push themselves harder. Moments of rest

---

44 www.news.cornell.edu/stories/1999/09/onscreen-break-reminder-boosts-productivity

and quiet anchor us on our hectic days and help us stay efficient and productive.

Skill 2 - Action Step

Set a timer for 3 minutes. Make yourself comfortable then stay silent and breathe deeply from your belly. Notice how your body feels when you finish. Try this exercise throughout your day and keep a record of your observations.

Skill 2 - Next Step

You can introduce Skill 2 into your life by making the time to practice as well as trying moments of quiet with other people who are of the same mind and willing to take moments of rest with you. The exercises in *Joy Starts Here: The Transformation Zone* will help as you practice with a few friends. Take the online JOYQ Assessment and measure your progress. Watch the *THRIVE Lectures* and participate in the *THRIVE-at-Home* online curriculum to take your theory and application to a new level.

If you are married, attend a *Joy Rekindled* marriage retreat or use the *30 Days of Joy for Busy Married Couples* exercise book which includes quieting steps throughout. Learn more about this and other Life Model topics by listening to the *Jesus In Mind: Talks on Kingdom Life* audio lessons. If you are serious about learning to rest and quiet, attend *THRIVE Training*. The three *THRIVE 52-week Skill Guides* will give you practice. The skill guides are *Mastering Joy and Rest*, *Mastering Returning to Joy* and *Mastering Applied Strategy*. Don't keep the good stuff for yourself; bring the *Connexus* program to your church and community. Learn more at joystartshere.com.

Conclusion

Similar to Skill 1, Skill 2 is the result of a chesed community where members value rest and encourage quieting as needed. We feel safe with people who use Skill 2 and recognize these individuals as "content," "peaceful," "non-anxious" and "refreshing." We feel drawn to those who use Skill 2, and chesed communities are formed when people are good at calming, quieting and breathing. Koinonia, our relational pocket of pooled resources, provides the examples and opportunities to help every member of the community to use, strengthen and repair Skill 2. Much like the wild, demon-possessed Gerasene cave-dweller who could not be restrained or contained, once Jesus healed him, the man was clothed and sitting in his right mind, to the surprise of people who knew him.[45] Peace, contentment and rest are all signs of a Skill 2 makeover; therefore, transformations always include and lead to Skill 2. One sign of resolved trauma is the ability to rest. As we see in the Application Step in a moment, transformations occur when Skill 2 is learned and used.

When I have Skill 2: I value rest and frequently take time each day to quiet and calm myself. I notice when I need to take a breather.

When Skill 2 is missing or underdeveloped: I stay busy and distract myself with games, gadgets, television, books and pretty much anything that keeps my mind busy.

45 Mark 5:1-20

Skill 2 Application Step - *Jen's Jumpiness*

When I first met my wife Jen she was on Federal Disability for depression and anxiety. Years, even months earlier, Jen had been a straight-A student who excelled in most areas of life. However, Jen eventually crashed and bottomed-out to the point she could no longer function, much less hold down a job. Jen will be the first to say that she lacked the 19 skills, but Skill 2 in particular was the missing key to her overall health and well being.

I remember one day Jen told me that it was a good day if she could get out of bed. To help Jen get back on her feet, some friends and I encouraged her to slowly start to practice Skill 2 in small increments of time: 30 seconds here, 30 seconds there. We sat with her in silence and soon we moved up to 45-second intervals, but even this small amount of time was difficult because her mind would not stop racing. Skill 2 became a part of Jen's daily regimen of things to do, and soon she started to notice a significant difference in her outlook on life with an increase in her emotional capacity and a renewed ability to function. I even started to see Jen smile!

I am glad that I am now not only her friend but her husband, and I am proud to say Jen is now a thriving young mother who is raising our sons to be secure and stable in the 19 skills. Jen helps them rest when they are tired and shows them how to recover when they are upset. Most of our friends cannot believe Jen was once so depressed and anxious that functioning felt impossible. She is my hero!

Chapter Five

Brain Skill 3 - Form Bonds for Two

Synchronize Attachments:
When we can share a mutual state of mind that brings us closer and lets us move independently as well.
We are both satisfied.

After taking a moment to ask God, "Why does this skill matter to You?" I found myself thinking,

> "I interact with My children in a language they will understand. I meet with My children in a way they can handle. Human relationships are a template for how I meet with My people. Bonds for Two is the beginning of relational life for mankind, and I designed it to be the start of something good, intimate and joyful. This is My gift, and it only grows and increases with time."

Skill 3 is the bond we share with one other person. When Skill 3 is successful we develop an inner security that shows up as an abiding confidence where we engage the world with expectation and curiosity. From the moment we are born, our bond with mom becomes the primary playing field to learn brain skills, especially Skills 1 and 2. In an ideal world mom is glad to be with us, which is expressed by her attuned engagement to our needs as she feeds us and regulates our temperature. We become bonded with her smell, presence, touch, voice, face and responsiveness to our ever-changing needs. Mom builds up our joy, then, with her comforting presence she calms us down so we can rest. With a mother's consistency and predictability, joy and rest will become our natural state. Here the world feels like a safe place.

In addition to the primary bond with mom, Skill 3 in general refers to the delightful, interactive dance between two people who share and respect each others signals and limitations. Expressions, feelings, thoughts and words move rhythmically between two people so both understand the thoughts and intentions of the other. Skill 3 looks like a lively game of Ping Pong or tennis where one player serves the ball over the net. In a flash the receiver returns the serve. If skillful, the two players volley until someone stops. Both parties momentarily catch their breath then start all over again. The fun continues within the range of expertise and abilities the two players possess. While a sports match focuses on winning, Skill 3 aims to keep the relational volley between two people safe and manageable. The more experienced of the two will work hard to respect the other (ideally the younger) person's limitations and abilities so that both feel protected and connected.

Skill 3 is the reciprocal sharing between two people that dynamically forms a mutual mind state. We are on the same page. This brain to brain coupling creates a cohesive mutual mind where we feel seen, valued and understood. Our emotional brains are connected. It feels as though you are the source of my joy. In reality ***we are the reason for our joy.*** When properly synched and executed early in life, the combination of shared thoughts, feelings and expressions provide lasting love and security. Our bond grows deeper with each new cycle of joy and rest. Skill 3, the bond between two people, provides us with the ideal foundation to fast-track the 19 brain skills.

In some ways we have forgotten or even lost the skills to start and sustain relationships. When relational skills disintegrate we no longer form lasting joyful, predictable bonds that mold our character and fashion our identity. As far as the brain is concerned, we are the sum of our relationships. This may be good or bad news depending on our personal library of faces and interactions. When relationships are a source of joy and stability we enter each new relationship with a foundation of wisdom and confidence. When relationships have been toxic we expect the worst out of people.

The failure to form a loving, secure bond with the people who raise us results in deep-seated pain that spreads into each new relationship we encounter. Isolation, abandonment, rejection and BEEPS hijack our reality instead of peace, security and joy. We can become better at preying than protecting, hurting than helping and killing than saving. At the least we become self-focused instead of people-focused. We want to win at whatever the cost rather than enjoy the game and play with integrity. This failure can lead to grudges, fear, resentment, disconnectedness and self-centeredness that painfully alter the landscape of our decisions and values. Skill 3 is an underestimated brain skill because when we have it we don't have to wear masks to pretend or placate. We become resilient, resourceful, playful and creative. Skill 3 prepares us for an adventure in a world filled with people.

A Father's Voice

From the onset of life, Skill 3 glues us to the person who loves, feeds, comforts, and protects us. In the womb baby knows mommy's voice, and research shows that baby can not only hear mom as early as the 16th week of pregnancy[46] but understands and learns language from her during the last 10 weeks of pregnancy.[47] Mother's voice is amplified, so baby bonds with mommy's voice. While many sounds can be heard inside of mommy's tummy, from her heartbeat to blood and water swooshing around, baby can hear and become acquainted with external sounds as well. This reminds me of the time Jen was pregnant with our oldest son. Early in the pregnancy I decided to take a few minutes each day to read, talk and pray over the developing baby inside my wife's belly. Each night I would read Psalms, pray

46 Association for Prenatal and Perinatal Psychology and Health
47 http://www.webmd.com/baby/news/20130102/babies-learn-womb

for his health or simply talk with him. Yes, it was awkward talking to my wife's belly in the beginning of this process, but I got over it.

When my son was born he was quickly placed on my wife's chest to feed and rest with the soothing sound of her heartbeat. After some time the medical staff wanted to measure and weigh the baby, so they took him to the other side of the room, away from his mother. He decided this was a bad idea and immediately started screaming and crying. Intuitively, I walked over to comfort my son and tell him he was not alone. I bent down to his ear and spoke to him in a soft voice. "It's ok, buddy; Daddy's here!"

In an instant his screaming stopped. My son quickly turned his head toward me then quieted down. The sudden reaction surprised the nurse who mentioned she had never before seen such a quick response. "What did you just do?" she asked. Initially, I was surprised as well until I remembered the moments each day where I would read, talk and pray over my son. I told the nurse my routine, and she was astonished. It should be no surprise that a child knows his mother and father's voice as Jesus talked about the sheep knowing the Shepherd's voice.[48] While this moment was meaningful for me, my son was much more interested in bonding with his primary attachment and lifeline, Mommy. Over time I would play more of a role in the bonding process when it was time for Skill 5, *Family Bonds.*

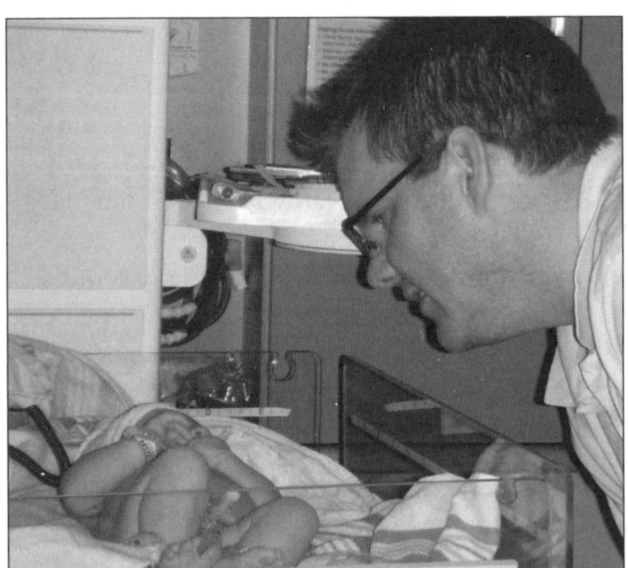

My mother-in-law took this picture of the moment I interacted with my son and he stopped screaming.

48 John 10:1-18

This biological foundation for a strong bond forms our identity, trains our brain and lays the framework for our view of the world. Problems that develop with Skill 3 can lead to a devastating shift in how we relate to other people. Because our personal reality as we know it is created by the people we are glued to, our deepest pain and greatest joys occur in loving, secure bonds. We are driven to connect, then reconnect. As we will explore later in Skills 17 and 18, the absence of a predictable, consistent connection creates some of the worst pain a person knows. We are built for human interaction that is anchored in joy.

The mutual exchange of verbal and nonverbal communication sheds light into the hidden recesses of our minds and identities. Interpreting visual cues is a skill that develops with Skill 3 and takes practice and time. The power of a look, glance, smile and frown makes all the difference between love at first sight, a first impression, a vote, a successful business meeting, even the health of a marriage. We do not easily forget the joy of an embrace or the sting of a loss.

Speaking of loss, we must exercise caution when it comes to using Skill 3, *Form Bonds for Two*. When we bond with another person our brain creates couple bonds. The risk of bonds turning sexual increases when we build joy with one other person, particularly members of the opposite sex.[49] Our bonding circuits are located near the sexual circuits in our brain, and when two people become one for life this is a great plan. However, because bonds create and change our reality, we must exercise caution when building joy with one other person because two-way bonds can be the source of affairs and relational shipwrecks. It is for this reason Skill 5, *Family Bonds*, provides the safest route to train communities, which is what the *Connexus* curriculum accomplishes for groups. Bonding with other people in strong emotions can bring up a variety of unexpected feelings in particular with people who have used sex to mask the pain of loss.[50]

The good news about Skill 3 is this: training with a bonded partner is the fastest way to learn and strengthen brain skills which is

49 In many cases affairs can involve sexual promiscuity with members of the same sex as well by people who profess no same sex attraction.

50 Learn more in Dr. Jim Wilder's book, *The Complete Guide to Living with Men*.

why attendees bring a person they already know to *THRIVE Training* such as a spouse, friend or prayer partner. Redemption is one joyful relationship away. Skill 3 is the canvas where we begin to develop emotional and relational intelligence. Attunement, recovery and face-to-face interaction with a primary caregiver forms the beautiful tapestry that builds our character, heals our wounds and propels our growth. While Skill 5, *Family Bonds*, will take our skills and growth to an entirely new level, it is important to note that the foundation established with Skill 3 anchors and sustains us throughout life.

How Skill 3 Is Normally Acquired, Practiced And Propagated

As mentioned above, the ideal for Skill 3 development happens in our natural families as baby bonds with mother. Once the bond is secure and strong, baby learns the world is a safe place and feels free to explore daddy; then, later in life, this security transitions to groups. Because of Skill 3 we feel confident interacting and building a group identity (Skill 5) after puberty. Here is the starting line to build strong bonds and establish deep friendships with meaningful connections. Once in place, we use Skill 3 as the bridge to introduce people to our families and communities using Skill 5.

How Skill 3 Is Remedially Acquired, Practiced And Propagated

Let's examine how transforming fellowship/koinonia can restore the missing *Form Bonds for Two* skill. The apostle Paul not only tirelessly traveled on his missionary journeys teaching, preaching and planting churches, he invested in and mentored individuals. Paul spent much time discipling Timothy and others in order to "duplicate himself" and on several occasions Paul tells the Corinthians to "imitate" him (1 Corinthians 4:16) and, "Follow my example, as I follow the example of Christ." (1 Corinthians 11:1) Paul understood the value of investing in others and using his example to further his message. Paul writes one of his spiritual sons named Titus and tells him,

> "Likewise, teach the older women to be reverent in the way they live, not to be slanderers or addicted to much wine, but to teach what is good. Then they can train the younger women to love their husbands and children…" (Titus 2:3-4, NIV).

Paul knew the value of Skill 3 as he taught people to invest in one another, specifically men to invest in young men and women to invest in young women. Here, the intersection of mentoring and discipleship meets Skill 3 in a one-on-one bonded relationship. Healing and growth happen in the framework of a healthy bonded relationship however; sometimes our ability to bond with another person is greatly diminished. When our bonds are insecure, we require a combination of a chesed environment, Skill 1, Skill 2, and Immanuel healing where God brings peace to the areas of our life where peace is missing and repairs cracks in our relational foundations. We strengthen Skill 3 when we get married, and build friendships with our peers. Except for couple or sibling bonds Skill 3 should lead to Skill 5, *Family Bonds*, as we express God's hospitality and welcome friends into our corporate group identity.

THRIVE Training started by using Skill 3 to train new skills. The primary requirement was for attendees to bring a spouse or a friend who is a same-sex, bonded partner they trusted and enjoyed. Rather than create new bonds, the exercises at *THRIVE Training* were designed to transform *existing* bonds using deliberate interactions in shared states of joy and quiet. Because Skill 3 creates couple bonds, without safety precautions in place, our bonds can be sexualized - especially when our brain has sexualized bonds in the past. It is not uncommon for affairs to start all because someone's face lit up or a sparkle glistened in someone's eye when they were looking at us, because we are especially vulnerable when our joy levels drop. Our secure relationships outside of marriage should naturally lead to shared joy within groups. For Skill 3 to develop to Skill 5 we must replace fear as a motivator with joy and love.

Skill 3 - Action Step

This step has two parts. First, in order to develop a general sense for how well Skill 3 was established in your life, think about the three options below then identify which one feels consistently true.

- I frequently feel comfortable giving and receiving. My general view of the world is one where I feel safe and secure. I have little difficulty expressing my needs and wants to my spouse or friends.

- I frequently feel like other people are too needy. My spouse or friends want me to be more expressive than I feel comfortable with. I find it difficult to depend on other people.
- I frequently feel like close friends do not initiate and reach out to me as much as I do to them. When my spouse or friends are away I fear they will find someone else who is more interesting than me.

Next, consider how well you stay engaged and feel like you have something to contribute when you are with a group of friends or coworkers. Do you enjoy the collaboration and wish more people could join the fun, or do you feel overwhelmed and wish you could be alone?

We will explore more about this foundation with Skills 5, *Family Bonds* and Skill 17, *Attachment Styles.*

Skill 3 - Next Step

One of the easiest ways to strengthen Skill 3 is to bring a friend to the intensive 5-day *THRIVE Training* where you practice 19 relational skills.[51] The *THRIVE Skill Guides* include preparation exercises to attend *THRIVE Training* and to maintain your joy momentum. Both resources provide exposure and practice using Skill 3. Take the JOYQ Assessment to measure your progress as you train the skills with your partner.

Watch the *THRIVE Lectures* and participate in the *THRIVE-at-Home* online curriculum. If you are married, attend a *Joy Rekindled* marriage retreat or use the *30 Days of Joy for Busy Married Couples* exercise book which includes additional interactive exercises for you and your spouse.

Conclusion

Skill 3 properly develops when we are planted in the garden of a chesed family and community where we grow joy through consistent and predictable interactions free from fear. The fruit of Skill 3 should

51 Tracks 1, 2 and 3 are designed for bonded pairs while *THRIVE: True Identity* is free from the bonded partner requirement.

be the development of Skill 5, *Family Bonds* with the formation of a group identity in a chesed community fueled by koinonia, the pooling of resources. With Skill 3 our closest relationships are characterized by joyful connection with the freedom to rest as needed. This reality is best summarized by a follower of Jesus who said, "There is no fear in love. But perfect love drives out fear, because fear has to do with punishment. The one who fears is not made perfect in love."[52]

When I have Skill 3: I feel comfortable and confident in my relationships with people. Others say I am easy to interact with and approachable. I do not create a lot of drama in my relationships.

When Skill 3 is missing or underdeveloped: I feel alone most of the time. I usually avoid people and I find people are irritants in my life. Fear and pain keeps me guarded from family and friends. My comfort zone is rigid and my feelings dominate my interactions with people.

Skill 3 Application Step - *Lisa's Loneliness*

Lisa frequently felt lost trying to connect with people. While she preferred to spend time alone she had a few friends she could connect with for fun or for prayer. When out with one of them she would inevitably feel alone and anxious. Lisa felt lost and didn't know why.

After learning about Skill 3 from one of her friends, Lisa recognized some of her difficulties bonding with people. After some prayer Lisa realized her relationship with her mother was not anchored in joy which set her up for some low-joy problems later in life. Lisa felt hopeful discovering she was not "broken" because here was something she could work on. Lisa started attending a women's group where people were trying to practice joy exercises together. While it was intimidating at first, over time she noticed more peace and joy. It would not be long before Lisa began reaching out for more opportunities to connect with her friends and community.

52 1 John 4:18, NIV

Chapter Six
Brain Skill 4 - Create Appreciation

Healthy minds are full of appreciation:
Appreciation creates belonging and
changes stress to contentment.

After taking a moment to ask God, "Why does this skill matter to You?" I found myself thinking,

"Skill 4 is the expression of My heart to and between My children. Here is another gift that helps My children know and remember Me. Creating appreciation soothes a sick heart and paves the way for My Spirit to bring comfort. Here is the lubricant to keep all the parts of My Body moving in unison with Me."

What are you thankful for today? What makes you smile? Pause for a moment, then reflect on something you appreciate.

What do you notice? Appreciation is packaged joy. This joy package is a gift we can share any time, any place, with any person we encounter. Puppies, babies, sunsets, ocean breezes, colorful autumn leaves, a warm bath, a compliment, an unexpected surprise, a hug, a kind gesture and special memories with loved ones give us reason to be thankful. Gratitude and appreciation go hand in hand. While enjoying special memories-in-the-making, we store, remember and share these moments for an even bigger boost of joy. In this way appreciation gives birth to joy that spreads to the people we encounter on a daily basis.

Appreciation is not rocket science; we can create appreciation with a simple compliment, "You look nice today!" We generate gratitude with, "I appreciate your service - thank you." This short but meaningful gesture can change the course of a bad day and bring a warm smile to sad faces and broken hearts.

When shared, appreciation activates our brain's relational circuits, resettles our nervous system and releases a cocktail of bonding hormones so we feel connected and peaceful. We are in our best form when Skill 4 permeates our interactions. The student of scripture will discover frequent reminders to remember, appreciate, enjoy and meditate on the good stuff. "Be thankful" in both good times and bad. An increasing amount of research tells us appreciation is a game-changer for life and relationships.

Gratitude boosts dopamine levels, which makes social interactions more enjoyable, and thinking of things you are thankful for boosts serotonin production in Level 3 of the control center, the anterior cortex.[53] When we use Skill 4 in our relationships, we train our brain to remember to look for things we are thankful for, and this is not only a sign of relational intelligence but it increases neuron density in one of the most complex regions of our brain, Level 4 of the control center.[54]

Skill 4 Before Bed

Years ago my wife Jen struggled to wind down after a busy day, so falling asleep proved to be a challenge. Her mind raced and raced. Because I am a light sleeper, guess what this meant for my sleep? So, partly out of concern and partly out of selfish ambition, we created

53 *The Upward Spiral* by Alex Korb, Ph.D. March 2015.

54 The brain regions are the Ventromedial and Lateral Prefrontal Cortex mentioned in *The Upward Spiral* by Alex Korb, Ph.D. March 2015.

the following exercise with the hope it would alleviate some sleep deprivation. Once snuggled in bed we would try the following steps for the exercise we called *3x3x3* or, *Three, Three and Three*. First, identify three things from your day that you feel thankful for. Give examples and take turns sharing. An example looks like this, "I am grateful for the opportunity to walk this evening. It was good to get outside and move around. I felt refreshed. What a beautiful evening it was!" Follow with two more examples from the day.

Next, identify three qualities you appreciate about the other person. Give examples from the day and take turns sharing. An example looks like this, "I appreciate your hospitality this afternoon when our friend stopped by. You were quick to offer her a drink and you checked to be sure she was comfortable. You work hard to help our visitors feel welcome in our home. I like this about you!" Follow with two more qualities and reasons for these examples. If you are single, improvise with a friend or use your journal to write about someone you know. You can read it to your pal later for an extra boost of Skill 4 goodness.

Last, name three qualities about God you feel thankful for. Give examples from the day and take turns sharing. An example looks like this, "I am grateful for the ways God cares for us. We have food at our table and I can look back on my life and see how God has led us here." Follow this up with two more qualities about God you enjoy.

By the second step of the exercise I consistently feel Jen's breathing slow down and her body relax. Once we finish the exercise Jen falls fast asleep within ten minutes - at the most. Jen sleeps better. I sleep better. The exercise is a win/win for both of us and it only takes about ten minutes to complete. I am struck by the simplicity of the exercise, but I feel grateful for the results! On the nights we skip the exercise Jen can toss and turn for 2-3 hours. With Skill 4 we feel better, lighter, calmer and safer.

We know Skill 4 is at work when laughter fills the air and people wear genuine smiles and hug. Yes, even hugs release chemicals such as oxytocin that reduce pain, reduce stress hormones and reduce reactivity of the brain's guard shack at Level 2 of the control center, known as the amygdala. This is the center for the fight/flight/freeze response. Oxytocin makes us feel peaceful, generous, calm and connected. This is why Jen and I will cuddle when we practice the appreciation exercise.

Dr. Jim Wilder further emphasizes the importance of Skill 4 saying that if we practice feeling appreciation for five or more minutes three times a day, any time of the day, our brain will reset normal to appreciation.[55] Can you imagine your "go to" state as appreciation instead of anxiety, anger, despair or some other negative emotion? As parents, Jen and I use this information to generate appreciation in our household. One of the ways we do this involves mealtimes. With my 93 year-old grandmother and our six and four year-old sons, we all take turns reflecting on special moments from our day. Watching joy and peace reduce and replace stress is incredible!

Skill 4 helps us feel seen and valued *as though we belong*. In fact, belonging can be created by a simple compliment. Unfortunately, for many of us, appreciation does not fit with our learned responses. It is all too easy to think about and expect pain, distrust, anger, resentment and bitterness instead of joy. We expect the worst, and this scratched lens filters our views and guides our behaviors. We become critical. Instead of being tender toward weakness we criticize the people around us. Because the brain uses the past to predict the future, the painful absence of Skill 4 increases rejection, depression, overwhelm and despair. We all know someone who is grumpy, bitter and unforgiving. The poor brain that lacks Skill 4 will focus on pain, problems, and the past instead of expecting good things. When this happens, negative emotions can define their personality. Thankfully, appreciation rewires the brain and restores vision for the downtrodden soul so we can go out today and give a hug, extend a compliment and find something good to remember and share. Neurons that fire together wire together, and how often you do something sets the tone for what your brain expects. Appreciation resets the thermostat for your nervous system.

Another unfortunate by-product when Skill 4 is missing is entitlement and pessimism. Instead of "I like this about you." we think to ourselves, "I want that!" or "She looks ugly in that dress." The glass is

---

55 *RARE Leadership: 4 Uncommon Habits for Increasing Trust, Joy and Engagement in the People You Lead* by Dr. Marcus Warner and Dr. E. James Wilder.

half-empty and we expect negative outcomes. Skill 4, therefore, brings people together. The presence of Skill 4 is a direct reflection of what a healthy and stable marriage, family and community looks like. Successful leaders start and end their day with appreciation while strong marriages are built on a foundation of appreciation. When appreciation levels run low a wellspring of bitterness starts to spill out which, as you can imagine, becomes toxic for any relationship - especially a marriage.

As with any sport or musical instrument, exposure and practice trains the body and brain. The more we play an instrument, the better we become. If we did not grow up playing a sport or an instrument, it may feel awkward and challenging to learn something new. Thankfully, the brain has a novelty detector, and learning something new is a good brain exercise. Your brain says, "Pay attention!" Learning something new changes your brain, and when we spend time with people who use Skill 4 we catch a glimpse of what appreciation looks and feels like. We enjoy interacting with individuals and groups who are well-versed in appreciation skills. Just think about someone who frequently expresses appreciation and someone who tends to be negative and critical. Which example would you prefer? With practice, appreciation becomes effortless.

Now, back to learning something new. Thanks to dopamine, learning something new builds memories, strengthens long-term memories and helps us grow closer with people.[56] In order to become a usable brain skill, appreciation must be practiced, enjoyed and shared on a daily basis. Thankfully, we can use appreciation any time we like, and it's free! Skill 4 keeps us focused on what is important when it comes to problems and people because it keeps the relational centers of our brain engaged. When we feel offline and overwhelmed we restore appreciation when we ask, "What am I thankful for today?" then spend three to five minutes feeling appreciation in our body and mind.
We can start and end our day with appreciation and quickly notice more energy and a positive outlook on life along with an increase in stamina.

---

56 *Scientific American Mind*, Learning by Surprise by Daniela Fenker and Hartmut Schutze. Dec. 2008/Jan. 2009.

How Skill 4 Is Normally Acquired, Practiced And Propagated

Because healthy marriages use Skill 4, we learn how to create appreciation by watching mom and dad use it as a normal part of their interactions. Parents coach children how to use Skill 4 much like teaching children to say "Thank You" at the right times. Parents demonstrate how to reflect on special moments and share stories about what they appreciate. A trained brain looks for opportunities to be thankful; therefore, every interaction becomes the chance to creatively practice Skill 4.

When learned, we highlight the people and moments we are thankful for with our friends, family members and even strangers. Research shows a "feedback loop" exists when marriage partners use gratitude with one another.[57] This means Skill 4 motivates partners to use it both to meet a need and to influence behaviors, perceptions and feelings. In this way Skill 4 becomes a trained habit partners rely on during interactions. People who learn Skill 4 can't help but spread it to children, friends, neighbors and others outside the home.

How Skill 4 Is Remedially Acquired, Practiced And Propagated

Let's examine how transforming fellowship/koinonia can restore the missing *Create Appreciation* skill. Skill 4 is a thread woven through both the Old and the New Testament books of the Bible. We find an insightful passage in Colossians that captures the significance Skill 4 has for the health and well-being of our chesed communities:

> "Let the peace of Christ rule in your hearts, since as members of one body you were called to peace. And be thankful. Let the word of Christ dwell in you richly as you teach and admonish one another with all wisdom, and as you sing psalms, hymns and spiritual songs with gratitude in your hearts to God. And whatever you do, whether in word or deed, do it all in the name of the Lord Jesus, giving thanks to God the Father through him" (Colossians 3:15-17, NIV).

---

57 http://www.bakadesuyo.com/2011/10/is-there-a-way-to-create-a-positive-feedback-98910/

It is important to notice God's people are called to peace, "Shalom", and a fundamental ingredient to peace is gratitude, giving thanks.[58] We see peace and thanksgiving connected in the offerings of the Old Testament, especially the fellowship offerings of thanksgiving mentioned in Leviticus 7. The sacrifice of thanksgiving is a peace offering, a "Shalem" which is the only sacrifice where the offerer is allowed to keep and eat the meat himself, and it was never used for sin or atonement. Through this offering the offerer is allowed to eat from God's table and have fellowship with God. Giving thanks is a core expression of God's people who are thankful for God's provision and presence. Paul tells us we should use Skill 4 all the time,

> "Rejoice always, pray continually, give thanks in all circumstances; for this is God's will for you in Christ Jesus" (1 Thessalonians 5:16-18, NIV).

When we weren't taught Skill 4 as children we must retrain our brain with some focused effort. Trying to learn Skill 4 can feel difficult at first because our brain wants to do what it has always done, which is focus on pain, problems, distractions, to-do lists and more. Thinking of appreciation moments and feeling appreciation requires practice. Most people can find something to be thankful for, but feeling appreciation requires some more practice. Thankfully, the hard work pays off. Not only do we enjoy the benefits of practicing Skill 4, but the mere fact we remember to look in the first place makes the entire process easier over time because a trained brain uses less effort and less energy to be grateful.[59] Keeping journals, telling friends and including Skill 4 in our prayer life are practical ways to acquire and practice Skill 4.

Both *THRIVE Training* and *Connexus* utilize Skill 4, and our chesed communities are filled with Skill 4 resources from the pockets of koinonia where we see, hear and experience Skill 4 during meals, in conversations and with reflection times. Once learned, we become messengers of Skill 4 into the world as we ask people, "What good

---

58 The *Passing the Peace* book by Life Model Works goes into great detail on the importance of Skill 4 for healing after a crisis.

59 http://motto.time.com/4225493/neuroscience-happy-rituals/

things are you thankful for today?" and we find qualities we can appreciate in others as well. The more we practice the better Skill 4 takes root in our character so we enjoy Skill 4 on our own with Jesus and, like a good meal, we enjoy it as we share it with people we encounter on a daily basis. There will be no shortage of opportunities.

Skill 4 - Action Step

Who or what are you thankful for at this very moment? Tell someone.

Tonight practice the 3x3x3 exercise with your spouse, a friend, Jesus or a journal. Notice how your body feels after the exercise. Try to practice five minutes of appreciation a day for thirty days and journal your observations.

What I feel thankful for right now:

Skill 4 - Next Step

Skill 4 is woven throughout all the Life Model Works resources. Start a small group study with *Joy Starts Here: The Transformation Zone One* or participate in the exercises from the book *Joyful Journey* to practice Skill 4 with Immanuel. This practice will change you!

Measure your joy levels with the JOYQ online assessment, learn about Skill 4 with the *Jesus In Mind* talks, practice Skill 4 with your spouse by attending a *Joy Rekindled* marriage retreat or use the *30 Days of Joy for Busy Married Couples* exercise book which includes additional Skill 4 exercises. Watch the *THRIVE Lectures* and participate in the *THRIVE-at-Home* online curriculum for more Skill 4 exposure.

Attend *THRIVE: True Identity* on your own or bring a friend to the intensive five-day *THRIVE Training* where Skill 4 is heavily used as well as in each of the *THRIVE Skill Guides*. Make Skill 4 a part of how your community works with the breakthrough *Connexus* curriculum. Learn more at joystartshere.com.

Conclusion

One of the tests for a chesed community is whether Skill 4 is present in conversations and felt during interactions. Skill 4 is the thread that is woven through chesed communities and is a natural part of prayer and worship. People who are not accustomed to using Skill 4 find a wealth of examples in a koinonia pool of resources and, at the end of the day, Skill 4 is the by-product of deep transformations because, simply, there is so much to be grateful for when our lives have been changed. In this way evangelism is the result of joyful transformation. We proclaim our gratitude from the rooftops when we experience sustainable transformation but we also find Skill 4 provides the bandwidth for healing. Skill 4 increases emotional capacity so it both leads to transformation and is the fruit of individual and corporate transformation. We have more to work with and more joy means an increase in our ability to process pain and better manage what we feel.

When I have Skill 4: I frequently find things to enjoy and appreciate.

When Skill 4 is missing or underdeveloped: I frequently find things that are wrong. I can be critical of myself and other people.

Skill 4 Application Step - *Bobby's Bad Mood*

Bobby spent much of his time at work isolated, frequently sitting alone at his desk. All around him people busily and joyfully interacted with each other, but they did not include him. Without realizing it, Bobby's body language was pushing people away. He often appeared defensive and frustrated. He slammed doors and gave dirty looks to people who were standing around talking. His coworkers sensed something was wrong, and they respected his nonverbal signals that screamed, "Leave me alone! Quit talking! Get out of here!" People gave him space.

One day Bobby turned to a coworker and asked, "Why doesn't anyone talk to me? Everyone seems to interact, but they ignore me. What did I do wrong?" The coworker replied, "Bobby, to be honest, you give signals that tell us you want to be left alone. You slam drawers. You grunt in frustration. You give us dirty looks. Your body language tells us to leave you alone, so we do." Bobby was surprised by his coworker's words, so he decided to practice Skill 4. Bobby began to reach out to his coworkers. "You look nice today, Helen." "Hey Curt, nice job on the project last week!" "Betty, I'm grabbing a cup of coffee. Can I get you one?" Soon Bobby was fully engaged with his coworkers, interacting and building joy. Appreciation provided the opportunity to start some meaningful, heart to heart connections.

Chapter Seven
Brain Skill 5 - Form Family Bonds

Bonds For Three:
Family bonds let us share the joy built
by the people we love.

After taking a moment to ask God, "Why does this skill matter to You?" I then had the image of Jesus carefully watching a young tree grow. He was focused and vigilant. Then, the following thoughts came to mind.

> "I delight watching My children grow. Families are the expression of My character and My love. As there is unity in My Presence, families and groups reflect Me when there is joyful unity among all members. Be perfect as I am perfect."

Family bonds provide the freedom to grow and explore the world. With Skill 5 we discover there is more than enough joy to go around. Thanks to Skill 3, the foundation for this relational house has been established. We are ready for a new surge in joy because the secure bond with our primary caregiver, usually mom, opens the door for dad to join the fun.

As long as the bond with mom is secure, infants readily turn their sights to dad with curiosity and the desire for connection. Babies become most interested in this third face who, up until about six months, has been in the back seat of the infant's focus and needs. There is no greater force than baby's need to bond with mom, so when a foundation is securely established between baby and mom, the infant gravitates toward dad with an expectation that more good stuff is on the way. This transition is successful when mom stays present and joins the fun. Mom's face shines with affirmation and delight while she observes baby and daddy building joy. Baby is keenly aware whether mom is giving permission for this new interaction.

Baby's brain is hard-wired for three-way bonds starting around seven months of life into the second and third year. Loving care from daddy from 12 to 18 months internalizes security for life.[60] As baby feels safe, she longs to be included in this delightful dance of interactive joy. Baby sees herself as an extension of this relationship that is now focused on "us." Family interactions become the playground for learning new skills. This three-strand cord, now securely established, is not easily broken. Skill 5 determines how the developing brain will approach life and relationships from this point on.

Joy increases as our community expands. After 12 years old, children begin their shift into the adult stage of maturity. Now the brain is ready to develop and build a group identity. Children want to be included in their "clan" and "tribe" where they have a place and role in the bigger picture of life. Problems now become "ours" to solve. How well this transition goes will determine the level of joy that is established with peers. New faces feel like an added bonus or, when bonds are insecure, a certain threat. All of us can relate to the pressures felt in school where we must conform and fit into a certain group in order to avoid feeling isolated and rejected. High school is the time we categorize peers according to the groups they spend time with. In my school we had the "Jocks" "Burn-outs" "Goths" and "Nerds." These categories have a negative connotation, but the quality of our Skill 5 foundation determines the comfort level we feel enter-

60 Learn more about this process with Dr. Jim Wilder's book, *The Complete Guide to Living with Men.*

ing and establishing a group that reflects our values. It also impacts the motivations we rely on during our participation in these groups. Groups can run on fear or joy and be life-giving or destructive.

Thankfully, I had enough security with Skill 5 by the time I met my friend James in grade school. James moved to the school well after the year started. By this time friendships are formed, groups are established, lunch room seats are claimed and hallway lockers are filled. It can be hard to be the new kid on the block! I remember James' first day when the teacher gave an introduction then brought James to the front of the class. I watched his face turn red then redder when the teacher asked for a volunteer to share his or her locker with the new guy. You could hear a pin drop as the class fell silent. No one volunteered. Feeling like there was enough joy to go around, I raised my hand and said with a smile, "He can share my locker!" I welcomed James to my established group of friends. This could have been a painful time for James since he left behind friends and familiarity with his previous school. Thankfully, James navigated the transition well as he met new friends and became part of a larger group who welcomed him with open arms. Thirty years later James is still one of my closest friends.

The prerequisite for a joyful, secure Skill 5 is a stable Skill 3. While there is a significant learning curve, we learn from one relationship how to interact and grow into the next. Early life patterns shape how well family bonds will develop. Rejection or belonging will set the tone for our interactions. We practice a number of exercises during *THRIVE Training* where attendees notice the difference between Skill 3 and 5.

Those who struggle with Skill 5 often feel alone at work, church and within group settings. It feels threatening to relate with more than one person at a time. Our comfort zone feels invaded when a new person enters the group. We may be guarded during gatherings and parties. Fear of rejection and anxiety surface when we interact with people. We count down the clock until it's time to leave. Computers, television, books and video games feel safer. Having one friend feels better than two or three so the motto, "Two is company, three is a crowd" fits well with our internal responses. When Skill 5 is missing, I simply do not know who I am in group settings. I feel the need to push, sell, fix, avoid, counsel and convince when my identity has not fully developed with secure family bonds. We are good at giving or receiving but not both in mutually satisfying ways. Who do you know that is always trying to fix someone or frequently feels left out?

Every child requires joyful three-way bonds between a mother and father. Three-way bonds provide the opportunity to express the best of ourselves, correct malfunctions and grow more joy. Where our biological family fails us, spiritual family and chesed community can supplement some of the needs for restoration. Trying to grow family bonds when unprocessed pain and unresolved ruptures hinder us can feel like stepping into a free fall at 15,000 feet. We expect the worst when Skill 5 is underdeveloped. We can grow, nurture and develop a secure attachment with one other person (Skill 3) that provides strength and confidence to explore and strengthen a group bond. We may be delightfully surprised to discover that the addition of people into our network grows rather than drains joy. But, the catch is, we must take the first step to find out.

Healing pain from disrupted bonds is not always easy but it happens when we turn to Immanuel (Skill 13) for guidance and restoration. Processing painful events leads to more joy so we can connect with confidence. We join small groups, churches, sport teams, clubs, and organizations to practice Skill 5. *THRIVE: True Identity* and the *Connexus* curriculum use Skill 5 so communities start joy, create belonging and grow in their relationships with people and with Immanuel, the God who is with us. These avenues become fertile ground to discover new ways to be ourselves in a group setting.

How Skill 5 Is Normally Acquired, Practiced And Propagated

As mentioned previously, Skill 5 forms after a secure Skill 3 is in place with mother. Over time with lots of practice, the infant learns the world is a safe place and explores the bond with daddy. This family bond is strengthened by watching mom and dad build joy, express their love and simply delight in each another. The three-strand chord of mommy, daddy and baby lays the foundation for Skill 5 that will carry the child throughout life especially when it's time to build a group identity starting at adult maturity. At this point, we welcome others into our tribe and our secure, welcoming responses to embrace new people demonstrates what a healthy family looks like.

How Skill 5 Is Remedially Acquired, Practiced And Propagated

Let's examine how transforming fellowship/koinonia can restore the missing *Form Family Bonds* skill. God the Father, Son and Holy Spirit make up the "three-in-oneness" we believers call the Trinity. The Godhead represents three distinct persons but one God in perfect unity. With Skill 5, *Form Family Bonds*, we have a group represented by closely-knit relationships but, unlike the Trinity, we are far from perfect. We function as distinct individuals who make up a unified family, group and community. The tribes in ancient Israel were made up of individuals who formed the larger group that defined their corporate identity.

The early church mentioned in Acts 2 practiced Skill 5 where it says, "All the believers were together and had everything in common" (Verse 44, NIV). Jesus had a mother named Mary and an earthly father named Joseph, He was born of the tribe of Judah and grew up in the small town of Nazareth with siblings and all. It is in a group context where individuals grow and blossom as personal identities shift from focusing on the individual to focusing on the group. Children experience this change starting at the age of 13 with the onset of adult maturity. We go from meeting *my own* needs to meeting *our* needs; at least this is the design.

When Skill 5 is missing or malformed we first recognize our difficulty forming belonging. Fear hinders our ability to securely attach and, to some degree, interact with groups. Skill 5 is dependent upon a stable Skill 3, so after developing safe friendships with peers we turn our sights to inclusion within a group of peers. We find opportunities to join groups that provide fellowship and activities that build joy. Our communities give us the opportunity to become part of something bigger than ourselves.

At *THRIVE Training* we take it a step farther with a number of exercises where pairs practice skills as part of a larger group. Attendees carefully evaluate the changes they notice when new people enter the bond. While many exercises strengthen Skill 3, pairs practice Skill

5 in a variety of ways including when all the training tracks come together after lunch for a group exercise which leads to excitement and group cohesiveness. We notice our reactions and invite Immanuel into areas of resistance or the lack of shalom.

Connexus focuses on Skill 5 throughout all of its curriculum and a profound change takes place after people begin interacting with others in the group. Participants feel connected, valued and excited. Skill 5 propagates as we invite others into our group to share the joy.

Skill 5 - Action Step

Invite two friends to do something fun together. Notice how you feel as you spend time with your friends and share what you are learning about Skill 5 and your journey with the nineteen skills.

Skill 5 - Next Step

Joy Starts Here: The Transformation Zone is a book designed for small groups to practice interactive exercises and Bible Studies along with assessments and discussion questions. Watch the *THRIVE Lectures* and participate in the *THRIVE-at-Home* online curriculum to learn more about Skill 5.

Joy Starts Here lays a foundation you can build on with *Connexus* curriculum for your community to start joy. Learn more about these Skill 5 options at joystartshere.com.

Conclusion

Skill 5, *Form Family Bonds*, is a fundamental skill for chesed communities where individuals belong corporately. Chesed communities demonstrate Skill 5 by extending themselves on behalf of those who lack community. Tender responses to weakness are the rule, the weak and the strong interact and people turn to Immanuel for shalom.

At one point Moses reminded Israel of God's character and how they are to be like God in their treatment to those who lack chesed,

> "He defends the cause of the fatherless and the widow, and loves the alien, giving him food and clothing. And you are to love those who are aliens, for you yourselves were aliens in Egypt" (Deuteronomy 10:18-20, NIV).

Healing and transformations lead to our being anchored in a chesed community where secure love casts out all fear. It is here where we create belonging for ourselves as well as other people.

When I have Skill 5: I easily interact with people whether I know them or not. I am comfortable in groups and I prefer to share joy with other people. Groups are fun for me.

When Skill 5 is missing or underdeveloped: I prefer one friend at a time. I feel left out and disconnected in a group setting.

Skill 5 Application Step - *Tanya's Tension*

Tanya grew up in a tense home where she feared her mother's anger. Mom's anger kept everyone on edge - even the family dog. This painful disconnect left her feeling alone and overwhelmed most of the time. Tanya did not fully understand how to relate to her father who, while physically present, was emotionally absent. As a teenager, Tanya found relationships confusing and unpredictable. As long as she had a good friend to interact with, Tanya felt safe but once other people joined the interaction, Tanya became guarded, jealous and envious. Watching her friend interact with someone else caused Tanya to feel hurt and rejected. Group interactions were anything but fun.

As Tanya began to look at her fear she realized a childhood pattern was emerging and she wanted to change this painful dynamic. With the encouragement of a trusted church friend, Tanya joined a women's group. This step was frightening, but over time Tanya started to learn how rewarding group interactions could be. Joy levels increased with each meeting. Tanya began to make more friends and spend time with other ladies from a number of groups. For the first time in her life Tanya felt hopeful and excited to be part of a group.

Chapter Eight

Brain Skill 6 - Identify Heart Values From Suffering

The Main Pain and Characteristic of Hearts:
Caring deeply can mean hurting deeply, but our deepest hurts hide our greatest treasures.

After taking a moment to ask God, "Why does this skill matter to You?" I found myself thinking,

> "When I design My children I gift them with qualities that reflect Me. These jewels are valuable, bright and shiny. Like any precious jewel, they attract the eyes of both good and evil. While the gifts I give My children come from Me and reflect Me, in this world they also produce pain."

Pain demands our attention. Left unchecked, pain is a thief that steals our most valuable resources. We are designed to avoid pain. The survival circuit deep within the brain's control center tells us in 1/10th of a second if we are to fight, flee or freeze when we feel threatened. The survival circuit is most interested in preserving self - to keep us alive. When pain goes unprocessed we start to hide, mask and run from pain. Unless the relational parts of our brain's emotional control center actively shift this response, we rigidly avoid pain, even when the threat of pain is long gone. Much like an uninvited house guest, pain that is not fully processed stays with us the rest of our lives.

The beauty of Skill 6 is what it conveys: *There is more going on than the pain that I feel.* Pain does not have the final word. Skill 6 provides some meaning and perspective for the distress we feel. We ask, "Why do I hurt like this?" With a little exploration we discover the gold in our identities. We find meaning in our hurts as we begin to see that we were uniquely created with specific heart values. We discover our purpose with the understanding, "There is something good in me that has been touched in a hurtful way. I am more than my pain."

All of us have issues that particularly hurt or bother us - issues that show up throughout life. Looking at these lifelong patterns helps to identify the core values within the DNA of our identity. We hurt the more deeply we care, so is the solution to stop caring? That would work about as well as trying to hold our breath because it hurts to breathe. It doesn't work well in the long run.

If we hold truth as a high standard for life and relationships, for example, we are deeply troubled when people lie, deceive, and advertise falsely. Because our core values lead to root pain we view these characteristics as liabilities not treasures. What things bother you? What has God placed within you that would cause you to be bothered by a particular issue? What inspires you? What gives you hope and makes you feel alive? The things that are important to us say something about who we are and what drives us. These also reveal our tender places.

We find peace when we recognize our heart values and embrace the gifts God has given each of us to reflect different aspects of His character. Would you leave a buried treasure untouched in your backyard? Pain leads to clarity on the uniqueness of our identity. A failure to learn Skill 6 reminds us we have not yet discovered the treasure in our identities. Without meaning and clarity on who we are meant to be life loses much of its color.

One of the reasons Skill 6 is not more common is simple. We are highly motivated to stop, fix and remove the effects of pain. We cannot imagine there is something valuable beneath the responses to what bothers us. Pain serves a purpose and informs our nervous system that something is wrong and needs to be corrected. The redemptive quality in pain is the reminder we are still alive. People who are alive should be bothered by anything that threatens or steals life.

One of the most practical ways to develop Skill 6 is to identify lifelong patterns, moments where we experienced something that bothered us. These patterns show up throughout life, in our relationships and even in major decisions. We can highlight sources of distress then prayerfully consider what our reactions say about us. What kind of person would be bothered by this?

Consider the non-negotiable issues that fuel, motivate and fire you up. What things excite you? What gets you out of bed in the morning? We can ask people we trust to reflect and share what they observe as our main pain and heart qualities. We can identify certain qualities in the people we know, even those we read about. Who values relationships? Who values justice? In the pages of the New Testament we see that Barnabus encouraged, Paul valued truth, John loved, Jesus forgave and Peter jumped out of boats (passion). While these attributes are merely the tip of the iceberg for the substance of a person's character, they demonstrate something essential within each person as they reveal qualities that caused each person pain and distress - even death on some occasions. What does your pain say about you?

How Skill 6 Is Normally Acquired, Practiced And Propagated

When people, particularly our families, see us as God sees us, Skill 13, they help us recognize some of the meaningful qualities God has placed within us. We feel understood, seen, valued and validated when the people who know us best say, "This bothers you doesn't it? I can see how much you care about how people are treated, and I like that you care this much!" We begin to see that our hurts say something important about us. With time we continue to have "mirrors" who know us and help us see what God has placed within us that can lead to some of the pain we experience. These people help us answer the question, "Why do I hurt like this?" Over time Skill 6 becomes a meaningful asset in our relational arsenal that we rely on to help others see some of what God placed in them as well.

How Skill 6 Is Remedially Acquired, Practiced And Propagated

Let's examine how transforming fellowship/koinonia can restore the missing *Identify Heart Values from Suffering* skill. In Mark 6:34 we read Jesus encounters a large crowd and responds with compassion because they "were like sheep without a shepherd" (NIV). It was like Jesus, with His values and love, to respond with compassion when He encounters people who are lost. His values motivate Him to teach, preach, perform miracles and, ultimately, die on a cross but not before praying, "Father, forgive them, for they do not know what they are doing" (Luke 23:34a, NIV). Jesus' love caused Him great pain and anguish. Should He therefore stop loving because it hurt too much? Of course not! John tells us love is essential to God's identity:

> "And we have seen and testify that the Father has sent his Son to be the Savior of the world. If anyone acknowledges that Jesus is the Son of God, God lives in him and he in God. And so we know and rely on the love God has for us. God is love. Whoever lives in love lives in God, and God in him" (1 John 4:14-16, NIV).

Saul of Tarsus was a man who valued God's love and expressed it in his pursuit of righteousness, truth and justice. Soon to be named Paul, he deeply cared about God's law but also God's people. At one point he declares,

> "For I could wish that I myself were cursed and cut off from Christ for the sake of my brothers, my own flesh and blood" (Romans 9:3, NIV).

Here is someone who cares – a lot. Skill 6 recognizes unique qualities that have been knit into the fabric of our being that both motivate and hurt us. The "weeping prophet" we know as Jeremiah loved his people as well and he once wrote,

> "Oh, that my head were a spring of water and my eyes a fountain of tears! I would weep day and night for the slain of my people" (Jeremiah 9:1, NIV).

Like Paul, here is someone who hurts because he cares. Our communities must help people recognize some of what God has placed in each person and learn how these "God qualities" also lead to redemptive suffering. This process begins when we notice the qualities that defined people in the Bible then we apply this lens for one another.

Lies distort the truth about who we are. Skill 6 corrects distortions and sheds light onto the reasons certain issues, people or events bother us. Truth sets us free[61] and seeing some of what God has placed in us leads to the deeper understanding about who we were created to be. People learn Skill 6 in two primary ways. One, our chesed communities practice Skill 6 so followers of Jesus value the process of helping people discover the gifts God has given them. Two, people experience Skill 6 as part of the training developed for *THRIVE Training* and for *Connexus*. People learn Skill 6 with a number of exercises in *THRIVE: True Identity* as well as Track One, then attendees train others in Skill 6 with Tracks Two and Three. Skill 6 exercises are one of the favorites for attendees during Track One.

Skill 6 - Action Step

What does your pain say about you? Ask three people to tell you the qualities they see in you that they admire. Check if patterns emerge.

Skill 6 - Next Step

Discover the richness of Skill 6 by attending *THRIVE Training* as well as practicing the *THRIVE Skill Guides*. Watch the *THRIVE Lectures* and participate in the *THRIVE-at-Home* online curriculum to learn and apply Skill 6 to your life.

Conclusion

The pockets of koinonia within our chesed communities provide mirrors to reflect back some of what God placed in us. People who know us can express the qualities they observe working in us and highlight the pain responses they experience. They say, "It is like you to be bothered by this thing because this is who God made you to be."

61 John 8:31-32

These trusted friends should confirm what we know to be true and suggest new possibilities as well. People who use Skill 6 are wise stewards who become strong pillars within chesed communities. Transformations include Skill 6 as we understand and embrace what God has placed within us that best reflect His love, character and nature. This reality leaves us feeling peaceful and hopeful.

When I have Skill 6: I know there is redemption behind my pain and suffering even when I can't see it at the time. I remember what is important when I or someone I care about is hurting. It is easy for me to see how my pain says something valuable and important about me.

When Skill 6 is missing or underdeveloped: I often feel punished by God when things go wrong. I work hard to avoid things going wrong in my life. When I am in pain I simply want to make it stop because I see no value in pain.

Skill 6 Application Step - *Tim's Turmoil*

Tim grew up believing something was wrong with him. As a child Tim felt a deep love and sadness for other people, particularly those who have suffered loss and hardship. Tim did not know what to do with these strong feelings and he felt vulnerable, even weak. He noticed how friends seemed to easily dismiss the needs of other people and yet Tim could not shake the compulsion that he needed to do something in order to help people in need. Unsure of what to do, Tim started asking trusted colleagues what qualities they appreciated in his character. Tim also began praying and reading God's Word. He read how the Good Shepherd leaves ninety-nine sheep to go and search for the stray. Tim discovered that the best seat at God's table is reserved for the "least" of God's people and compassion was not a bad thing.

Over time Tim began to embrace his "weakness" as he called it. Freedom and a newfound peace emerged in Tim's life as he discovered compassion was a gift he could share with the world. Tim no longer felt like he needed to fight or resist his gift. The more Tim embraced his need to show others compassion, the greater his peace. While Tim's gift over the years brought him a lot of pain, his gift has richly blessed his life and enriched his relationships.

Chapter Nine
Brain Skill 7 - Tell Synchronized Stories
Four-plus (4+) Story Telling:
When our minds work together our stories come together.

After taking a moment to ask God, "Why does this skill matter to You?" I found myself thinking,

"Stories paint pictures. Not only do My children internalize My gifts to them, they share My gifts when they tell their stories. My Son used stories to share Kingdom truths and realities in ways people could understand and remember. These stories are a gift to pass on My goodness to one another."

Fountain Of Living Water, Sort Of

I heard a loud crash while sitting at my desk. I knew my son Matthew was supposed to be taking a nap, but the noise led me to believe he was not sleeping. "What in the world is he doing?" I wondered as I took a deep breath and stepped away from my desk to investigate. I noticed tension increase in my stomach and shoulders, so I took another deep breath. I gasped as soon as I opened the door to my son's room. I saw the bathroom sink overflowing with water. The sight and sounds of water spilling onto the floor made me cringe. I then saw my son sitting on the floor sobbing; he looked distressed. I felt a surge of adrenaline overtake my body, telling me to act. My heart raced. I rushed over to turn off the water and comfort my son. "What happened? Are you okay?" I said as I picked him up. Because his room was upstairs I envisioned water coming through the ceiling into my grandmother's room below. This added some dread to the situation so I called for back-up and soon my wife rushed in to help.

After some quieting, cleaning and comforting, my 3-year old son shared that he was making a waterfall by putting his pajamas into the sink then turning on the faucet. He accomplished his goals as the clogged sink was certainly transformed into a spring of water, but in the process of creating his masterpiece he slipped on the wet floor and bumped his head on the wall, which was the sound I heard. After a short time the three of us returned to joy as we felt quiet and peaceful and the tension left our bodies. It was good to be together and we could breathe deeply again, even laugh at the ordeal. Thankfully, the water remained upstairs and did not leak into the lower level of the house and, more importantly, my son was not seriously injured. This moment has now become a Skill 11 return to joy story we pass on and tell our friends and community.

If you were to watch me tell this story, you would see the authentic emotion, in this case fear, on my face. You would hear it in my voice. My body language would tell you I was genuinely afraid, and then you would see me relax at the end with a smile on my face. I would make eye contact with you, and you would feel what was going on in my mind and body as you shared this moment with me. I would be sure to keep it at a low level of intensity in order to avoid overwhelming you.

Stories do more than captivate our listeners. The quality of our stories tell us how well our brain is functioning. If the water fountain episode was still unprocessed and unresolved in my brain, I could not tell you a coherent narrative about the event. I would have the information but no feelings or unregulated feelings with choppy details. When the brain is well trained, our capacity is high, we are not triggered by the past, and our whole brain works together the way it is supposed to. Unresolved pain and the lack of storytelling by our families hinder our ability to create coherent narratives of our life.

Four-plus stories are a specific kind of story that offer a glimpse into the workings of our internal world. Four-plus stories are strategic, carefully crafted stories that require all four levels of the nonverbal right-hemispheric control center to work together. When this happens the bonus of our words in the left hemisphere match our experience and emotions in the right. The combination of words and nonverbal signals produce a most meaningful, coherent narrative. Telling and listening to four-plus stories brings people together, resolves conflicts, propagates brain skills and provides healthy examples of responses to emotions and upsets. Four-plus stories require time, practice, skill and emotional regulation.

When emotional and spiritual blockage is resolved, our whole brain works together in a unified way. By carefully selecting our stories we can test and train our brain's ability to handle specific aspects of life and relationships. We use four-plus stories to celebrate the special moments that create our legacy for our loved ones to remember us. These brain-based stories demonstrate secure bonds, regulate emotions and allow us to train brain skills in an effective manner.[62]

What Makes Up A Four-Plus Story

Several ingredients make up a successful four-plus story. With eye contact, four-plus stories should be shared at a moderate level of emotion. Too much intensity overwhelms our listeners. An overwhelmed brain is not a trainable brain. We want people engaged so they enter in to share our emotions and feelings. Four-plus stories are packaged in three formats: *Return To Joy* (Skill 11), *Acting Like Myself* (Skill 12) and *Share Immanuel* (Skill 13). Each story must illustrate a specific feeling for maximum efficacy. We show the authentic emotion on our face and in our voice. We rely on feeling words for emotions and body sensations. We use stories we have told before, and we keep our

62 https://www.sciencedaily.com/releases/2013/03/130327103054.htm#.VtEroy6cEmc.facebook

stories concise - anywhere from ninety seconds to five minutes. As with all learned skills, our stories improve with practice.

Now that we have the details, four-plus stories do not happen naturally unless family, friends and community members spontaneously and frequently told us stories in everyday life. Thriving marriages and joyful families automatically do this. As mentioned before, unprocessed trauma, lack of examples, insecure attachments and few *stories of us* during childhood lead to difficulty with Skill 7. We may simply be untrained to tell stories. Possibly we are too consumed with pain and problems. Without practice, it can be difficult to create a narrative using words to describe our feelings much less our body sensations. It takes training to tell an autobiographical narrative, one where *we are involved* in the story. This step requires activation of the highest regions of the prefrontal cortex, Level 4, in the right hemispheric control center. When the control center is working together, what we refer to as "synchronized," the left hemisphere creates coherent narratives with input from the right hemisphere. The left brain explains everything and makes logical connections while the right brain is concerned with emotions (what I feel), identity (who I am) and the landscape of the body (what's happening in my body).

As relational brain skills become less prevalent because of our increasing dependence on technology, entertainment, and changes in family and community structure, we have an urgent need for Skill 7. Let's face it; our families and communities simply do not communicate like we used to. We no longer use meal times to converse - at least for very long. And, when was the last time you told someone a story about your day/week/month?

Some of the changes are useful while others are detrimental to face-to-face interactions. For example, I enjoy the opportunity to "see" my family when I am traveling out of the country thanks to video options on my phone and computer, but I should not rely on my phone to replace my relationships. Computers, cellular phones, texting, tweeting and online media minimize the frequency of face to face communication. It takes a trained brain to use Skill 7. What's happening in your body right now? Even this task requires a bit of training.

Speaking of a trained brain, the human brain is a most remarkable learning machine with 100 billion neurons, 1,000 to 10,000 synapses for each neuron and over 100,000 blood vessels.[63] We grow new skills, strengthen weak skills and change unwanted patterns that hinder our growth when we have examples, practice and feedback. As mentioned previously, we must take time to notice our bodies in order to shift Skill 7 to the forefront of everyday life. Sound strange? That's because we rarely pay attention to our bodies until we discover something we don't like, notice something we want to change, or find something that is wrong and needs attention. Paying attention to our bodies is a key step in sharing the content of our minds. Remember, our body is the canvas for our brain. We ask, "What is happening in me?" "How do I feel when I am joyful, angry, sad, hopeless, ashamed, disgusted and afraid?" "How's my breathing right now?"

With practice and input from the left hemisphere we find words to describe these sensations so others better understand our personal experience. We insert these details into a coherent narrative that clearly conveys what it's like to "be in my shoes" at this very moment.

Like any good gift, four-plus stories should be shared with other people. Listeners become relational mirrors to help us gauge the effectiveness of our stories with suggestions and feedback. "You were smiling when you were talking about feeling mad." "I would have enjoyed hearing more how you felt in your body when you perceived God was with you." It helps to have a four-plus checklist nearby during practice so we can first write out our stories. Next, we share our stories using our words, senses and body. Joy is amplified, emotions are shared, then quieted. Four-plus stories weave together our history with the present then prepare us and our listeners for the future. All of us notice a refreshing difference in our relationships when we add Skill 7 to our relational tool belt.

How Skill 7 Is Normally Acquired, Practiced And Propagated

Most of us learn Skill 7 because family members tell stories about their day and recollect special moments from the past. Hearing and

---

63 Learn more about your amazing brain. http://www.nursingassistantcentral.com/blog/2008/100-fascinating-facts-you-never-knew-about-the-human-brain/

telling personal, engaging stories not only improves the brain's memory systems but these stories also become ingrained as part of "how we do things" in our families. Children enjoy stories. My young sons are captivated listening to my 93 year-old grandmother tell her stories! Hearing stories on a regular basis turns us into story-tellers because we are given the opportunity to share stories from our day that include how I feel and what's happening in my shoes when this moment occurred. Four-plus stories are not only fun and engaging but an integral part of our interactive fellowship. Just think about a time you couldn't wait to tell someone a story. With practice, we become more proficient story tellers and we spread Skill 7 by our example as we demonstrate this skill with others who are watching and listening. We invite them to join the fun and share their mind with us.

How Skill 7 Is Remedially Acquired, Practiced And Propagated

Let's examine how transforming fellowship/koinonia can restore the missing *Tell Synchronized Stories* skill. From Genesis to Revelation the Bible is a profound, inspiring love story between God and mankind. Each of the characters play an important role and this love story includes triumph and tragedy, birth and death, love and hate, good and evil. It is filled with sobering moments of costly redemption.

God must clothe His disobedient children after the fall of humanity in the Garden of Eden and then again clothe His children with righteousness and everlasting life by sending His Son to die on a cross where He arose on the third day conquering death. Gripping, personal stories fill the pages of Scripture and these stories paint the masterpiece we know as our history and our future. Every one of us has a place in God's story and each of us has a story to tell for how we got here and where we are going.

Stories are fundamental to fellowship, evangelization and discipleship. In many ways we take stories for granted yet the Bible is one big story comprised of many smaller stories. Stories make up our traditions and it is the story as a testimony that will one day be part of the strategy the Lamb uses to overcome the accuser of the brethren.[64] Believers should be the world's best storytellers because stories are our

64 Revelation 12:11

heritage. We have a redemptive story to tell the world because our story and God's story are intricately intertwined. Jesus taught using stories and parables that would stick in the minds of His listeners. Paul and Peter frequently told stories about their experiences to provide a context for their message.

Stories create a legacy because they allow something important to live on for future generations. We know people by the stories they tell. The mistreated younger brother, Joseph, when he could no longer contain his emotions before his brothers in Genesis 45, tells his redemption story during an emotional reunion. Joseph's mind processed the trauma of his experience and he could now share his life narrative coherently and include some of what God sees, Skill 13,

> "And now, do not be distressed and do not be angry with yourselves for selling me here, because it was to save lives that God sent me ahead of you" (Genesis 45:5, NIV).

In the Old Testament God asked Israel to recount and tell stories about the miraculous ways He provided for His people. In Exodus 12 and 13 is the Passover story that is still told at every Passover table to this day:

> "On that day tell your son, 'I do this because of what the Lord did for me when I came out of Egypt…" (Exodus 13:8, NIV).

It was during another Passover seder service, filled with stories and symbols, where Jesus instituted communion, a story packed full of meaning and richness. In Luke 24:19 Jesus said "do this in remembrance of me" and this is a living story that continues to this day all over the world. When children hear stories of remembrance and deliverance they expect God will also deliver and dwell with them as He did for previous generations. Just imagine all the stories Jesus and the disciples must have shared during their time together!

Skill 7 stories become opportunities for us to share our minds with other people in our community. When four-plus stories are not in our relational repertoire we need purposeful practice with like-minded friends who are willing to give us useful feedback. Because four-plus stories are an effective way to train relational brain skills, Skill 7 is woven through the flow of *THRIVE Training* and *Connexus* to equip participants with the necessary skills to use Skill 7 and pass this skill on to others. We practice with a clear goal for the kind of story we are telling, we use story sheets to guide us and we practice with others who reflect back to us the elements of our stories. We also keep a close eye on the time since too much information diminishes the training value of the stories. With practice we find ourselves using Skill 7 to interact with family, friends and strangers - without realizing we just used the skill! As with all the nineteen skills, once we learn and use the skill we can't help but pass it on to those we encounter on a daily basis. All we need is a few minutes to share our gift.

Skill 7 - Action Step

Tell someone a joyful story about one meaningful event from your day or week. This will be an *Acting Like Myself* story where you focus on how you managed to stay yourself (or how you would have wanted to respond if you had a Do-Over next time) while feeling the specific emotion, joy. For example, "It is like me to smile when I feel joyful." Use the story sheet included at the end of this chapter as your guide.

Skill 7 - Next Step

Skill 7 is woven through much of the training Life Model Works offers. *THRIVE Training* uses Skill 7 throughout the training tracks as well as in each of the three *THRIVE Skill Guides*. *Connexus* uses Skill 7 to train communities. If you are married, the *Joy Rekindled Marriage Retreats* offer a variety of Skill 7 exercises for married couples to build joy. Watch the *THRIVE Lectures* and participate in the *THRIVE-at-Home* online curriculum. Learn more at www.joystartshere.com.

Conclusion

Skill 7 is a healthy form of communication that chesed communities rely on to build joy, create belonging and train relational brain skills. Some of us are better than others at using Skill 7, but we all need practice to stay sharp. We come to know one another through four-plus stories and in this way the weak and the strong both benefit from hearing and sharing stories. The pocket of koinonia provides a refreshing blend of mastery with Skill 7 so everyone increases their ability to use the interactive skill. The result of a deep transformation is the ability to "share the good news" of what happened through a four-plus story that honors God, increases our faith, inspires our listeners and helps our brain to process information and emotions.

When I have Skill 7: Telling stories that include my emotions and body feel natural and easy. I like telling stories about my day/week.

When Skill 7 is missing or underdeveloped: I do not tell stories and I feel like people should simply know that I care about them. I avoid recounting my day, whether it was good or bad. I often feel "grilled" by people who ask me questions about myself.

My Four-Plus Story Preparation Checklist

1. This story has a moderate feeling level and is not too intense
2. I have told this story before
3. I do not need to be guarded in telling this story
4. This story is autobiographical (I am involved in the story)
5. This story illustrates a specific feeling

Ideas To Include In My Four-Plus Story

6. Briefly describe the situation:

7. Feeling words for my story:

8. During this story my body felt:

9. The things I did in this story that demonstrate how I like to act in this emotion are:

Follow-up Checklist

- I showed the authentic emotion on my face and in my voice.
- I maintained eye contact while storytelling.
- I used feeling words for my emotions.
- I used feeling words for my body sensations.
- I told the story like I was involved (autobiographical).
- I kept my story concise.

Skill 7 Application Step - *Eric's Erroneous Thinking*

Eric needed to work on his marriage. One of the difficulties Eric's wife expressed to him was his inability to communicate, to "share his heart." Eric felt like he was trying hard to be a good provider and a loving husband. Shouldn't his wife and children just know that he loved them? Eric felt like his wife was asking him to do something he didn't know how to do.

After some thought and consultation with his prayer partner, he recognized something was indeed missing. After learning about Skill 7 from his friend, Eric realized his father was "the silent type" and Eric was following his father's example. Along the way Eric developed the deep-rooted assumption that expressing himself was pointless, so why bother? This painful absence was not the legacy Eric wanted to pass on to his wife and children.

Eric began to practice four-plus stories with his prayer partner and his family. Eric noticed a drastic shift in himself and his marriage. Skill 7 became an avenue for joy as Eric used four-plus stories to highlight events from his day, share special moments from vacations, and convey the qualities he appreciates about his wife and marriage. Skill 7 was a foundational skill that improved Eric's ability to communicate and stay relationally and joyfully connected with the people he cared about.

Chapter Ten

Brain Skill 8 - Identify Maturity Levels

We need to know where we are, what we missed and where we are going. Without a map we keep falling in the same holes.

After taking a moment to ask God, "Why does this skill matter to You?" I found myself thinking,

> "I desire abundant life in all of My creation and I want My children to fully blossom and be ripe so they can experience more of Me at each stage of life. I am grieved to see My children robbed from the fullness of life that I long for them to receive. Intimacy with Me should always produce joyful growth, much like the tree planted near rivers of water."

Whenever we take a family trip Jen and I inevitably end up lost trying to reach our destination. Sometimes the confusion is momentary and our GPS quickly redirects our route. Other times the seconds turn to stressful minutes as we wait for our GPS system to guide us back to where we need to be. It is no fun driving blind and feeling lost.

It is especially miserable to feel lost and hindered in life and relationships with no idea where we are going or what we are missing. This brings us to the crucial topic of maturity. We want to identify our ideal level of maturity so we know if our development is impaired. Knowing our general maturity, our "baseline of operations," informs us what the next developmental task will be in our growth. Recognizing our immediate level of maturity from moment to moment reveals if we have been triggered into reactivity by something that just happened or if we encountered a "hole" in our development that needs remedial attention. Watching when our maturity level is slipping tells us when emotional capacity has been drained in us or other people. Skill 8 helps us stay the course for a fully thriving life expressed with earned maturity where we respect our limitations and function within our earned capacity.

Six Life Stages

The Bible mentions six stages that define the ideal developmental road map for life. The Unborn, Infant, Child, Adult, Parent and Elder stages cover the full range of our potential for emotional, mental, physical and spiritual growth. At Life Model Works these six life stages have been carefully sequenced to bring clarity to the process of joyfully growing and reaching our God-given potential. How tragic it is when a tree is cut down before it reaches its prime. Millions of babies are not given the opportunity to finish the Unborn stage of life while three-quarters of men are estimated to be stuck in the Infant stage of maturity with three-quarters of women still in the Child stage of development.[65] What this means is our bodies continue to grow but somewhere along the way we have missed what we needed to continue increasing and growing in step with our bodies. We are emotionally stunted, even malnourished. In most cases our families and communities lacked what we needed, and children do not grow beyond the maturity of their parents unless mom and dad address their hindrances and resourcefully advance in their own growth.

65 Learn more by reading Dr. Jim Wilder's, *The Complete Guide to Living with Men* book.

While I have a 41 year-old body I can be emotionally stunted as a 5 year-old. Stunted growth may be amusing on sitcoms where big people act like children but the loss of potential is tragic in real life. Families and communities are often missing essential ingredients that hinder their growth. We learn from ancient wisdom literature that one of the reasons the earth shakes, rattles and rolls is when an unprepared, unqualified person becomes a leader. *Catastrophe strikes when we do not have the training and maturity to match the role and responsibilities we are given.*[66] Have you seen or heard someone in a position of authority respond in a way you would expect a child to behave?

Speaking of running on fumes, when my wife Jen and I both learned about Skill 8 we quickly noticed we were stuck at Infant maturity, which meant we had some work to do. "How could this happen?" we asked ourselves. When I first assessed my maturity I felt like I flunked a test. I thought, "I should be at adult maturity, but I'm still an infant!" While there were good reasons for why we were stuck and stunted, once we removed the roadblocks and added necessary ingredients for growth, our lives drastically changed for the better. We could handle more pressure and strain than ever before. We could quiet ourselves, return to joy and regulate our emotions, ask for what we need, learn what satisfies, take care of two or more people at the same time and give life without requiring anything back. Now we are both, for the most part, functioning at Parent level maturity where we can feed others instead of the Infant stage where everything must feed us. While we have more work to do, this transformation has been glorious!

We can only give what we have. No matter how hard we try we can only train someone to play the violin or hit a baseball if we know how. We cannot give what we are missing. For this reason Jesus said that those who first believe in Him will then release rivers of living water.[67] Skill 8 provides the framework for the essentials to grow from a developmental, sequential perspective. What we need changes at any given time, especially as we age, so families and communities must stay attentive to one another's changing needs. We address our

---

66 Proverbs 30:21-23

67 John 7:37-39

stunted growth when we recognize what is missing that keeps us from moving forward. Skill 8 shows us where our maturity is secure or slipping and gives us the clarity to earn the maturity that matches our age and stage of life.

When embraced, Skill 8 changes our life and relationships because it recognizes our emotional capacity and reminds us to respect our limitations. We recognize the urgency for maturity formation when we reflect on moments we responded in a rigid, "childish" way that does not line up with our personal values. We may have a hard time resting or returning to joy, or we make too many decisions out of fear.[68] Regardless of the symptoms of stunted maturity, all of us can reach our God-given potential starting today.

While there are six life stages, we may not complete every life stage because everyone does not become a parent or an elder in their community. Each of us, at the very least, should aim to function at an adult level of maturity where we learn to use power wisely, achieve mutual satisfaction and develop a personal style that reflects our heart. These few qualities alone would disqualify many leaders in churches, governments, schools and offices who simply lack the maturity for their responsibility.[69] Each life stage includes a set of very specific needs and tasks to complete. When undeveloped, we risk wearing a "pseudo-maturity" mask where we look more mature than we really are. Inside we are running on fear and fumes while we appear "all together" to onlookers. With each stage of growth we increase our capacity to care for ourselves and other people. Stunted maturity means we only care for ourselves and cannot consistently care for other people. At one point God condemned the false shepherds in Israel because these rulers fed themselves rather than care for the flocks under them. These ill-equipped, bad shepherds filled their own mouths and failed to strengthen the weak.[70] We know the health of a group and the maturity of the leadership by their response to weaknesses in themselves and those they serve.[71]

68 Dr. Jim Wilder's, *The Complete Guide to Living with Men* book is the best resource to view the entire list of needs and tasks for each maturity stage.

69 Read *RARE Leadership* by Wilder and Warner for more.

70 Ezekiel 34

71 *Joy Starts Here: The Transformation Zone* by E. James Wilder, et al.

By identifying maturity we develop greater wisdom because we see why we or other people are not functioning at their full potential. We add substance to our character when we face our weaknesses with courage. The lack of maturity does not mean I have less value, rather it means I can carry less weight from the demands and pressures of life before something gives and I break. Recognizing limitations means we avoid passing on our problems and the same painful absences to our families and communities. By making corrections to our stunted growth we increase our emotional capacity and experience new resiliency for life. We literally change generational patterns; now this is a legacy!

Skill 8 explains why we keep falling into the same holes, often in spite of attempts to do otherwise. We discover why our will power, better choices and good intentions fall short of lasting change. Skill 8 offers clear steps for progress. Practice with Skill 8 fosters a clearer understanding of personal and corporate maturity. This step addresses immaturity, so we avoid burn-out and prevent blow-outs with our families, communities and organizations.

By 12 years old, children should have learned to tame their cravings. This task prepares them for the pressures of adulthood. Church, business, education and society as a whole provides countless examples where educated, talented, successful, even godly leaders fall prey to behaviors associated with untamed cravings. Like Esau with a pot of stew, they lose everything to fill their bellies, pockets or fantasies. Many confess with deep remorse to behavior contrary to their most cherished values. These moments may be chalked up as a mistake or interpreted as a poor decision. In many cases more rules are added into the equation to prevent similar mishaps in the future. Without a clear understanding and application of Skill 8 we fail to recognize *that developmental deficits, if addressed, could have prevented the disaster in the first place*. While a lake may be frozen and look good on the surface, it takes only one weak spot to plunge us into the icy cold water. Weak spots in our maturity and character frequently appear during times of strain and pressure. Without systematic effort to correct weaknesses we risk relational plunges that leave us and others wondering, "What just happened?"

For the wise, distress becomes an opportunity to find weaknesses and strengthen areas that require patching and repair.

Skill 8 reflects the health and resources of our families and communities. Gaps and deficits that are not addressed are passed on like every other unwanted pattern. There is a remarkable shortage of mature maps and guides within our communities. The lack of elders with earned maturity as well as missing multigenerational communities leave a gaping hole in the fabric of a family and community. For the church in general, it is easy to spiritualize maturity and miss the need for earned emotional maturity where people learn to do hard things and recover from upsetting emotions.

When I was a child, I assumed people in big bodies, especially those with grey hair, should automatically be mature. After all, they were big and I was small! My assumption proved faulty when I observed big people acting like children in a way that I, a young child, would act. The spiritual among us tend to assume maturity is a natural progression from salvation or that church attendance equals spiritual maturity. We may believe holes in our maturity are a reflection of our value and self worth. Subscribing to these beliefs can create resistance to an honest assessment of maturity and produce shame for those of us seeking to identify our true, earned maturity.

We minimize relational casualties when we assess obstacles that keep us stuck. Unprocessed traumas and painful events stunt our maturity at the age they happen. While my body keeps growing, emotionally I stay stuck and malnourished. We can ask, "Do I need more mature examples in my life?" "Do I have unprocessed pain robbing me?" "What skills am I missing?" "Where does fear run my life and dictate my decisions?" Acknowledging our weaknesses is the first step toward joyful change. We increase our maturity with an honest appraisal of our earned maturity. "What areas of my character need some work?"

Asking For Help

I remember the time my character needed some work. One day I picked up some large rolls of carpet to deliver to my office building. These heavy rolls of carpet were loaded onto my trailer by very big and strong workers. Instead of asking for help I decided to off-load the carpet myself when I arrived at the office. At the time it seemed like a good idea and after 45 minutes of sweating and straining I finished the job and wondered if I was going to have a heart attack! My body was hurting. I felt exhausted. I wondered why I pushed myself so hard at the risk of my own peril when I could have asked friends to help me.

Using Skill 8 I realized I was not good at asking for help; this was an area of weakness for me. At some level I did not like feeling "needy" or vulnerable to rejection. I noticed a pattern in my life and relationships where I frequently took matters into my own hands - at the cost of my well being. Trying to be strong made me weak, and I had not learned the child maturity task of asking for what I needed. If something did not change, this unmet need could be the end of me, especially if I ever had to move carpet again! From that point on, I began looking for examples in my community to practice this new task. I cannot begin to tell you how good it feels to ask for what I need in my relationships. I have experienced freedom and joy in a whole new light that would have been absent without Skill 8. Fear no longer has the last word in this area of my life.

Similar to the development of a house that starts from the foundation, we search for holes and unfinished tasks beginning with infant maturity. We fill gaps then we reinforce needs and tasks with the help of others who already have maturity, particularly where we lack it. All of us have something to give and something to receive. We start to remove fears that hinder forward progress. We seek Immanuel's guidance to process painful events that keep us stuck (Skill 13). We locate guides to encourage, pray and oversee our journey. We create belonging where the weak and strong mix. We increase our joy. Each step propels us forward. As we fill in gaps we explore next steps at the child then adult stages. Some steps require little effort while others need more. Maturity does not add to our value; rather, maturity helps us better express and share ourselves with the people we love. We no longer live within the confines of a rigid comfort zone that keeps us from embracing life to the fullest. After all, who wants to stay in a prison of low-joy when we can walk in green pastures with abundant life?

How Skill 8 Is Normally Acquired, Practiced And Propagated

We grow best in the gardens we are planted, assuming mom, dad, family and community members provide the necessary ingredients to thrive. When family members are attentive, consistent and predictable to our ever-changing needs, we naturally increase and develop earned maturity. Healthy families repair when things go wrong and stay relational as they learn and grow together.

Family members give what is needed at the right times and teach their children the road map for life. This road map means parents help children understand where they are, where they are going as they grow, and where they have been. Children learn family history and the history of God's family.

As we grow, we search for opportunities to give some life where life is needed. We find satisfaction in both giving and receiving. One sign of earned maturity is that we do not fearfully keep all the good stuff for ourselves and build bigger and bigger barns; rather, we look for places and people to feed and share our wealth of resources.

In the story Jesus tells in Luke 10 we see an example of this with the Good Samaritan who stopped and served the battered traveler who had been left for dead. In this parable a priest and a Levite both pass by the wounded man without assisting. While helping the man would have made them ritually unclean and unable to serve in the Temple, the sages taught there was no excuse to neglect a person in need - even if it means burying a corpse and even if it makes the helper unclean. These two leaders had no excuse; they should have inconvenienced themselves on behalf of the traveler. However, the Samaritan responds compassionately - even at great cost and inconvenience. Skill 8 provides the emotional resources needed to both care for ourselves and serve others in spite of the price it may require. We give because we first received.

How Skill 8 Is Remedially Acquired, Practiced And Propagated

Let's examine how transforming fellowship/koinonia can restore the missing *Identify Maturity Levels* skill. Maturity is the process of becoming more and more complex over time as we stay mindful of our capacities and limitations. Unless our character is tested we easily forget that we can stay emotionally stunted as an infant or a child. It is under distress that our deficits show up the clearest. Growth, in all its challenges, is beautiful. Jesus provides an example of personal transformation where He "grew in wisdom and stature, and in favor with God and men" (Luke 2:52, NIV). The boy Jesus grew into a man.

Paul understood maturity and the lack of it when he wrote the Corinthians,

> "Brothers, I could not address you as spiritual but as worldly — mere infants in Christ. I gave you milk, not solid food, for you were not yet ready for it. Indeed, you are still not ready. You are still worldly. For since there is jealousy and quarreling among you, are you not worldly? Are you not acting like mere men?" (1 Corinthians 3:1-4, NIV).

And,

> "When I was a child, I talked like a child, I thought like a child, I reasoned like a child. When I became a man, I put childish ways behind me" (1 Corinthians 13:11, NIV).

Jealousy and quarreling were behaviors Paul associated with immaturity in the Corinthians. Having a 4 and 6 year-old son I can attest to the process that takes place where children must learn how to share and get along - especially during big emotions. I can also attest to the frustration when jealousies and quarreling happens. How much more so when seeing this in people with adult bodies! Paul understood he could not "feed the people meat" while they were still drinking milk. We see this again in Hebrews 5:11-14,

> "We have much to say about this, but it is hard to explain because you are slow to learn. In fact, though by this time you ought to be teachers, you need someone to teach you the elementary truths of God's word all over again. You need milk, not solid food! Anyone who lives on milk, being still an infant, is not acquainted with the teaching about righteousness. But solid food is for the mature, who by constant use have trained themselves to distinguish good from evil" (NIV).

While this passage may sound harsh, the reality is these words are a gift for the listeners to receive because when God's people do not know or respect their limitations the results can be catastrophic. When we attempt tasks or responsibilities that we do not have the maturity for, it inevitably sets us up for problems. To have the appearance of maturity when essential ingredients are missing not only hurts us but it hurts others and can lead to the abuse of power, fearful living, addictions and, as in the case above, poor discernment. These are but a few casualties. While we know that with God all things are possible, God does not call us to do all things at the same time.[72]

Skill 8 is one of those skills that naturally develops because the correct ingredients are mixed together. Unfortunately for many of us, one or more of these ingredients were missing at specific times when we were growing up, and we developed distorted growth in our development. Many of us experienced bad things that stunted our growth at the age the bad things tragically happened and we therefore missed essential nutrients to help us keep growing. Skill 8 brings into focus our limitations and our next steps for growth.

Good resources are available to guide maturity formation and to give a clear road map for where we need to go. While these are mentioned in the *Next Step* section, starting with *The Complete Guide To Living With Men* by Dr. Jim Wilder is by far the best resource. Here we find the guidance needed to identify earned maturity as well as the elements needed to fast-track Skill 8 progress. We must identify missing needs and tasks in order to propel our growth. We find people who have the skills in pockets of koinonia where we lack them within our chesed communities. We stay intentional about filling gaps and we stay prayerful with Immanuel about our needs, fears and necessary resources.

In this way, the solutions are relational as family, community, prayer partners and trusted colleagues play a role to strengthen areas of weakness. We focus on small steps, we diligently practice to strengthen our growing maturity skills, and then we start training others. We stay strategic and resourceful as we learn and receive then strengthen and spread the good stuff to others. When the pieces are in place to grow, one of the common responses to Skill 8 develop-

72 Mark 10:27

ment is, "I thought this would be a long, drawn-out process but I am discovering that it is not as difficult or time consuming as I thought it would be!" We look back on our progress with delight for how much ground we have covered, and we celebrate every step forward as joy levels increase.

Skill 8 - Action Step

How would you describe the relational legacy you want to leave? In other words, what do you want your family, friends and coworkers to say about you when you are gone? Write out a few of your thoughts and consider how fear or the painful lack of maturity hinders you from achieving your desired legacy.

The relational legacy I want to leave:

Skill 8 - Next Step

Relational joy is the number one fuel for the formation of maturity, and Life Model Works has a number of great resources to start joy and learn more about Skill 8. Begin by reading *The Complete Guide to Living with Men* book by Dr. Jim Wilder and *Living From The Heart Jesus Gave You* book by Wilder et. al. Take 20 minutes to complete the online JOYQ Assessment to measure your progress while you practice joy and go through *Joy Starts Here: The Transformation Zone* book for a perspective on maturity with exercises and Bible studies. Listen to *Jesus In Mind: Talks on Kingdom Life* for even more on Skill 8. Utilize the *THRIVE Lectures* and participate in the *THRIVE-at-Home* online curriculum.

THRIVE Training uses Skill 8 with a variety of exercises in each of the three training tracks as well as each of the *THRIVE Skill Guides*. For the married among us the *30 Days of Joy for Busy Married Couples* book includes Skill 8 in some of its exercises. *Connexus* uses Skill 8 to train communities.

Conclusion

Skill 8 is a reflection of my community and the resources that were or were not present. One sign of maturity is how many people I can take care of. One sign of stunted maturity is the fear that runs my life and relationships. Chesed communities produce mature members who build relationships based on love and joy. People who have Skill 8 and value the formation of maturity become pillars in chesed communities that hold up well under the weight of strain, overwhelm and pressure. Koinonia provides ongoing opportunities to correct distortions and strengthen weaknesses. It is here we find examples with ample opportunities to both give and receive life. Transformations pave the way for Skill 8 by removing stumbling blocks that impede growth. Transformations are also the by-product of Skill 8 because this skill builds capacity and my ability to heal and sustain my healing over time is connected to the safety net of mature relationships in a multigenerational community where the weak and strong interact. Skill 8 requires pioneers who have traveled the road before us and road maps to show us the big picture of maturity formation from beginning to end.

When I have Skill 8: Growing up is important to me. I want to be more mature than I already am. It hurts me to see people stuck and stunted in their own growth. People would say I value growth.

When Skill 8 is missing or underdeveloped: I do not know how to develop maturity. Something in me prefers to stay where I am at and I make a lot of my decisions out of fear. It is important to me to stay within my comfort zone.

Skill 8 Application Step - *Sue's Stunted Growth*

My friend Sue spent much of her childhood years getting into trouble. Most of her teachers assumed she was a troublemaker because her relational skills were deficient. Without knowing it, Sue lacked the maturity skills to quiet, return to joy from negative emotions and do hard things she did not feel like doing. This made navigating the classroom environment a real challenge for both Sue and her teachers.

Several of her teachers, however, believed in Sue, and these women saw something valuable in her so they invested in the teenage girl. Sue's teachers took time to meet and encourage Sue to pursue her dreams. These interactions were seeds that would sprout joy and hope.

Sue found a counselor who taught her about Skill 8 and how stunted maturity creates pain. Sue learned she was reacting to missing ingredients that her family just did not have to pass on to her. Hoping to fill gaps, Sue plugged in to her church community and started connecting with people at different stages of life, some with more maturity, some with less. With purposeful effort, Sue developed the maturity to better live from her heart instead of her hurt. After high school Sue signed up for classes at the local college and found a job at a local community center mentoring troubled kids. She continues to blossom and is now an active member in her community, both giving and receiving life. Skill 8 provided the foundation for Sue to thrive.

Chapter Eleven

Brain Skill 9 - Take A Breather

Timing When to Disengage:
Skillfully take short pauses before people become overwhelmed. We read the non-verbal cues so we can build trust.

After taking a moment to ask God, "Why does this skill matter to You?" I found myself thinking,

> "I know what it feels like when people go too far. As I set boundaries for the ocean, I smile when My children respect weaknesses and limitations in themselves and one another. As I protect You from Myself, I want to see My children protect each other from going too far. My Spirit respects limits."

One morning I was sitting at a table having breakfast with several attendees at one of our events when I noticed someone standing over me. I turned to greet the mystery guest. Recognizing the woman as one of the attendees, I greeted her with a warm smile, "Good morning; nice to see you!" The look on her face told me it was not a good morning and she was not glad to see me. She responded with, "I have a bone to pick with you." I took a deep breath and felt a knot form in my stomach.

In a loud voice she questioned me about a short video I played the previous day about a family who was standing firm for their faith in a country that was hostile to followers of Jesus. Part of their testimony included how they were standing and witnessing amidst severe persecution. It was an inspiring video but a sobering testimony because this family had children. As you can guess, this story reminded the woman of painful times in her own life where she felt unprotected. "How could you show this video?" "What's the matter with you?" she yelled. My attempts to clarify and answer her questions only made the situation worse. Her face turned red. Her energy levels climbed. She was loud. She was obviously hurt and overwhelmed. She was overwhelming me and my breakfast guests. I took a quick look at the attendees sitting next to me at the table. They looked stunned. Their shocked expressions reminded me of deer frozen by the headlights of an oncoming car.

After a few moments with her intense questioning, I motioned to the woman with my hands, making a T sign - the signal for Timeout. Surprised by my response, she turned as though she might walk away. My heart was racing and I took a deep breath. "No, please!" I said. "Let's pause, just for a moment. I want to hear what you have to say, but first let's catch our breath." Even though she looked bewildered by my request, she agreed. We paused. No one said a word for about 30 seconds. It felt like an eternity.

The attendees at the table still looked like deer frozen by headlights. I broke the silence. I looked her in the eyes and, with a soft tone, I said, "I am so, so sorry you were offended by this video. If I had known this story would bother you like this, I would not have shown the video - or I would have warned you. This was an awful experience for you!" In less than 2 minutes she was smiling. She felt understood, valued and validated. She walked away feeling protected.

I turned to the attendees sitting at my table and asked them if my words and more information fixed the woman's problem. They quickly shook their heads with a resounding, "NO." I then asked them if the interaction improved once we took a moment to pause and quiet ourselves. They nodded with an animated, "YES!" Though intense, this interaction turned into a helpful teaching moment for the group - all because of Skill 9.

Later in the week the woman's husband thanked me for the *THRIVE Training* and shared how the event changed their lives. I knew he would not be saying this to me if the interaction with his wife would have ended badly. Skill 9 saved the day.

Have you ever felt overwhelmed by another person? Of course you have! We don't have to spend much time on this planet before we are overwhelmed by someone or something. Many of us live in an overwhelmed state. We hear phrases such as, "Settle down, you are too loud." "Get out of my face!" "Lower your voice!" "Back off!" "If you don't stop I'm going to _." Verbal and nonverbal warnings are sirens that signal our personal limits have reached maximum overload. By the time most of us recognize overwhelm cues it is too late. We or someone else has already plowed through the need for a breather. Pushing past the threshold of our limitations comes at a cost.

Trust deteriorates when our limitations are disregarded. We avoid people who do not protect us from themselves. We feel guarded when others accelerate and drive through the red lights of our personal space. Teasing, bullying and violence occur when Skill 9 drops out of our relational repertoire. This results with us and others feeling violated, unprotected, even dishonored. Sustained closeness and trust requires us to stop and rest before people become overwhelmed. These short pauses to quiet and recharge take only seconds. Those who read the nonverbal cues and let others rest are rewarded with trust and love.

Skill 9 is the safety net for our interactions. Behaviors, sounds, silence, facial expressions, words and responses can push us to the edge. These are moments we feel run over. Our limits are not respected when our body cues are dismissed, minimized and ignored. People who fail to attune with us and our limitations do not increase our joy. All the brain-developing and relationship-building moments that create understanding and produce mutual-mind states require paired minds to stop a moment (pause) when the first of the two gets tired, near overwhelm or too intensely aroused. Those who disengage quickly and briefly allow the other to rest. This moment to recharge feels rewarding.

Tender responses to weakness allow joy to increase. Family members who pause and "tone it down" when we show overwhelm signals give us the chance to catch our breath. Tickling is fun but damaging when pushed too hard beyond the brink of our ability to rest and recharge. The momentary pause keeps an interaction safe and joyful. How well do you recognize overwhelm in yourself and other people?

A common scenario of a Skill 9 failure is when the skill was not used with us so we did not learn to use the skill in our relationships. When we or others fail to pause and slow down we may frequently hear "Stop!" "Back off!" "Chill" "Settle down!" "You're too hyper!" when interacting, playing and communicating. When these nonrelational moments are not processed by the brain our survival circuit at Level 2 of the control center can work too hard and become overactive. Now our Level 3,the cingulate cortex, fails to regulate energy levels. We become reactive, restless, irritable and intense. The brakes of our nervous system no longer work properly when triggered. At this point it will be difficult to regulate what we feel. Sadly, the most vulnerable among us will pay the greatest price when Skill 9 is missing in our families and communities.

We learn Skill 9 because people used the skill with us. Dad knew just the right amount of wrestling before it became too much. Mom kept a close eye on our signals for quiet when correcting us for not doing our chores. Our family members, teachers and coaches demonstrated how to pause when energy levels climbed. They toned down their intensity at just the right times. They recognized our weaknesses but they protected and strengthened us rather than pounced.

Training Skill 9 is a delicate process because most of us have pain resulting from the nonrelational moments people failed to recognize our overwhelm cues. In this case we must turn to Immanuel (Skill 13) for peace and our trusted friends (Skill 5) for support. At *THRIVE Training* and in the *Connexus* curriculum for communities we are careful to provide strategic exercises so people effectively learn Skill 9.

Next, during our interactions, we search for signs that we are overwhelmed or that we are overwhelming others. We notice and regulate our responses. We invite friends and family members to offer suggestions in case we miss important cues. We ask, "Did I just overwhelm you? You looked overwhelmed." in order to update our minds about people and situations. We check for subtle cues in ourselves and others that were overlooked. We practice noticing moments our relational engine is "in the red" and take some time to quiet. We review, "How is my breathing?" "Where do I feel tension?" "Do I have racing thoughts?" We keep our relational circuits on and notice when we relationally go dim in order to quickly return to our ideal state of joy and peace. Skill 9 lays the groundwork for the more demanding brain skill we will learn shortly, known as Skill 15, *Interactive Quiet.*

How Skill 9 Is Normally Acquired, Practiced And Propagated

We learn Skill 9 because family members use the skill with us. They respect our limitations, back off and lower their voice at just the right times because they observe we are overwhelmed. They give us a language when, after stopping, they name the moment then repair with, "Wow, I just scared you didn't I? I am sorry; are you ok?"

As children we practice Skill 9 with play, usually through wrestling, splashing, chasing and tickling games where we have to regulate our energy levels all the while noticing how the other person is doing. We propagate Skill 9 when we interact with our peers and community members. Similar to a referee during a basketball game, we point out when people "travel with the ball[73]" or foul other players, and we stop the game momentarily. We help people learn to pay attention to subtle body cues that scream, "Stop. I'm overwhelmed!" Parents, teachers, coaches and service providers are in ideal positions to train Skill 9.

73 Traveling in basketball means you failed to dribble the ball and took one or more steps.

How Skill 9 Is Remedially Acquired, Practiced And Propagated

Let's examine how transforming fellowship/koinonia can restore the missing *Take a Breather* skill. God's people should be protectors because God is a Protector. Skill 9 is the protective, momentary disengagement response to the need for a break. Skill 9 says, "I see this is too much for you. Let's stop and rest." In the Bible God frequently has to shield and protect us from Himself or in some cases, protect us from ourselves.

After sinning, Adam and Eve were removed from the Garden of Eden in order to protect them from the tree of life that was still standing in their midst. Another time God places Moses in a rock cleft then covers Moses with His hand while God's glory passes by.[74] Moses must have learned something about God's protective care because after spending time in God's presence on Mount Sinai he walks down the mountain with two stone tablets and people fearfully run away from him. This is not the response Moses must have been expecting! At this point Moses covers his glowing face with a veil because his shining face frightened everybody.[75] Rather than justify his glowing face with, "Hey, I was just in God's presence. How can I help it that my face is shining? You can just deal with it!" Instead, Moses humbly respects their limitations and shields them. Skill 9 notices and responds to physical/mental/emotional/spiritual limitations.

There are times God's silence and perceived absence become overwhelming for the authors of the Psalms. When this happens we find the psalmist crying out for God's face to return.

> "Answer me, Lord, out of the goodness of your love; in your great mercy turn to me. Do not hide your face from your servant; answer me quickly, for I am in trouble" (Psalm 69:16-17, NIV).

Here we see Skill 9 is the *return to connection* after silence and disconnection. In 2 Timothy 1 Paul tells how he was deserted by his friends but it was the household of Onesiphorus who stayed, comforted and joined him in his vulnerable moment.

---

74 Exodus 33:22

75 Exodus 34:29-35

> "You know that everyone in the province of Asia has deserted me, including Phygelus and Hermogenes. May the Lord show mercy to the household of Onesiphorus, because he often refreshed me and was not ashamed of my chains. On the contrary, when he was in Rome, he searched hard for me until he found me. May the Lord grant that he will find mercy from the Lord on that day! You know very well in how many ways he helped me in Ephesus" (2 Timothy 1:15-18, NIV).

In this case connection is the gift Paul needed in order to be refreshed. Skill 9 is the pause in connection that says, "Let's rest" and it is also the return to relational interaction that says, "Let's continue."

A couple of factors must come together to train Skill 9. First, we stay mindful that Skill 9 is a difficult skill to train because when people don't use the skill with us these are not our most peaceful moments. Abuse and trauma result from moments people fail to respect our overwhelm cues.[76] When we try to train Skill 9 without safeguards in place we reinjure people. Second, remedial training means we need to keep our relational brain circuits active during the training because once our relational circuits go offline we cannot effectively learn Skill 9.[77] Third, we need observers as a safety net to watch for overwhelm cues who can intervene and say, "Pause" and "Stop" at the first signs of overwhelm. Finally, we use easier emotions with low stimulation in order to avoid too much overwhelm in the early phases of training.

Skill 9 is woven through the *THRIVE Training* by starting out with simple exercises with easier emotions such as joy for joy smiles where we must look away at the right times to rest in order to sustain joy levels. We then increase the training with more demanding exercises and emotions from there. In some cases, pairs tell stories to their partners while looking for overwhelm and pause at the first sign of overwhelm. These exercises are most redemptive because the environment is safe and the people have a unified goal to protect others from

76 In many cases perpetrators, bullies and sociopaths watch for overwhelm cues then increase their intensity and cruelty.

77 Learn more about relational circuits from *THRIVE Training*, *Belonging* in *Connexus* and Dr. Karl Lehman's resources at kclehman.com.

themselves. *Connexus* trains Skill 9 with creative, safe exercises so that communities practice this essential skill.

As we begin to learn Skill 9, we practice under safe conditions with like-minded friends until we become "masters" who can train other people. At *THRIVE Training* our Track Two and Three attendees learn how to propagate Skill 9 through a number of creative exercises where they instruct others how to connect and disconnect at just the right times. Our masters use stories and personal examples to demonstrate how Skill 9 works. Ironically, propagating Skill 9 is the easier part of the sequence since learning the skill is the hard part of the process for most of us.

Skill 9 - Action Step

How would you describe what overwhelm feels like in your body?

In what ways do you overwhelm people?

Start noticing your interactions to see if you can identify overwhelm cues in yourself and others.

Skill 9 - Next Step

As mentioned, *THRIVE Training* and *Connexus* are the best ways to practice Skill 9. Bonded pairs practice several Skill 9 exercises in each of the three training tracks at *THRIVE* while groups practice Skill 9 in some fun, creative ways with *Connexus*.

The *THRIVE Skill Guides* and *Joy Rekindled* marriage retreats are another practical way to increase your ability to use Skill 9.

Conclusion

Skill 9 is foundational for chesed communities where people start and sustain joy. The character of Christ is one that respects limitations and remains tender toward weaknesses. After an overwhelmed Peter denied Jesus three times, a resurrected Jesus restores Peter thus demonstrating the ministry of reconciliation. In this way, chesed communities are anchored by Skill 9 as they stay mindful of one another's limitations. Members guide each other to learn this most basic human skill that reflects love and respect. Repair and restoration should always follow moments Skill 9 was missing in our conversations. In this way we keep one another's limitations in the forefront of our minds. When we repair we begin to restore trust.

Koinonia provides the "trained brains" with examples to show community members how to recognize overwhelm cues and back off when intensity arises. For this reason Skill 9 results in deep transformations because we learn to sustain our healing and protect others from ourselves. We remove the log from our own eyes with healing so we can see others as God sees them (Skill 13). Our life is a living testimony to demonstrate what Skill 9 looks like during interactions.

When I have Skill 9: I notice when I feel overwhelmed. I also notice when people look overwhelmed. I try to stop when I see I am overwhelming people by my words and actions.

When Skill 9 is missing or underdeveloped: I do not notice overwhelm cues in myself or in other people. People usually tell me I am overwhelming them.

Skill 9 Application Step - *Dawn's Desperation*

Dawn knew she needed Skill 9. Her intense reactions, usually anger, were scaring her children and creating distance with her husband. Dawn was living in overwhelm. Inevitably, Dawn would feel ashamed and guilty after a blow-up over what seemed to be minor issues. The look on her family's faces during her outbursts was hard to forget. Dawn confided in her husband Rob that she was afraid. Dawn feared she did not know how to stop this painful pattern - but she was highly motivated. Dawn found hope in the training she heard about from a friend. This training, called THRIVE, was designed to equip people in brain skills, including Skill 9. Dawn couldn't wait to sign up.

After attending THRIVE Training and practicing Skill 9 exercises, Dawn realized it does not take long for her to feel overwhelmed, nor does it take much time to overwhelm her husband - merely seconds! The training and the examples helped Dawn learn what she was missing. Dawn was ready to transform her painful patterns into protector qualities, so she shared with her children what she learned at THRIVE. Dawn repented to her family for the ways she hurt them. The family came up with words and signals to use when someone needed a breather during interactions. Soon there was more peace and joy. Dawn's children commented on the changes and how much they enjoyed seeing Dawn rest and calm down instead of blasting others. Dawn and Rob's marriage was filled with a fresh dose of joy and intimacy. Smiles replaced sad faces.

Chapter Twelve
Brain Skill 10 - Tell Nonverbal Stories

The nonverbal parts of our stories strengthen relationships, bridge generations and cross cultures.

After taking a moment to ask God, "Why does this skill matter to You?" I found myself thinking,

> "A visual story is impactful for My children. It is for this reason an example is one of the best ways to express My love and My character. The sheep watch attentively and listen carefully, so the nonverbal story becomes a mirror to demonstrate My qualities and reflect My heart. In this way, nonverbal stories are carried and available to My people during upsetting moments where useful examples of My character are needed."

I walked into the room when a friend approached me with a look of concern on her face. Nearly panicked she asked, "Chris, are you angry with me? Did I upset you?" Surprised by her question, I replied, "Angry? No, I'm not angry with you! Why would you ask this?"

She clarified, "Because you looked mad when you walked into the room." I responded with, "Oh no, not at all! I'm not angry with you. Actually, I just ate an entire pepperoni pizza by myself. I'm feeling very full at the moment! You probably saw 'full belly misery' from the pizza I just consumed!" with a lighthearted laugh. My friend was misreading my facial cues; her internal interpreter was malfunctioning. Thankfully, she checked with me before assuming I was angry at her. All of us have an internal interpreter in charge of what researchers call *mindsight.* Mindsight is our ability to see and simulate what is happening in another person's mind based on what we see on their face. Skill 10 is the skill that helps us correct this interpreter when it is not working properly.

If you've ever been told by a parent, teacher or spouse, "Watch your tone!" or, "It's not what you said, it's how you said it!" you already know a little something about Skill 10. During a conversation, the content we convey is first assessed by *how* we say the words not by the words themselves (Hughes & Baylin, 2012). The brain processes words and nonverbal cues in different ways. In a foot race the nonverbal brain always wins over the verbal brain. The brain processes nonverbal content much faster than words so the nonverbal pieces of our conversations carry more weight in the brain than words alone.

Our brain relies on words and a vast collection of nonverbal signals to effectively communicate and attune with other people. Eye contact, facial expressions, voice tone (prosody), posture, gestures, timing and intensity all contribute to the interactive dance we know as communication. One UCLA study reported that 93% of effective communication is nonverbal. It has been said that 10% of conflicts are due to difference of opinion while 90% are due to the wrong tone of voice. Words, while weighty, have their limitations. If you ever visited an area where you did not speak the language, or enjoyed some good old fashion fun playing Charades, you practiced Skill 10. Reading emails, text messages and media postings give us words to read but no emotional content to correctly gauge the mind of the writer. This absence creates problems for the emotional brain.

Misunderstandings and conflicts arise when there is a lack of voice tone and facial expressions. Let's say you receive an email from your boss that says, "I want to speak with you. Come to my office now." This may be somewhat unsettling unless you can simulate what is happening in your boss's mind because you have a secure bond. If you enter the office to see your boss wear a big, warm smile and hear an inviting voice tone with accepting, open body language, you may have a more welcome response to these words and feel less guarded. The brain searches for emotional cues with every interaction. Skill 10 is what helps us interpret other people and correctly convey the emotional content of our shared minds. Overall, women tend to be better at interpreting facial cues than men.[78]

Our body is the canvas to express our thoughts, feelings, desires, fears and our most prized memories. Skill 10 allows us to share our emotions and express the rich content of our minds through our face, voice and body. When used, Skill 10 conveys our internal world, brightens our stories, anchors our relationships and creates mutual understanding in our interactions. Using a conglomeration of the limbic system, vagal nerve, anterior insula and more, our body informs us, often in compelling ways, when something is going right or wrong. The amygdala, part of the limbic system's survival circuit, what we refer to as Level 2 of the control center (Skill 18), detects a threat in 1/10 of a second. This response is much faster than the time it takes for our brain to create a conscious thought.[79] We know this emotional control center as the fast-track system in the brain. Skill 10 is what helps us use both our brain and body to bring clarity to our conversations and create mutual understanding in our relationships. Our face and body signal the quality of our day, the tone of an interaction, how rested we are, even how much we enjoyed a recent meal of pizza. The brain and body have an intimate, interconnected relationship that improves with Skill 10. When working together, our brain and body tell a story that shows up on our face and in our voice. What story is your face telling today?

---

78 Based on the research of Simon Baron-Cohen (2003).

79 Hughes & Baylin, 2012 and RARE Leadership *RARE Leadership: 4 Uncommon Habits for Increasing Trust, Joy and Engagement in the People You Lead* by Dr. Marcus Warner and Dr. E. James Wilder.

TED Talks

Research on TED talks by Vanessa Van Edwards and her lab demonstrates the power of Skill 10. In one trial she asked participants to watch and rate TED talks while the videos were on mute. After viewing the talks and watching the body language of the presenter, the team rated each video. Interestingly, the highest rated TED talks by her team matched the viewer counts on the video. The videos with the most view counts at TED.com are the most popular. By watching the nonverbal cues then ranking these speakers, the participants voted on talks that, without knowing it, were the most popular talks rated by viewers watching the videos online with sound! As Van Edwards puts it, "This tells us that when viewers tune in to listen to a TED talk, they make a lot of their decisions about the speaker's charisma, intelligence and credibility based on their nonverbal actions."[80]

Skill 10 not only enhances our ability to communicate effectively, but it helps us interpret what we see on someone's face to better understand the content of their minds. We learn to read if someone is joyful, engaged, bored, tired or, if we are TSA agents studying human behavior in airports, up to no good. We improve our stories the more we practice Skill 10 because nonverbal stories require the body to be involved. This takes practice. Our face, voice, body language and personal space comprise the story-telling package. While we are accustomed to words as our primary mode of communication, our body engages the content of our minds to tell its story for others to view.

The use of our body adds flavor to our stories. As Van Edwards and her group noted during her research to find nonverbal differences between the TED talks, how people used their hands told another story. She writes, "The bottom TED talks had an average of 124,000 views and used an average of 272 hand gestures. The top TED talks had an average of 7,360,000 views and used an average of 465 hand gestures — that's almost double! Hand gestures seem to keep your audience more engaged."[81] With practice we discover nonverbal stories are fun,

80 http://www.chicagotribune.com/bluesky/hub/ct-bc-learning-from-ted-talks-bsi-hub-20150929-story.html

81 http://www.chicagotribune.com/bluesky/hub/ct-bc-learning-from-ted-talks-bsi-hub-20150929-story.html

engaging and invigorating. Remember to use your body and, yes, especially your hands when you interact with people.

How Skill 10 Is Normally Acquired, Practiced And Propagated

Skill 10 is a skill that, while at the forefront of every interaction, remains hidden behind the words and analytical content of our conversations. In other words, we tend to focus our attention on *what people are saying* all the while our emotional brain is tracking and deciphering the nonverbal elements the speaker is conveying through a message.

We learn Skill 10 because our families and communities have words, emotions and actions that line up. When they talk about how excited or sad they feel, their face, voice and body match their words. They respond according to what we expect excited or sad people to do. We know this as a genuine response that becomes internalized within our emotional brain. When there is an incongruity between words, emotions and actions, our brain picks up this distortion and has difficulty believing what people are saying. "Your words are right but your face and voice tell a different story" is what we feel. With Skill 10 we will trust our gut over the words we hear - which can be bad news for politicians.[82] Consider the rebuke from Jesus to the Pharisees who were compared with whitewash tombs where the outside actions did not match the inside motivations.[83] The leaders were hiding their true intentions and feelings which is what happens when we fail to utilize Skill 10 as part of the rich repertoire of our character.

The example of our family members and friends show us how to use Skill 10. We practice Skill 10 every time we communicate and tell our stories. We spread this hidden gem with every opportunity to convey our internal world using our face, body and voice tone. We invite others to "show us" what their words mean.

---

82 Obviously not every politician is manipulative, but those who are use words to mask true intentions.

83 Matthew 23. The term hypocrite means "mask-wearer, performer, pretender and actor" in the Greek. NT 5273.

How Skill 10 Is Remedially Acquired, Practiced And Propagated

Let's examine how transforming fellowship/koinonia can restore the missing *Tell Nonverbal Stories* skill. Early in the narrative of Luke we learn the angel Gabriel appears to a devout priest named Zachariah who is serving in the temple. Gabriel shares the good news that Zachariah's prayers have been answered; he and his wife Elizabeth are going to have a son. This news is a big deal. Zachariah and Elizabeth have not been able to have children for a very long time. They are old. They believed Elizabeth was barren. Imagine for a moment that an angel appears to you then tells you something big is about to happen. Something you have been waiting and praying for is going to take place. How would you respond? How would you feel?

Zachariah must have been overwhelmed. He hears this exciting news, quickly does the math, and is a bit perplexed. "We are old. We do not have children even though we have tried. My wife is barren. Here stands an angel before my very eyes!" These thoughts must have raced through his mind. With the painful history and the numerous limitations in his scenario, Zachariah questions the angel and asks for proof, a sort of deposit to ensure things will pan out.

Gabriel responds with proof by telling Zachariah that he will be unable to speak until his son is born. In all likelihood this was not the response Zechariah was hoping for; however, the priest was about to get really good at using Skill 10. Once Zachariah loses his voice he is unable to recite the joyful priestly blessing over the Israelites waiting for him to finish his work. Onlookers would have expected this blessing once he finished his service in the temple but this time Zechariah cannot use his voice and must use gestures and signs to convey, "Something big just happened here!" and seeing his excitement and probably his panic, the people assume he saw a vision.[84]

Zachariah's voice returns months later on the eighth day during the newborn boy's circumcision. What a long time! The priest's voice returns during the naming of his child and this time his response is much better - he sings a praise to God.[85]

84 Luke 1:22
85 Luke 1:67-79

Skill 10 is a fundamental ingredient for effective communication between people and groups. Skill 10 is not simply the absence of words it is the addition of the colorful and flavorful ingredients that enhance our communication and enrich our interactions. Skill 10 uses our facial expressions, eye contact, voice tone, posture, gestures, timing and intensity to improve how we communicate, increase our ability to attune with people and better understand the minds of people during conversations.

When Skill 10 is missing we tend to minimize emotions and miss the richness of joyful interactions. Our emotional intelligence becomes dulled. We do not know the story our face and body is telling others nor do we correctly gauge the content of other people's minds. Because of this disconnect we need the mirrors in our communities where people reflect back to us what we are saying and to help us update our internal interpreter known as mindsight. This means we take turns telling nonverbal stories then retell the stories back with words (Skill 7). We ask people what they are feeling and we compare their response with our best guess based on what we are seeing when we look at them.

In the *Next Steps* below a number of available resources train Skill 10 but one common way to practice with a peer is to start by thinking of a story we want to tell someone. We act out the story nonverbally and retell the story back with words. In the beginning this skill feels clunky, but over time with practice we become keen observers who effectively interpret and convey nonverbal skills. We practice and strengthen the skill with our peers until the skill becomes a natural part of our interactions.

Skill 10 - Action Step

Find a friend and practice telling a nonverbal story about something from your day. See if your friend can figure out what you are sharing. Don't leave your friend hanging; be sure to tell the story again including words and the elements of the four-plus story from Skill 7.

Skill 10 - Next Step

Skill 10 is a fun skill to practice! Make it a game with Charades or use some of our more focused resources to further your Skill 10 progress. You and your spouse can practice during a *Joy Rekindled* weekend or with the *30 Days of Joy for Busy Married Couples* book. *THRIVE Training* uses Skill 10 throughout the week including a bonus day during lunch and, if you are one of the lucky ones in Tracks Two and Three, breaks and breakfast as well. Watch the *THRIVE Lectures* and participate in the *THRIVE-at-Home* online curriculum for more information on Skill 10.

Conclusion

Zechariah, John the Baptist's father, lost his voice on account of unbelief in what the angel Gabriel told him concerning his son who was going to be "great in the sight of the Lord" who would "go before the Lord in the spirit and power of Elijah."[86] Zechariah practiced Skill 10 for nine long months, but thankfully we don't have to wait to lose our voice before practicing Skill 10. Chesed communities use Skill 10 to understand each other through shared mutual mind states where people rejoice and weep together. Skill 10 forms the fabric of chesed communities as members interpret what is happening on one another's faces, update and correct distortions, then convey genuine thoughts, feelings and motivations. Koinonia pockets provide additional resources to practice and learn Skill 10 where the weak and strong interact. With healing and transformation, we are able to remove the log from our own eyes and share thoughts and feelings with one another where we feel seen, valued and understood.

When I have Skill 10: I am expressive when I communicate with other people. It feels easy for me to notice what a person is feeling based on their face and body language.

When Skill 10 is missing or underdeveloped: I have a hard time understanding other people and people have a hard time understanding me. I tend to feel that people do not listen to me.

86 Luke 1:11-21

Skill 10 Application Step - *Owen and Amelia's Game Night*

Owen and Amelia learned about the nineteen skills and immediately went to work practicing the skills in their marriage. Their focus was two-fold: enrich their marriage and help their children learn new skills, especially Todd, their son with Asperger's, who has a limited ability to read body language.

Trying to keep skill training fun, they used Skill 10 for a variation of Charades which proved to be a meaningful family time where everyone was engaged and enjoying themselves. This fun night would turn into a family tradition where one night of the week they play games and do something fun. They noticed small but meaningful changes in Todd, which was another blessing.

Next, Owen and Amelia focused on their marriage with Skill 10 by telling nonverbal stories about their favorite moments. This simple exercise helped both of them feel more connected and more understood. It wasn't bad that their joy levels increased as well.

Chapter Thirteen
Brain Skill 11 - Return to Joy from the Big Six Feelings

We return to shared joy as we quiet distress.
We stay in relationship when things go wrong.

After taking a moment to ask God, "Why does this skill matter to You?" I found myself thinking,

> "I don't want My sheep to get lost or stranded. I am a God who provides and rescues; Skill 11 is My provision for My sheep to find their way back when they are lost in the wilderness of their emotions and turmoil. I know how it feels to have emotions and I want relationships to stay intact during upset."

The human brain is wired to feel six unpleasant emotions. Fear, anger, sadness, disgust, shame and hopeless despair are each signals of something specific going wrong. We need to learn how to quiet each of these different circuits separately while maintaining our relationships. This process sounds easy, but it requires practice and a trained brain to stay connected with us to show us the way back to joy. Training under these six emotional conditions covers the full range of our emotional distress.

You and I are designed for glad-to-be-together joy. Joy is our natural state. The longer we stay stuck in a negative emotion the weaker we become. Just six minutes in a negative emotion leaves the stress hormone cortisol in our bloodstream for 24 hours.[87] We are highly motived to return to a joyful state when distressing emotions arise. Feeling angry for 20 seconds is a much different experience than staying locked in anger for 20 hours or even 20 days. The failure to learn Skill 11 leaves us avoiding, side-tracking and disconnecting from the very emotions our brain is wired to feel. If we have not learned Skill 11 after the second year of life our emotions become unregulated. As we grow older we rely on non-relational strategies to manage what we feel rather than quiet our emotions back to joy. Relationships blow out. We justify our responses with, "She made me do it!" We start to blame others for our upset or we simply shut down. Many of us turn to artificial means of quieting, known as BEEPS, for comfort. Skill 11 is a relational life-preserver because we stay connected with the people we love even when we are genuinely upset with them.

Parents who have not learned Skill 11 cannot show their children how to properly manage and quiet big feelings. At this point "behavior-management" strategies shut children down from expressing themselves and hinder children from learning the path back to joy. Power-plays intensify. Parents try to modify behavior and soon problems become bigger than the relationship as parents revert to emotions like anger to *stop the noise*. There is a better way. We must learn how to quiet big feelings and return to joy with one another.

Once I became a father I quickly realized how well I stay connected and guide my sons was largely determined by my ability to manage my own emotions. It did not take long for me to have some practice in this area in the form of a dirty diaper. Somehow, up until the time my son Matthew was born, I managed to avoid things that disgusted me - like dirty diapers. One day my son needed a diaper change and, for whatever reasons, my wife was unavailable to intervene. It was

87 Dr. David Levy, MD. Neurosurgeon, author of Gray Matter: A neurosurgeon discovers the power of prayer...one patient at a time. Tyndale House, 2011.

my turn. I gently placed my son on the changing table then prepared myself for the adventure.

Matthew's deep blue eyes were staring back at me as he smiled and made cute gurgling sounds that babies make. While interacting, smiling and keeping our eyes connected, I managed to strip him down to his dirty diaper then I began to carefully remove the diaper. The smell was bad, but the contents were worse. I felt squeamish as my face grimaced. While holding my breath, I lifted my son's legs and tried to clean his legs, back and bottom. This task proved to be more demanding than I initially realized; this was no ordinary dirty diaper. I took a deep breath and what happened next would not easily be forgotten.

No one ever told me what happens when you lift the legs of an infant with diarrhea, how it puts pressure on the tummy, which turns the toddler into a loaded cannon. While holding my son's legs in the air, apparently too close to his belly, I was giving him a good cleaning when waste-matter suddenly flew across the room, all over my arm, the changing table, even hitting the bedroom wall several feet away! I shrieked then panicked. A string of prayers, pleading and indistinguishable utterances flew out of my mouth before I yelled for reinforcements. "Jen, HELP! We have a serious problem here!"

My disgust reaction was intense and my son felt some shame as he intently watched my revulsion. His bottom lip quivered, shaking like a leaf on a tree. He was on the verge of crying. I once again locked eyes with him then started a mutual dance of interactive joy smiles including glad to be together sounds. I stayed connected with him as I tried my best to clean the mess. As we recovered to joy Jen arrived on the scene. We worked together to restore peace and order. My son recovered from his shame and I recovered from my disgust. I knew at some level my wife enjoyed seeing my misery, but more importantly, the three of us stayed connected. We were glad to be together in the midst of some good old fashioned disgust. Because my feelings of disgust were shared then quieted, the ordeal was manageable for me, and in a short time we were laughing about the events. We returned to relational joy and with this experience under my belt my diaper-changing skills significantly increased. I would change many more diapers as disgust became a bump in the road compared to a pothole that could cause me to relationally "bottom-out."

Emotions we have not learned to manage will be avoided. For example, we people-please to avoid making someone mad. In this way we use fear as a motivator to avoid our shame and rejection (loss). When Skill 11 is missing in action, our friendships, families and churches do not resolve conflicts because who is right or wrong remains the focus. Rules and tasks steer people and conversations. Leaders end up avoiding situations that create specific emotions. We justify and spiritualize our non-relational responses and call them normal. No one considers the brain skill that returns us to joy and glad-to-be-together states.

Marriages, families, communities, even cultures develop strategies to avoid certain emotions. Who do you know avoids a shame message? Who amplifies fear? Who stays stuck in hopelessness? Who avoids disgust? Who is a road-rager? Who is a people-pleaser? As we look at the relational landscape of our networks we start to see the urgency for Skill 11.

How Skill 11 Is Normally Acquired, Practiced And Propagated

Our brain has to learn that negative emotions will not kill us. Negative emotions do not have the final word and ideally we learn this as infants after the first year of life because mommy and daddy share the emotion with us and help us calm down. After repeated episodes this cycle becomes internalized so the practice equips our brain to know what to do when feeling upset. Baby learns upset leads to connection with mommy which includes comfort and validation. Baby has no reason to fear negative emotions because her experience tells her that mommy is always around the corner ready to bring joy anytime joy is absent. Over time mommy is internalized and the developing brain will remember and simulate mother's care and comfort when feeling upset.

With repeated practice at higher levels of intensity, Skill 11 is strengthened as baby grows older. Interactions with parents then family and friends strengthen returning to joy from upset. Skill 11 is used while interacting with others within our chesed communities and returning to joy becomes a natural response to "how we do life" particularly during times of conflict and upsetting emotions. We show others how Skill 11 works in "live time" under real conditions when our emotions signal something has gone wrong internally or externally. In this way, Skill 11 propagates one relationship at a time. We do not think much about the ability to return to joy and stay connected until we encounter others who are stuck and unable to use the skill. Here we see problems become bigger than relationships as people use non-relational strategies to deal with their feelings. When stuck in negative emotions, our personalities can form around the specific emotion. We know people who are always sad, angry, depressed, etc. Relational casualties are around the corner wherever Skill 11 is missing, but the trained brains among us demonstrate how to quiet big feelings and stay relationally connected, which propagates Skill 11.

How Skill 11 Is Remedially Acquired, Practiced And Propagated

Let's examine how transforming fellowship/koinonia can restore the missing *Return to Joy from the Big Six Feelings* skill. King David was a man of great faith with many talents who loved God. God Himself said that David was a man after His own heart.[88] All we have to do is remember David standing up to Goliath, review David's war exploits or read the Psalms where he pours out his heart in order to gain respect for the man. King David was a remarkable leader who could be tender, courageous, inspirational and eloquent - but also fierce. The shepherd boy grew to become a successful warrior who at times displayed a bit of a temper.

We catch a glimpse of David's temper during the time he was fleeing from Saul. David hears about a wealthy man named Nabal who is sheering his sheep. This activity would have been a festive occasion for Nabal, his family and his servants. David sends some men to ask Nabal for help, namely, provisions for his men. David's men justify their request by reminding Nabal that David and his men protected Nabal's sheep and shepherds; his men did not mistreat Nabal's work-

88 1 Samuel 13:14, Acts 13:22

ers.[89] Nabal, whose name means fool, responds with a less than gracious reply:

"Nabal answered David's servants, "Who is this David? Who is this son of Jesse? Many servants are breaking away from their masters these days. Why should I take my bread and water, and the meat I have slaughtered for my shearers, and give it to men coming from who knows where?" (1 Sam 25:10-11, NIV).

Nabal's response is offensive, which infuriates David who responds to the news with, "Put on your swords!" David is appalled. David has some very big feelings. The time for talking is over. With 400 men at his side, David leaves in a fury to solve the Nabal problem. Nabal's wife Abigail hears what happened and quickly responds by gathering food and supplies to take to David and his men. We can't help but notice the contrast between David and Abigail. One person has shifted into a non-relational predator response and wants to decimate a village of people. The other stays relational and protective; she wants to preserve the village.

Abigail encounters David on his way to slaughter Nabal and all his men. Abigail falls at David's feet then pleads with David by validating and comforting David in his upset.[90] David accepts her intercession and offering then sends Abigail home in peace. David returns to joy from his anger and a cooler head prevails. Had David remained stuck in his upset incredible violence would have rained down on Abigail's family and community.

While we see examples of returning to joy throughout Scripture, a few beautiful Psalms capture the process of returning to joy. Psalm 30:4-5 says,

"Sing to the Lord, you saints of his; praise his holy name. For his anger lasts only a moment, but his favor lasts a lifetime; weeping may remain for a night, but rejoicing comes in the morning" (NIV).

---

89 1 Samuel 25

90 1 Samuel 25:24-31. Note, This is what Wilder and Warner call VCR to help people return to joy. VCR stands for Validate, Comfort and Repattern. When we are validated and comforted our brain is retrained to return to joy, Skill 11.

Here we see God's anger is no match for His favor and rejoicing follows weeping. In Psalm 126:5-6 joy follows sadness,

> "Those who sow in tears will reap with songs of joy. He who goes out weeping, carrying seed to sow, will return with songs of joy, carrying sheaves with him" (NIV).

In the New Testament Jesus prepares the disciples for their future trials and troubles by saying,

> "I have told you these things, so that in me you may have peace. In this world you will have trouble. But take heart! I have overcome the world" (John 16:33, NIV).

There is something greater Jesus wants the disciples to remember and hold onto. Returning to joy does not mean we avoid pain and upset but we stay relationally connected with the ones we love during our emotions and upset. It is with this lens we can read Peter's admonition in 1 Peter 4,

> "Dear friends, do not be surprised at the fiery ordeal that has come on you to test you, as though something strange were happening to you. But rejoice inasmuch as you participate in the sufferings of Christ, so that you may be overjoyed when his glory is revealed" (Verses 12-13, NIV).

Our communities give us plenty of practice with Skill 11 and if we want to learn and strengthen Skill 11 we must first identify the emotions we need help with. From there we focus on learning Skill 11 for each negative emotion the brain knows. Using the pockets of koinonia within our chesed communities, we locate people who have some ability to return to joyful relationship from anger, fear, disgust, sadness, shame and hopeless despair. These resources give us examples so we see and feel what it looks like to navigate a negative emotion back to joy. We identify our weak emotions then ask friends who have Skill 11 where we are weak to tell us four-plus return to joy stories about times they felt a negative emotion and returned to joy. We also watch people spontaneously react under stressful moments and see how they return to relational joy. Their example speaks volumes to our nonverbal relational brain. Here the strong members within our chesed communities stay connected with us when our relational brain falls out of relational mode and we need someone to validate, comfort and show us how to manage what we feel. As with all the skills, we don't keep the good stuff to ourselves. With practice we become the experts who have the skill and we help others. We use our example and stories to spread Skill 11 to those around us. Effective return to joy stories can be told in anywhere from 90 seconds to three minutes.

Dr. Jim Wilder and I designed Track Two of *THRIVE Training* to strategically train return to joy skills after a year of practicing the basic skills, including Skill 1 building joy and Skill 2 learning to rest. By Track Three, attendees are training Skill 11 to Track One and Two members. While we much prefer to see Skill 11 spread naturally because chesed communities already have the skill, the truth is our networks have a severe shortage of Skill 11 "trained brains" within our families and communities.

Big Six Emotions

Sadness - *I lost some of my life.*
Anger - *I need to protect myself and make it stop.*
Fear - *I want to get away.*
Shame - *I'm not bringing you joy and/or you are not glad to be with me.*
Disgust - *That's not life-giving!*
Hopeless Despair - *I lack the time and the resources for this.*

Skill 11 - Action Step

How well are you able to feel then quiet the "Big Six" emotions and return to glad-to-be-togetherness with people? Rate your Skill 11 ability for each emotion on a scale of 1 to 5 with 5 being the strongest and 1 the weakest. Try to remember real-life scenarios when you encountered each emotion. What helps or hurts your ability to return to joy from each emotion?

- When I feel sad. (I can do it) 5 4 3 2 1 (Not so well)
- When I feel angry. (I can do it) 5 4 3 2 1 (Not so well)
- When I feel afraid. (I can do it) 5 4 3 2 1 (Not so well)
- When I feel ashamed. (I can do it) 5 4 3 2 1 (Not so well)
- When I feel disgusted. (I can do it) 5 4 3 2 1 (Not so well)
- When I feel hopeless. (I can do it) 5 4 3 2 1 (Not so well)

Share your observations with a friend over a shared meal or cup of tea/coffee. Talk about what you learned as it relates to Skill 11 and invite your friend to identify how he/she handles the six emotions, then share stories about times you both returned to relational joy using the following elements from the four-plus story sheets:

- Show the authentic emotion on your face and in your voice.
- Maintain eye contact while telling your story.
- Use feeling words to describe emotions.
- Use feeling words for body sensations.
- Tell the story like you are involved (autobiographical).
- Keep your story concise.

Skill 11 - Next Step

THRIVE Training and *Connexus* are ideal steps to take in order to learn and practice Skill 11. Each of the three *THRIVE Skill Guides* build joy capacity and give additional practice returning to joy. Watch the *THRIVE Lectures* and participate in the *THRIVE-at-Home* online curriculum to apply and learn more theory behind Skill 11. *The Bridges of Chara* book by Deni Huttula is a great allegory of the brain's emotional landscape which is helpful for adults and children.

Conclusion

Trying to avoid negative emotions is like trying to run through an active mine field. Eventually we will encounter the negative emotion and something explodes. Without proper training the brain's emotional control center loses synchronization and this means we are stuck in our negative emotions, unable to stay connected with the people we love. Being stuck is no fun!

God designed the human brain to learn how to quiet and manage big feelings early in life so that we return to relationship with one another as we grow older. There is no faking Skill 11; either we can or we cannot return to joy from negative emotions. People who cannot return to joy either stay stuck, avoid upset or use left-brain strategies to cope with the absence of skills. This means people tell us what they think, what we should do, and how to do it rather than joining us in our upset. Proper training takes place when we feel and share the emotion as well as demonstrate how joy feels after the storm of negative emotions.

Learning Skill 11 happens in three primary ways: Someone in our chesed community shows us by their example during a negative emotion, we strategically exchange stories from moments we encounter big feelings using the four-plus story sheets as a guide, and Immanuel meets us in our distress. Immanuel is an excellent resource for all of these skills; however, we must practice and strengthen the skills with our communities that are rich in koinonia, the pooled resources where each member of the Body is indispensable and we suffer well and grow together.[91] Transformations result when we can navigate our own emotions. Transformations are incomplete until we can quiet our emotions and return to relational joy with those around us.

Chesed communities have learned Skill 11 and specialize in keeping relationships bigger than problems. In this way Skill 11 flows from chesed communities while chesed communities are created from people who are good at returning to joy together. Sharing distressing emotions and getting back to joy builds and strengthens bonds between people. We bond with the people who share our emotions and show us the way back to joy! The next brain skill we will explore is similar to Skill 11, only this time we focus on *staying our relational selves during the negative emotion*.

---

91 1 Corinthians 12:21-26

When I have Skill 11: When something bothers me I stay connected with people and quickly calm down.

When Skill 11 is missing or underdeveloped: I avoid certain emotions. Some emotions do not go away when I feel them. I find it difficult to stay connected with the people I care about when I feel angry/afraid/sad/disgusted/ashamed/hopeless.

Skill 11 Application Step - *Pastor Daniel's Dilemma*

Pastor Daniel loved God and people. The beloved pastor devoted his life to visiting the sick, serving the poor and praying for the hurting. People who knew Pastor Daniel for any length of time quickly respected the man. In spite of his devotion, one issue continued to hinder Pastor Daniel's joy; he ran his life on fear. His decisions and relationships were anchored in fear. Pastor Daniel tirelessly worked to keep the elders of his church happy, his congregation happy, even his family happy. Pastor Daniel was burning out because of his non-stop appeasement. To avoid disappointing people, he was running on fumes. While he was doing many good things, overwhelm and exhaustion were consuming the beloved leader.

During a lunch conversation, Pastor Daniel's friend Jack suggested he look at Skill 11, Returning to Joy, and consider this skill as a solution to his troubles. After some reading and research, Pastor Daniel recognized his pattern of evading negative emotions and using fear as a fuel for his life. A new-found hope was ignited. He now recognized what was missing! Pastor Daniel attended THRIVE Training with his wife and started using Skill 11. Pastor Daniel learned to face his fears because he now knew just what to do when feeling anxious and afraid. He learned to care for himself (Skill 8) and discovered that negative emotions like fear and shame would not be the end of him. In a short time his joy levels increased. Pastor Daniel started to blossom instead of burn out.

Chapter Fourteen
Brain Skill 12 - Act Like Myself in the Big Six Feelings

When we find our design we will be life-giving - whether we are upset or joyful.

After taking a moment to ask God, "Why does this skill matter to You?" I found myself thinking,

> "When My children discover their identities they find buried treasure. I designed My children to express their identities under every emotion and condition. It grieves Me to see My children lost in lies about who they are and unable to be themselves under good times or bad. I am a God of unity. I long to see My people function in the wholeness and completeness of mind that comes from Skill 12."

Now that we explored *returning to joy* from negative emotions we look at staying our relational selves *during* a negative emotion. We may wonder how staying relational <u>and</u> negative emotions can go together in the same sentence. We may be curious how someone can feel a negative emotion yet remain their true relational selves with God and others at the same time. It is time to explore Skill 12.

One crucial step to maintaining our relationships when we are upset is learning to act like the same person we were when we had joy to be together. A lack of training or bad examples causes us to damage or withdraw from the relationships we value when we become angry, afraid, sad, disgusted, ashamed or hopeless. I remember one time I watched a family member stay his relational self under stressful circumstances where I would have lost it.

Uncle Rich

One day Jen's aunt, uncle and cousins were driving up to visit Jen and meet me for the first time. After driving up most of the day to visit us, the family's van developed some problems and was malfunctioning. Something was not working the way it was supposed to work and strange sounds along with smoke emanated from under the hood. Thankfully, they arrived safely to visit us. While I know very little about car engines, I offered to assist Uncle Rich - more for moral support than anything else.

Uncle Rich propped open the van's hood then spent some time troubleshooting, patiently looking around to figure out where the problem originated. At first it seemed more was going wrong than right, but I was impressed by how patient he was. Uncle Rich used the work project as an opportunity to teach me about engines and how they should work. Uncle Rich scrupulously explained details about engines I never knew existed. When Uncle Rich would drop the flashlight or hurt his hand loosening a bolt, I expected a litany of profanity and yelling to ensue. I braced myself for the intense tirade, and much to my surprise, Uncle Rich stayed grounded. He did not raise his voice nor did he lash out. He stayed relational and continued troubleshooting and teaching. I could see he was visibly frustrated at times when things went wrong, but I was stunned by his ability to remain his relational self. "How can this man keep his cool?" I wondered while watching him work. I knew that I would have blown my gasket several times over while dealing with the frustrations he encountered. It was clear Uncle Rich had something I was missing.

At first I wondered if he was faking it because of my presence, but after two hours of close observation under difficult circumstances, I knew Uncle Rich was the real deal. Here is someone who stayed himself while feeling negative emotions and, after years of knowing the man, I have grown to admire his ability to stay himself when joyful, tired, overwhelmed or feeling any of the *Big Six* emotions. He is both consistent and predictable. Uncle Rich eventually fixed his van, but his example using Skill 12 demonstrated something new and profound for me: *it is possible to be upset and stay relationally connected with the people around us.*

Life throws us curve balls. Unexpected problems interrupt and plague our day. We live in a world where people hurt us and relationships create distress. Instead of trying to isolate ourselves from the many disappointments that can derail our relational brain, we can learn how to stay our true selves as God designed us when emotions arise. At the end of the day, *we are as good as our ability to manage what we feel.* How well we navigate upset largely determines the level of trust and closeness we create with other people. How well we attune and comfort others is a reflection of our ability to manage our own emotions. Do we stay relationally connected? Do we isolate? Do we attack? Our reactions tell a story. Skill 12 is what equips us to express our faith and values under increasingly difficult and ever-changing circumstances.

Skill 12 equips us to live relationally and respond gracefully as we navigate upset, pain, fatigue, distress, misunderstandings and loss. Our emotional brain must learn to feel unpleasant feelings and stay engaged, relational, kind, caring and attentive to ourselves and the people we come across on a daily basis. Avoiding upset is impossible. The greater goal must be placed on the values we want to express when we respond to ever-changing circumstances in a world where fiery trials show up on our doorstep.[92] A few moments of reflection tell us we have work to do in the area of staying the same person under varying emotions and conditions. This learning curve can feel

92 "Dear friends, do not be surprised at the painful trial you are suffering, as though something strange were happening to you. But rejoice that you participate in the sufferings of Christ, so that you may be overjoyed when his glory is revealed" (1 Peter 4:12-13 NIV).

like having a tooth extracted or more like an adventure to discover the buried gold hidden in our hearts. A bit of curiosity will go a long way as we seek the treasure-trove Skill 12 offers. We can ask, "Jesus, who did you create me to be and how should I best reflect this reality?"

How Skill 12 Is Normally Acquired, Practiced And Propagated

We learn Skill 12 because family members stay relationally connected with us when we or they feel a negative emotion. Family members stay the same people when upset so they are approachable, recognizable and relational. When this happens we learn negative emotions do not have the final word and it is possible to be ourselves when feeling upset. Otherwise, we act like a different person when encountering a negative emotion.

Babies learn to manage emotions and receive guidance from parents on how to regulate feelings and stay relationally connected. We learn from our clan what is acceptable or unacceptable during moments of upset. The best guidance comes from caregivers sharing emotions to help baby learn how to stay herself when feeling upset. Our shared experiences provide the resources to navigate upset. In this way we internalize helpful examples and carry them with us.

A trained brain has no reason to fear distress when our experience tells us distress leads to validation, comfort and attunement. Skill 12 connects us together as we express the best of ourselves and repair as necessary when things go wrong. This consistency to be ourselves under ever-changing variables creates safety and inspires others. We practice with our peers who have shared group values that, like mom and dad, instruct one another on who it is like us to be during upsetting emotions. People become mirrors to reflect our true hearts and guide us to be ourselves when big feelings erupt. Like Skill 11, our example and our stories provide the fuel to spread Skill 12 into our communities. Immanuel moments update our brain on who God created us to be and guide us to express the life of Christ in both good times and bad. Once learned, we become the mirrors to reflect back to others both who God created them to be and how to express that life during negative emotions. Our example speaks volumes to observers while our "acting like myself" stories train others in Skill 12.

How Skill 12 Is Remedially Acquired, Practiced And Propagated

Let's examine how transforming fellowship/koinonia can restore the missing *Act Like Myself in the Big Six Feelings* skill. Who in the Bible do you read about and think to yourself, "That's just how I would like to respond!" Or maybe you find those sections where you say, "That's not how I would respond!"

Skill 12 is what we use to relationally live from the heart Jesus gave us. Jesus spent a lot of time showing the disciples, mostly by His example, how to live and fully express their true identities. At one point Jesus corrects Peter after the zealous disciple cuts off the high priest servant's ear.[93] The sword Peter would have used was known as a "skull crusher" and was designed to cut through the helmet of a Roman soldier. We can imagine Peter was not aiming for the ear yet, Jesus stayed relational under difficult circumstances and restored Malchus' ear.

Later on Jesus prayed and forgave those who crucified Him.[94] Without Skill 12, unregulated emotions run rampant and dictate our behaviors and responses - often contrary to our faith and values. Can you think of anyone in the Bible who was afraid and landed in the belly of a fish or someone who was angry and struck a rock with his staff?

Paul is another person with a lot of Skill 12 practice. In 1 Corinthians 4 he writes,

> "For it seems to me that God has put us apostles on display at the end of the procession, like men condemned to die in the arena. We have been made a spectacle to the whole universe, to angels as well as to men. We are fools for Christ, but you are so wise in Christ! We are weak, but you are strong! You are honored, we are dishonored! To this very hour we go hungry and thirsty, we are in rags, we are brutally treated, we are homeless. We work hard with our own hands. When we are cursed, we bless; when we are persecuted, we endure it; when we are slandered, we answer kindly. Up to this moment we have become the scum of the earth, the refuse of the world" (Verses 9-13, NIV).

93 John 18:10
94 Luke 23:34

How about this for a job description? There is more. Hebrews 11 talks about the men and women who were faithful to God in spite of overwhelming oppression and obstacles.

> "And what more shall I say? I do not have time to tell about Gideon, Barak, Samson, Jephthah, David, Samuel and the prophets, who through faith conquered kingdoms, administered justice, and gained what was promised; who shut the mouths of lions, quenched the fury of the flames, and escaped the edge of the sword; whose weakness was turned to strength; and who became powerful in battle and routed foreign armies. Women received back their dead, raised to life again. Others were tortured and refused to be released, so that they might gain a better resurrection. Some faced jeers and flogging, while still others were chained and put in prison. They were stoned; they were sawed in two; they were put to death by the sword. They went about in sheepskins and goatskins, destitute, persecuted and mistreated— the world was not worthy of them. They wandered in deserts and mountains, and in caves and holes in the ground. These were all commended for their faith, yet none of them received what had been promised. God had planned something better for us so that only together with us would they be made perfect" (Hebrews 11:32-40, NIV).

Our life stories and examples within chesed communities provide fertile ground for the seeds of Skill 12 to grow and spread. Speaking of Skill 12 stories, here is where the remedial work happens. In addition to the power of an example and real-life experience with someone who remembers who they are during upsetting emotions, we learn Skill 12 when we listen and share "acting like myself" stories that include genuine emotional responses and focus on "here is how I did or did not act like my true self when feeling upset." With practice, we learn Skill 12 and the skill is both strengthened and propagated by our telling Skill 12 stories to friends, family and community members. Like every other skill, we find no shortage of opportunities to practice. *THRIVE Training* uses Skill 12 throughout each of the training tracks while Tracks Two and Three specifically demonstrate what Skill 12 looks like by personal stories and examples.

Skill 12 - Action Step

What area of your life today could use some clarity to better understand who you were meant to be?

List the top 5 qualities you would like to express when you feel upset. These are not necessarily the qualities you currently exhibit when you are upset, but what you would like to express. Next, categorize how you currently respond to each emotion and use the 3 categories to identify your responses: Protector, Predator and Possum.

I would like to express these qualities when I feel angry, afraid, disgusted, sad, ashamed and hopeless.

Quality #1 -

Quality #2 -

Quality #3 -

Quality #4 -

Quality #5 -

What I do when I feel emotions:

	Protector Traits	Predator Traits	Possum Traits
Angry			
Afraid			
Disgusted			

What I do when I feel emotions:

	Protector Traits	Predator Traits	Possum Traits
Sad			
Ashamed			
Hopeless			

Skill 12 - Next Step

Similar to Skill 11, you can meet with friends who are good at staying their relational selves during negative emotions. Tell your friends or family members what you learned about Skill 12 and invite them to tell you stories about times they felt a specific emotion and how they stayed themselves during the emotion. Offer some suggestions for what you are looking for in these stories.

THRIVE Training and *Connexus* are the ideal steps to take in order to learn and practice Skill 12. Each of the three *THRIVE Skill Guides* offer additional practice using Skill 12. Watch the *THRIVE Lectures* and participate in the *THRIVE-at-Home* online curriculum to deepen your understanding of Skill 12.

Conclusion

We find great satisfaction when we discover who God created us to be and we relationally express this reality to the world. Our chesed communities equip individuals with Skill 12 by providing mirrors to reflect back what is or is not life-giving during upset as well as offer helpful examples to demonstrate Skill 12. In this way people develop this important relational skill. Likewise, people who stay themselves not only demonstrate Skill 12 but provide the foundation for chesed communities because they have the needed stability chesed communities require.

We learn Skill 12 by interacting with people who already have the skill. Their example and presence guide us to effectively use the skill in our own lives. "Acting like myself" stories let us learn, strengthen and spread the skill to others around us. In this way transformations must include Skill 12 as people begin to see clearly who they are and live this reality in their relationships. Immanuel moments provide additional clarity on who God created us to be with direction for how to express this revelation under ever-changing circumstances and emotions. Acting like our true selves lines up with the characteristics, qualities and values of Jesus who said,

> "...the Son can do nothing by himself; he can do only what he sees his Father doing, because whatever the Father does the Son also does" (John 5:19b, NIV).

When I have Skill 12: I remember what is important to me when I am upset. Family and friends say that I am consistent. People would say I act like the same person whether I feel happy/angry/afraid/sad/disgusted/ashamed/hopeless.

When Skill 12 is missing or underdeveloped: I am inconsistent and inflexible when I feel upset. I respond like a different person once something bothers me. My personality changes with different emotions. I try to avoid negative emotions.

Skill 12 Application Step - *Julie's Jam*

While in the middle of a home remodeling project, Julie received news her job was coming to an end. This news came as a shock and added strain to her already full life. With three children in school and incoming bills beginning to pile up, Julie and her husband Mike were feeling a hailstorm of pressure coming down on their heads. Conflict ensued. Slamming doors, the "silent treatment" and overwhelm defined their existence. The normally joyful family was coming unglued.

Knowing something needed to change, they decided to see a marriage counselor to discuss the strain in their lives. Julie and Mike learned about Skill 12, Acting Like Myself, and a light bulb went on. Julie and Mike were feeling consumed by the onslaught of negative emotions, and they had no idea who they were during negative emotions. Their pattern was to simply avoid negative emotions which caused them to lose sight of what's important. Their new goal was to learn how to stay themselves in the midst of negative emotions. This would take some purposeful effort.

Julie and Mike started sharing Skill 12 stories in addition to inviting their friends and family members to tell Skill 12 stories. Julie and Mike started running Connexus in their community which gave them resources, skills, joy and hope. A lot of hope. Eventually Julie found a new job, but her marriage and family, just like her house, received a refreshing makeover.

Chapter Fifteen

Brain Skill 13 - See What God Sees: Heartsight

Seeing people and events from God's perspective yields a life filled with hope and direction.

After taking a moment to ask God, "Why does this skill matter to You?" I found myself thinking,

"I want My children to see clearly as I see clearly. False-seeing leads to deception and destruction. While the enemy manipulates, I restore heart vision. Listening to My voice and seeing as I see guides My children into My presence. You will have many trials in this world, but be of good cheer, I have overcome the world.[95] Here is true heart vision."

Heartsight, Godsight and *i*Sight are all terms to describe a simple but profound reality: *seeing what God sees.* Pick the word that works best and embrace a new skill that will bring peace and alter the landscape of your life.

95 John 16:33

Without Skill 13 Jim Elliot would not have attempted to evangelize the Huaroni people of Equador which cost him and his friends their lives but planted a seed that would sprout and bear remarkable fruit for countless lives. Skill 13 provides the lens to see that there is more going on than our eyes tell us.

Hope and direction come from seeing situations, ourselves and others the way they were meant to be instead of only seeing what went wrong. This spiritual vision guides our training and restoration. Even forgiveness flows from seeing people's purpose as more important than their malfunctions and makes us a restorative community instead of an accusing one. Through our hearts we see the spiritual vision God sees.

Without Skill 13 people become problems to solve, commodities for personal gain and enemies to avoid. We miss the beauty of redemption when Skill 13 is absent. With Skill 13 we see there is more to a person and situation than our limited vision allows. We are reminded that God is with us and at work, even when fears and feelings say otherwise. With Skill 13 we turn to Immanuel for perspective and comfort. Speaking of perspective, let's look at the well-known story of a dead man who came back to life.

Lazarus

At one point Jesus receives news his friend Lazarus is ill, but he stays on across the Jordan for two more days before leaving for Bethany, just outside of Jerusalem. Upon arriving, Jesus discovers his good friend has been buried in a tomb for four days. Lazarus' two sisters, Martha and Mary, who previously opened their home to Jesus as a place of hospitality, were in deep despair. The distressed sisters, along with their grieving community full of hurting people, were a short distance away from Jesus as He approached. From all appearances this grieving community did not expect to see their beloved friend again this side of heaven.[96] Yet, for the author who tells this story, the eternal life Jesus offers is something to be entered into immediately, not something to look forward to some day down the road.[97] Skill 13 says there is more to this story.

---

96 This story takes place in the Gospel of John Chapter 11.
97 Parashat HaShavuah Chukat, Torah Club Volume 4, Page 813.

In Judaism during Jesus' day, it was common for grieving family and community members to sit on the floor for seven days. During this period of time, the mourners neither washed nor worked, nor did they greet people who arrived on the scene to comfort them. It was customary that mourners would give permission for the comforters to offer words of condolences.[98] In the middle of this seven-day process, Martha breaks tradition, gets up, and greets Jesus and His travelers while Mary stays behind.

Once she reaches Jesus, Martha confronts Him about what she sees. If only He had been there, the bad thing would not have happened. Soon, Martha returns to grab her sister Mary, who then comes to Jesus with her mourners close behind. Mary approaches Jesus and expresses similar sentiments as her sister, "If you had been here, my brother would not have died" (Verse 32). All of us can relate to the pain and bewilderment the women must have been feeling that day: *If only God was with us, our circumstances would be different.* Yet, Skill 13 tells us there is more we do not see.

As only a good comforter would, Jesus attunes with the mourners and shares their feelings (Skill 18). Jesus then asks for the stone to the tomb to be removed. Martha quickly objects, knowing that all hope of resurrection was gone. After all, the sages wrote and the rabbis taught that three days was the absolute maximum amount of time a resurrection could take place. After the third day they believed the person's spirit left the body for good.[99] All other resurrections Jesus did took place on the same day, but this one is different. Onlookers watch with anticipation, wondering what will happen next. Skill 13 says there is more going on here.

The stone is removed. Jesus prays to the Father and calls the dead man back to life. Lazarus walks out in his grave clothes. People are stunned. Some believe; others flee. It is a sad bit of irony that Jesus, after giving life, is, from this very moment, marked for death by the high priest and religious leaders of the day. These leaders even added Lazarus to their hit list.[100] Skill 13 says there is more to this story as well.

98 This process is known as a Shiva. Parashat HaShavuah Chukat, Torah Club Volume 4, Page 815.

99 Genesis Rabbah 100:7

100 John 12:10

Skill 13 reminds us we see but a fractured view of reality, a painting only partially finished. When using Skill 13, we discover the beggar on the street has a story, our annoying coworker needs some love and the people around us are a few quarts shy on joy. We find that we are put in a situation for a reason. We seek wisdom when we ask, "Lord, what do You see in this frustrating situation?" and, "Lord, help me see my child/spouse/friend with Your eyes." We find peace when we ask, "Lord, how do You see this painful moment from my day?" Skill 13 opens the door for a broader perspective that extends beyond the scope of our limited understanding and explanations.

Skill 13 Brings Comfort

Skill 13 tells us there is more going on when pain, problems and upsets disrupt our day. We discover what is important in a given situation as Skill 13 provides perspective and restores our peace. I remember the day Skill 13 brought me some much needed peace. I was feeling deep despair because of ongoing chronic back pain that was limiting my life. After months of searching for solutions I was still in a lot of pain most of the time. I felt spent. Unsure what to do next, I turned to Skill 13 during prayer.

After a few minutes of remembering moments God was with me, I said, "Lord, I feel tired and overwhelmed because of my back. I see no way out nor do I feel relief. I am so helpless!" I shared out loud while peering out the window looking into my backyard. Because it was winter, all I could see were bare trees and an empty forest. There was no life. I then expressed my thoughts and feelings with, "Lord, this is how I feel! There is no life in these woods and the leaves have fallen to the ground. The animals have long disappeared. Lord, what do You want me to know about this?"

After a few moments I sensed God was with me. I felt nudged to keep looking out the window. Soon I noticed squirrels playing on the trees. I watched as birds flew around. I remembered how the bare woods would soon transform in the springtime when flowers and trees burst forth with new life. At this point I sensed Immanuel say, "Chris, what you see is death, but what I see is an opportunity for My life to be revealed. I can use your weaknesses and your limitations for

My glory." Wow! I thought to myself. God can use my weaknesses for some greater purpose! I remembered the times in Scripture when Jesus encountered hurting, disabled people and He touched them. Now I felt seen, valued and understood. I felt hopeful and peaceful. I carefully got up from my chair to share this special moment with Jen.

This Skill 13 moment is now something I remember and cherish whenever I feel stuck in back pain. Skill 13 works well to quell the flames of upset, but it can be used as a way of life to help us navigate good and bad times. We watch beautiful sunsets and sense that Immanuel is with us, orchestrating the moment as a gift for us. We feel thankful (Skill 4). Seeing what God sees guides our faith and restores our relationships.

How Skill 13 Is Normally Acquired, Practiced And Propagated

We learn Skill 13 because our family and community show us some of what God sees in and around us. As mom and dad see us through heaven's eyes we start to see ourselves through heaven's eyes. This seeing translates to our seeing others and seeing life from God's lens. We learn and practice Skill 13 within our family and community, then we pass it on relationally. Interactions and conversations provide opportunities for Skill 13 to spread.

How Skill 13 Is Remedially Acquired, Practiced And Propagated

Let's examine how transforming fellowship/koinonia can restore the missing *See What God Sees* skill. Skill 13 says there is more going on than what our eyes and ears tell us. Peter, James and John experienced Skill 13 in a most profound way when Jesus led the men up a mountain. Imagine this scene:

> "His face shone like the sun, and his clothes became as white as the light. Just then there appeared before them Moses and Elijah, talking with Jesus. Peter said to Jesus, "Lord, it is good for us to be here. If you wish, I will put up three shelters — one for you, one for Moses and one for Elijah." While he was still speaking, a bright cloud enveloped them, and a voice from the cloud said, "This is my Son, whom I love; with him I am well pleased. Listen to him!" When the disciples heard this, they fell facedown to the ground,

terrified. But Jesus came and touched them. "Get up," he said. "Don't be afraid." When they looked up, they saw no one except Jesus" (Matthew 17:2b-8, NIV).

There was more going on and Jesus shared this reality with His friends. The three men caught a profound glimpse of a heavenly reality while still dwelling in their earthly bodies. While Skill 13 may not always be as exciting as this mountaintop experience, we really do not know what will happen until we use the skill. Colossians 3 tells us we should direct our attention toward and seek this heavenly reality:

"Since, then, you have been raised with Christ, set your hearts on things above, where Christ is seated at the right hand of God. Set your minds on things above, not on earthly things. For you died, and your life is now hidden with Christ in God. When Christ, who is your life, appears, then you also will appear with him in glory" (Verses 1-4, NIV).

We see the prophet Elisha teaching his servant Skill 13 during a situation where they were surrounded by an enemy army of soldiers on horses and chariots. Naturally, the servant was alarmed, and the prophet assures the servant there is more to the story. The prophet prays for the Lord to open the eyes of the servant who then sees hills full of horses and chariots of fire around Elisha.[101] The chariots of fire were always there, but the servant was unable to see them.

Like Elisha's servant, we learn Skill 13 from others who have the skill; they pray with us and help us practice interacting with Immanuel to see some of what God sees. The skill is strengthened when we have the confirmation of witnesses who also sense some of what we sense God is doing/seeing/thinking about a situation. Our trusted friends help us practice Skill 13 using the test of shalom (peace), Scripture and what we know about the character of Jesus. We learn to silence the flesh, or in Greek sarx (Skill 14), and soon we develop the confidence to use Skill 13 as a lifestyle in our relationships and interactions.

---

101 2 Kings 6

Skill 13 is woven throughout *THRIVE Training* so that attendees practice seeing some of what God sees each day. In Tracks Two and Three, Skill 13 soars to new heights as attendees train Track One members using Skill 13; this is the propagation step in the training sequence.

Skill 13 - Action Step

Identify a low-intensity moment from your day where you lost your peace or you simply were not aware of having peace. For example, *as I was sitting in traffic today I felt frustrated and did not feel peace.*

Moment from my day where I was missing peace:

Next, write out a special moment or a gift you feel like God has given you at some point then spend three minutes remembering appreciation (Skill 4) or focusing on a time you felt like God was with you. For example, *I feel like my small group is a gift from God. My friends in the group help me feel seen and valued.*

My appreciation moment and/or time I felt like God was with me:

Invite Immanuel to show you what He wants you to know about His presence during that window of time. For example, after your three minutes of appreciation/God moment, ask or journal, *Lord, what do you want me to know about Your presence when I was sitting in traffic today?* Notice the thoughts that come to mind and whether the thoughts restore some peace. If you feel stuck, simply return to your appreciation moment and talk with Jesus about anything that hinders you from perceiving Him. This is practice so do not be discouraged if you cannot notice any "God thoughts." Sometimes we need to try this several times to keep our relational brain circuits active.[102]

Possible Immanuel's thoughts:

Skill 13 - Next Step

In addition to practicing Skill 13 in your prayer life, one of the best resources to practice Skill 13 is the *Joyful Journey, Listening to Immanuel* book. Additional resources include *Share Immanuel: The Healing Lifestyle* book and CD, *Joy Starts Here: The Transformation Zone, 30 Days of Joy for Busy Married Couples, Joy Rekindled* weekend marriage retreats, *Jesus In Mind: Talks on Kingdom Life* lessons and the premiere resources, *Connexus* for communities and *THRIVE Training* for bonded pairs.

102 Learn more about relational brain circuits from the resources at Life Model Works (joystartshere.com) and Dr. Karl Lehman at (kclehman.com)

Learn more about hearing God and the availability of the Kingdom of God by reading anything written by Dr. Dallas Willard especially *Hearing God: Developing A Conversational Relationship With God* and *The Divine Conspiracy, Rediscovering Our Hidden Life in God*. Also consider the work by Dr. Karl and Charlotte Lehman at kclehman.com and the ministry, *Alive and Well* at alivewell.org expand on Skill 13.

Conclusion

Skill 13, *See What God Sees*, is a crucial ingredient that separates chesed communities from any other kind of community because people see one another as God sees them which keeps relationships bigger than problems. Skill 13 resolves conflicts and maintains relational homeostasis because, at the end of the day, people turn to Immanuel for guidance and clarity rather than amplify pain and problems. Skill 13 is the glue that binds chesed communities together and leads to deep and profound transformations that hold up with the test of time. Deep transformations occur when people utilize Skill 13 in what we call the Immanuel Lifestyle where we value joy and talk to God about everything.[103] Pockets of koinonia have the potential to change the world because Skill 13 is essential for the spreading of the Good News that we have a loving God who is available, present and delighted to be with us.

When I have Skill 13: It is normal for me to talk with God about my life. I usually feel more peaceful after talking and listening to God. I feel as though God is a helpful resource in my life.

When Skill 13 is missing or underdeveloped: I spend very little time talking with God or I simply do not talk to God about my life. I feel like God is angry and/or disappointed in me most of the time. I do not perceive God as a helpful resource throughout my day. It feels like God is distant and powerless, as though He doesn't care about me.

103 "Be joyful always; pray continually; give thanks in all circumstances, for this is God's will for you in Christ Jesus" (1 Thessalonians 5:16-18, NIV).

Skill 13 Application Step - *Lydia's Lack of Connection*

Lydia was feeling rejected by her coworkers. Not knowing what she did wrong, her so-called friends were treating her poorly and ostracizing her. When she approached a group of coworkers talking together, they would walk away. Something was going on and Lydia had no idea what or why. Feeling confused and upset, Lydia's distress was mounting. On the verge of quitting her job, Lydia decided to reach out to her prayer partner Dalia for help and perspective.

Dalia prayed with Lydia and invited Immanuel to show what she needed to know about the painful work situation. After a few moments, Lydia remembered Jesus' words about being persecuted because of Him and she started to feel some compassion for her coworkers. "I sense they are treating me how they were treated at some point in their lives" she told Dalia. Lydia felt she needed to pray for each of them and soon she was crying as she sensed they were living out of their hurt and immaturity instead of the heart Jesus gave them. She sensed from Immanuel this is also how they were treating Him. Skill 13 started a shift in Lydia that changed both her behavior and her perspective toward her coworkers. In coming weeks her cold work environment thawed as Lydia practiced the nineteen skills to create belonging and joy. More than anything else, Lydia found hope and peace the more she used Skill 13 in her prayer times.

Chapter Sixteen

Brain Skill 14 - Stop The Sark

False "Godsight" may seem true to us at the moment but leads to blame, accusation, condemnation, gossip, resentment, legalism, self-justification and self-righteousness. The sark requires active opposition.

After taking a moment to ask God, "Why does this skill matter to You?" I found myself thinking,

> "Skill 14 is like the shepherd's staff that protects the sheep from predators and from falling off cliffs or plunging into pits. The seed of Adam and Eve poisons My people and I have come to set the captives free. Skill 14 provides the safety net for My people to stay by My side without straying due to destructive forces guiding their hearts and minds."

Just as Skill 13 is seeing what God sees that guides us to a peaceful destination, Skill 14 is the skill that turns us around when we are lost. Sometimes we think we are heading in the right direction when in fact we are going the wrong way. This Greek word sark (also rendered sarx) refers to seeing life according to our view of who people are and how things should be. This conviction, that I know or can determine the right thing to do, is the opposite of Skill 13, *Seeing What God Sees*. For the sark, people become what they have done (the sum of their mistakes) or what we want them to become for us. Blame, accusations, condemnation, gossip, resentment, legalism, self-justification and self-righteousness are all signs of the sark. We feel judged, alone and misunderstood when others fail to see us as God sees us.

Skill 14 sustains joy in our spiritual communities by stopping destructive, painful behavior. All of us are susceptible to hallucinating and seeing a mirage as we walk through the desert of this life. Instead of drinking sand in our desperate search for water, we must learn to discern reality from fantasy. We may think we are seeing clearly when in truth our reality is not reflecting what God sees. The brain can only use old information for its evaluation of good and bad. When the past does not include God's shalom, we predict the future using old, faulty information from the past. Faulty information from the past comes in and colors our predictions and conclusions. "I just knew you would hurt me like everyone else!" we hear from the sark. Self-fulfilling prophecies come true as we end up far from our intended destination.

Some of Jesus' most ardent accusers were the most devout teachers who studied and memorized the Torah scrolls better than anyone. The sark, my own understanding, says that I know the right thing to say or do. The sark says that picketing funerals of soldiers who have lost their lives is what a follower of Christ would do. The sark says that being right is more important than keeping our relationships intact. The sark leads to toxic hope about the future, "If only this changed I would be happy!" The sark burns bridges with the very people we care about and want to stay connected with. Without Skill 14, unprocessed pain, fears and contempt guide our lives and direct our decisions. The more Biblically trained the sark is, the more dangerous it becomes because we use scripture to justify our actions. I remember a time I encountered a "Biblically trained sark" in a group of church leaders.

The Sark Attack

My wife Jen and I traveled over one hour for what we felt was a good opportunity. We were to meet an influential leadership team interested in starting joy in their church. Once at the restaurant we placed our food orders and the team raised several questions about a specific scenario with a woman who was trapped in an abusive marriage. Feeling compassion for this woman, I expressed the importance of a married couple creating belonging by surrounding themselves with community. I included a word of caution about the need for protection and shelter when danger arises, then I shared some inspiring success stories about similar situations.

At this point one leader in particular asked to hear my theology on divorce. While the question surprised me I responded with my desire to see couples fully restored to joy but this does not always happen when violence is in the equation. Trying to be helpful, Jen and I offered specific steps they could take to provide protection and adequate intervention for their situation. Now red-faced and looking more like a tomato, the leader intensely pressed in, asking to talk about whether divorce was allowed or sinful in Scripture. He raised his voice then sharply asked, "Do you believe God would encourage a marital separation?" He became abrasive and I noticed a knot in my stomach. The team adjusted uncomfortably in their seats as tension filled the air. I took a drink of water and used Skill 18 to mentally conclude his control center's fast-track processor was starting to unravel as big emotions intensified. Our words and responses increased his irritability. He began to cite Scriptural passages and tossed them like detonated grenades. He stopped relating to us as human beings and started attacking. His demeanor was piercing and his approach crushing. After a few more minutes the meeting ended.

"What was that all about?" Jen asked on our drive home. We felt like we were blind-sided by a Mack truck. The leader's urgency to debate theology while the rest of the team sought to examine options for the endangered woman seemed unbalanced. Jen and I felt compassion for the woman and her situation. We compared our meeting to a group of life guards debating the best rescue techniques while a swimmer splashes and drowns before their eyes. We took a moment to pray and practice Skill 13 for some perspective into the situation. It was at this moment I remembered the angry synagogue ruler who rebuked Jesus for healing a crippled woman on the Sabbath.[104] We suffered a sark attack over lunch and, sadly, I knew that I was just as susceptible as the man who wanted to challenge us. Discussing theology is a good thing to do but the timing was off. It seemed we missed what was important to do at that moment because we did not listen to God's Spirit.

Speaking of timing, the wise King Solomon once wrote there was a time for everything under heaven, a time to search and a time to give up, a time to keep and a time to throw away.[105] Unless we are anchored and interacting with Immanuel, how do we know what time it is?

The sark is active when we believe we are doing right when in fact we are producing death. It is common to confuse the sark with intellect and to misunderstand this concept that is found in over 150 places in the New Testament alone. Apart from three occasions where sark refers to carnal or carnality, every case where sark is used refers to man in his fallen state. We can say the sark is the unredeemed part of man. As 1 Corinthians 15 tells us, "For since death came through a man, the resurrection of the dead comes also through a man. For as in Adam all die, so in Christ all will be made alive."[106] Because we are victims of Adam's poison, we need the antidote that is only found in a genuine relationship with Jesus Christ where we listen and interact.

Every one of us has fallen from glory and all of us are bent mirrors that reflect distortions of who we were meant to be. Historically there are many examples when the people of God thought they were doing right but the outcome was catastrophic. Some used quotes from the great apostle Paul to justify slavery and abuse. Murder and injustice against Jewish families has happened since the time of Christ, with many Jewish people slandered, "Christ killers." Even Stephen, the first Christian martyr, was stoned to death by leaders using Scripture to justify themselves. Spirituality without maturity (Skill 8) is similar to giving children the keys to a Formula One race car. They really do

104 Luke 13

105 Ecclesiastes 3:1-8

106 1 Cor 15:21-23 (NIV)

not have what they need to drive, and when they try to be big they end up crashing in a glorious pile of debris that harms the driver and innocent bystanders.

Skill 14 is what helps us remove the log in our own eyes to correctly gauge what is going on around us, especially what is happening inside the minds of other people. We prevent ruptures and spiritual abuse by applying the brakes to what Scripture calls "the flesh" or "meat." All of us at some point have been convinced we knew the right thing to do as we think to ourselves, "If only people listened to me, the results would be good!" A wise man once said, "There is a way that seems right to a man but in the end it leads to death" (Proverbs 14:12, NIV). The "way that seems right" is the sark that must be stopped. Much like a cowboy lassoing a stubborn bull at a rodeo, we must engage Immanuel and invite God's Spirit to reveal to us the ways we think we are giving life when in truth we are bringing death through the sark. We may think we are building joy when in fact we are robbing joy and spiritually "kicking" the people around us in a most unhelpful way using our complacency, spirituality and the number one killer of communities, self-justification.[107]

How Skill 14 Is Normally Acquired, Practiced And Propagated

Skill 14 is the counterpart to Skill 13. When we learn to see things as God sees them, we are better able to recognize when God's influence is missing and people are using their flesh/own understanding/sark rather than following God's heart.

Skill 14 is best learned in families and churches that value both truth and relationships. We best learn truth from personal relationships where people have an interactive relationship with Immanuel that guides their life and decisions. Skill 14 develops in two primary ways. First, we watch others humbly live while taming the sark's influence; these are people who are correctable and who repair with us after realizing they had a "sark attack." Second, we receive guidance and feedback from mature, trustworthy people who have Skill 14 experience. They help us check our intentions, notice our blind spots, and correct our distortions.

107 Learn more with JIMTalks audio lessons Volumes 24-25.

Skill 14 is strengthened with prayerful discernment where we learn to "listen to our gut" when something has the signature of God's peace versus moments something sounds religious with the signature of the sark. This can only happen in the presence of chesed communities where koinonia pockets guide, correct and walk with us as we grow. Much like carrying a flashlight into a dark room, we begin to propagate Skill 14 when we use it to guide others who are lost.

How Skill 14 Is Remedially Acquired, Practiced And Propagated

Let's examine how transforming fellowship/koinonia can restore the missing *Stop the Sark* skill. The need for Skill 14 entered the picture the very moment Adam and Eve ate from the tree of the knowledge of good and evil. Their eyes were opened, death and "the flesh" now became the thorn humanity would have to deal with. Scripture tells us the offspring of the flesh is flesh but the offspring of the spirit is the Spirit.[108] In this context we learn the Spirit gives life while the flesh counts for nothing[109] and flesh cannot inherit the Kingdom of God.[110] Scripture does not hold "the flesh" in high regard and for a good reason. There is a real battle going on between our flesh and our spirit and Galatians provides some insight into how these two warring members fight against each other in a fierce tug of war contest.

> "So I say, live by the Spirit, and you will not gratify the desires of the sinful nature. For the sinful nature desires what is contrary to the Spirit, and the Spirit what is contrary to the sinful nature. They are in conflict with each other, so that you do not do what you want. But if you are led by the Spirit, you are not under law. The acts of the sinful nature are obvious: sexual immorality, impurity and debauchery; idolatry and witchcraft; hatred, discord, jealousy, fits of rage, selfish ambition, dissensions, factions and envy; drunkenness, orgies, and the like. I warn you, as I did before, that those who live like this will not inherit the kingdom of God. But the

108 John 3:6
109 John 6:63
110 1 Corinthians 15:50

fruit of the Spirit is love, joy, peace, patience, kindness, goodness, faithfulness, gentleness and self-control. Against such things there is no law. Those who belong to Christ Jesus have crucified the sinful nature with its passions and desires. Since we live by the Spirit, let us keep in step with the Spirit. Let us not become conceited, provoking and envying each other" (Galatians 5:16-26, NIV).

There is a strong contrast between the flesh and the Spirit and on this side of glory we must strive to maximize life in the Spirit and minimize life out of the flesh. We are not talking about extreme asceticism where we severely neglect our bodies, rather, Skill 14 is the skill that furthers the process of living in the Spirit. We remedially learn Skill 14 in a similar way as the natural process: *we rely on people who have the skill to guide us.* With trusted friends and family members, we turn to these lampposts for "a witness" in our decisions and relationships. There is wisdom for Skill 14 in the passage where Jesus says, "Again, I tell you that if two of you on earth agree about anything you ask for, it will be done for you by my Father in heaven. For where two or three come together in my name, there am I with them" (Matthew 18:19-20, NIV). This is not simply a verse about finding people to agree with us so we get what we want; it is an example of mutual mind between people and the Living God where we are "on the same page." It is the result of a chesed community with like-minded people who gather to engage the Living God. In this way we practice Skill 14 in the safety of our relationships where people share our values to follow the Father's will and live from the heart Jesus gave us. We check our reality and intentions with one another. We remain open to correction and invite others to help us identify our blind spots.

Practice strengthens Skill 14 and with humility and a receptivity to God's nudging; we begin to walk with others who are on the same learning curve. Skill 14 spreads like helicopter seeds carried by the wind toward new destinations when we walk with one another and worship the King in spirit and in truth.[111] *THRIVE Training* includes Skill 14 practice in each of the training tracks to equip attendees to both practice and propagate this valuable skill.

111 John 4:24

Skill 14 - Action Step

Answer the following questions:

First, how would you summarize your feelings from an interaction with someone who thought they knew the right thing for you but their responses left you feeling misunderstood?

Second, what examples from the Bible come to mind where people thought they were doing right but later discovered they were missing God's intended desire?

What areas of your life can you recognize the signature of the sark?

Skill 14 - Next Step

Learn more about the sark by listening to *Jesus In Mind: Talks on Kingdom Life* lessons, Volume 8 on the heart and sark. Practice the *THRIVE Skill Guides* and attend *THRIVE Training* for more hands-on practice with Skill 14. Watch the *THRIVE Lectures* and participate in the *THRIVE-at-Home* online curriculum to learn more about Skill 14.

Conclusion

Skill 14 preserves our relationships and protects our church communities from the toxicity that arises when people think they know the right thing apart from God's Spirit and will. Skill 14 gives us the discernment to notice when people seem to be missing God's heart and intentions and are pursuing their own agendas. Chesed communities rely on Skill 14 to stay anchored in mature love that is expressed when weak and strong members interact, tender responses to weaknesses are the rule, and an interactive relationship with Immanuel leads to peace.[112] Koinonia pockets bring calm and produce clarity as members use Skill 14 to guide their fellowship, relationships and worship. Transformations result once sark activity stops. Actively opposing the sark leads to transformation in members much like the time Ananias prayed for Saul and scales fell from his eyes so he could see again.[113] Removing sark activity results with clear vision, Skill 13, where healing occurs and joy levels continue to increase.

When I have Skill 14: People would say I am quick to listen and slow to speak. I give people the benefit of the doubt most of the time. Relationships are more important to me than being right. I am careful with my judgments toward other people because I know that I can be wrong. When I realize my mistakes I am quick to apologize.

When Skill 14 is missing or underdeveloped: Being right is more important to me than staying relational with people. I believe people need me to correct them. I have no problem telling people what I think they need to do in order to live a better life. I know the Bible better than most people.

---

112 *Joy Starts Here: The Transformation Zone* by E. James Wilder, Ed Khouri, Chris Coursey and Shelia Sutton. Shepherd's House, Inc. 2013.

113 Acts 9:17-19

Skill 14 Application Step - *Frank's Furnace*

Frank was a pillar in his church who loved God and felt compassion for hurting people. With the blessing of his pastors Frank started a class that would bring discipleship and healing to the congregation. After months of success and much good fruit resulting from the Christian program, some of the church members believed there was not enough Scripture in the curriculum to justify keeping the program. Even though these members were not part of the program, they pressured the leaders to put a stop to Frank's work. After weeks of painstaking conflict, Frank's pastors put a pause on the program. This setback confounded Frank and many church members. People asked Frank if he was going to leave his beloved church.

It was during this time Frank learned about relational skills and particularly how Skill 14 identifies and disarms sark activity. Frank looked at his situation with new eyes. After some prayer Frank perceived Jesus was with him and he felt like Jesus gave some insight into how big a fire the sark can create. Frank remembered examples in Scripture where Jesus was accused of doing wrong, even being accused of casting out demons by the prince of demons. Frank sensed in some mysterious way that Immanuel was using this as an opportunity to draw him and his community closer to Jesus and that there was more to this story. Frank could now see his leaders and accusers with eyes of compassion.

Frank has been working to keep relationships bigger than problems. He invited people to share testimonies from the class and spoke with the church congregation to see how the training is both Biblical and useful for the fellowship. Today, Frank is still in his church and is now teaching on ways to grow gentle protector skills and how to live an Immanuel lifestyle. With his leaders blessing, Frank's classes are running again. Lives are being changed.

Chapter Seventeen

Brain Skill 15 - Quiet Interactively

Skilled reading of facial cues allows us to operate at high energy levels and manage our drives without hurting ourselves or others.

After taking a moment to ask God, "Why does this skill matter to You?" I found myself thinking,

> "I am the Good Shepherd who likes to play with His sheep. Because I care for My sheep, I am careful to protect them from My strength. I interact and play at the level they can handle in order to avoid going too far. I desire all My children to know their strength and avoid overwhelming each other during interactions. Skill 15 keeps My people in the boat, together, during stormy seas."

Using the ventromedial cortex that is part of Level 4 of the control center, together with the intelligent branch of the parasympathetic nervous system, allows us to control the upper end of arousal states. Instead of taking us all the way to quiet/peace, Skill 15 allows us to operate at high levels of energy and quiet just long enough to avoid going into overwhelm. This system controls aggressive, sexual and predatory urges so we can avoid harmful behaviors. This means that our brain learns to control high-energy emotion states while keeping an interaction going without flying "over the top." Without training, this brain system will go over the top in a scary way. Who have you seen lose it and go over the top? Pretty much all the villains in our superhero movies lack Skill 15 and, in most cases, the good guys don't have it either.

Skill 15 prevents some of the more violent, aggressive responses a person can develop. Skill 15 keeps us from going over the top during fits of anger, fear, excitement, sex and arousal. Based on early life experience, particularly with the father between 12 and 18 months, children learn to regulate fear responses and control the two types of aggression known as "hot" and "cold" reactions. Interactive quieting enables us to resist "hot" reactionary impulses and avoid premeditating "cold" revenge responses. We have no shortage of tragedies where Skill 15 was missing in people who use violence in order to solve a problem. Our schools and work places are now some of the more susceptible settings for this deficit to show up and, as Skill 15 drops out of society, we will see an increase in violence as a statement to punish others in a narcissistic style. When children fail to learn Skill 15 there is no mechanism in place to alert the nervous system that it is now time to stop before the interaction goes too far.

Coffee Shop Catastrophe

All of us have gone too far at some point, and we have witnessed someone going too far. The results are not pretty. I remember a time Jen and I were sitting in a coffee shop when an acquaintance walked in. I already knew this woman was not glad to be with us because of a previous misunderstanding; however, by the look on her face it was clear she was really not glad to see us. In fact, she was searching for us and after spotting us she darted our direction and yanked a chair from our table to place her foot on. She leaned in a mere handbreadth from our faces. I had the thought about how far south this interaction was going to go when she let it fly.

The woman screamed and unleashed her fury at Jen about a perceived slight that recently took place. The customers and workers in the coffee shop stopped what they were doing and turned to see the commotion. The intensity on the woman's face and the tone of her voice was overwhelming. I noticed my wife frozen in fear, and I felt my body tense up. There was no pause from the barrage of angry darts. "Who do you think you are?" "How dare you!" I quickly stepped in and caught her eyes. I diverted her attention with a Time-Out gesture and in a calm but high-energy voice I said, "This is important, you are upset! Let's calm down." Then we took a moment to catch our breath. Our friend paused, but her body language told us she was not finished. After a few short rapid-fire outbursts, I suggested we take a break and soon the woman left. It was intense!

Our friend did not have Skill 15 which would have kept the interaction going at a higher level of energy without going over the top. We could have stayed connected and avoided plunging into the depths of overwhelm. In many cases, episodes like these quickly turn violent as "hot anger" lashes out or people walk away in their "cold anger" and calculate how to best exact revenge. We know how commonplace the absence of Skill 15 can be with popular sayings such as "revenge is a dish best served cold." People with Skill 15 see no need for revenge as a solution to solve a problem; they simply recover from their upset and do their best to stay connected with the people they love.

As mentioned in Skill 9, tickling is a common experience that stays fun as long as overwhelm cues are respected. When pushed beyond our ability to manage intense feelings, the brain's evaluation center at Level 2 quickly shifts into "Bad and Scary" mode. Now our brain suspends its highest levels of processing in order to deal with the lack of attunement and mutual mind where we feel connected and understood. We now feel alone and overwhelmed. The fun quickly fades.[114]

Skill 15 is best learned when dad plays tickling and wrestling games, including "I'm going to get you." Dad intuitively relies on

114 Learn more about the pain processing pathway at Dr. Karl Lehman's website, www.kclehman.com.

interactive facial fear experiences to identify fear signals then pause. Skill 15 can be practiced later in life by going on extreme adventures such as camping and backpacking. During *THRIVE Training* we use carefully designed exercises to effectively train Skill 15. These training exercises are impactful and delicately balanced so people can practice the skill in a safe environment. Because our most painful experiences arise from moments involving people who lack this skill, we must train slowly and methodically.

The brain region responsible for Skill 15 is Level 4 of the control center which oversees real-time updates and predicts negative outcomes. These functions were missing in my friend who could not see our overwhelm cues and adjust her responses accordingly in the coffee shop. She failed to put herself in our shoes to figure out how we may feel based on her approach and adjust her method of solving the problem. This part of the brain at Level 4 also calms the fight/flight/freeze response at Level 2 so we return to our relational selves after a melt down. When working correctly, we rapidly update a situation in "live time" to avoid going over the top. We can observe a person's face switch from fun to fear then alter our responses accordingly. With damage to this circuit or a lack of training, problems quickly arise because cues are not recognized. It is like accelerating your car down a hill when the brakes quit working. Relational casualties loom on the horizon.

While experience and genes play a role, we see some of the more severe personality disorders develop when Skill 15 is not acquired in the brain's development process during the first year years of life. We can see anything from borderline personality disorder issues and disorganized attachments to sociopathic and violent personalities. The good news is Skill 15 can be learned; it is a trainable skill that can be practiced under the correct conditions. Prison ministries and organizations around the world are starting to catch on to the need for key personality skills such as Skill 15, *Interactive Quieting*. Just imagine a world where people know how to keep their relationships going under high energy emotions - without going over the top!

How Skill 15 Is Normally Acquired, Practiced And Propagated

As mentioned in the previous section, we learn Skill 15 because it shows up in our families and the community members who are close to us. Family members and friends use Skill 15 to keep interactions safe and manageable so we feel protected during moments of high energy and intensity. The father is especially crucial to train children how to use Skill 15. Dad tickles, wrestles, chases and plays at high energy levels without pushing too far. Those short pauses are the key to Skill 15 and much like dogs who play together by gently nipping and biting each other, we will use play to gauge when we are going over the top and correct our behavior as we navigate mutual play times. We strengthen Skill 15 in adolescence and we spread it as we interact with parents, grandparents, siblings, our friends, even strangers. Because we experienced Skill 15 growing up, our ability to sustain interactions without going over the top is simply part of our character. When we have this fast-track ability we find it perplexing why others cannot notice they went too far and modify their behavior.

We pass on Skill 15 by our example during personal interactions. We coach others who are missing or weak in the skill. Like the playful dog who yelps when another dog bites too hard during play, we relationally sound the alarm when others need to "catch their breath" and take a breather during intensity.

How Skill 15 Is Remedially Acquired, Practiced And Propagated

Let's examine how transforming fellowship/koinonia can restore the missing *Quiet Interactively* skill. In Mark 3 we find Jesus in a synagogue on the Sabbath along with a man with a shriveled hand and some Pharisees who were looking for an opportunity to accuse Jesus. As good predators do, the Pharisees "watched him closely" to see what Jesus would do with the man and his shriveled hand. A shriveled hand was a hopeless state; an incurable condition. The sages had rules against physicians working on the Sabbath but there was no problem with God healing someone on the Sabbath. The Pharisees, taking God's Torah to the extreme, disputed in those days as to whether prayer for the sick was permitted on the Sabbath.[115] These radical

115 IVP Background Commentary: NT

teachers were looking for trouble and Jesus knew it. Let's look at what goes down in this built-for-Hollywood drama.

> "Jesus said to the man with the shriveled hand, "Stand up in front of everyone." Then Jesus asked them, "Which is lawful on the Sabbath: to do good or to do evil, to save life or to kill?" But they remained silent. He looked around at them in **anger** (Orge) and, deeply distressed at their stubborn hearts, said to the man, "Stretch out your hand." He stretched it out, and his hand was completely restored. Then the Pharisees went out and began to plot with the Herodians how they might kill Jesus" (Mark 3:3-6, NIV).

As a sign of rabbinical respect Jesus provides the Pharisees an opportunity to answer and, at face value, it sounds like Jesus is simply mad and sad at their stubbornness or "thick and callous skin" surrounding their heart. When we examine the Greek words behind Jesus' reactions we see intense emotions were present. The Greek word for anger is *Orge*,[116] which implies violent passion, justifiable abhorrence, anger, indignation, vengeance and wrath. Orge is not simply frustrated or perturbed, it means if you are feeling this intense reaction you want to kill someone as in the state of "hostile vengeance." Orge is something to "put away" because of where it can lead, and Orge is used in Ephesians 4:31-32,

> "Get rid of all bitterness, rage and **anger** (Orge), brawling and slander, along with every form of malice. Be kind and compassionate to one another, forgiving each other, just as in Christ God forgave you" (NIV).

We are to "get rid of," "loose" and "sail away" from Orge. We see it show up again in Colossians 3:5-9,

> "Put to death, therefore, whatever belongs to your earthly nature: sexual immorality, impurity, lust, evil desires and greed, which is idolatry. Because of these, the **wrath** (Orge) of God is coming. You used to walk in these ways, in the life you once lived. But now you must rid yourselves of all such things as these: **anger** (Orge), rage, malice, slander, and filthy language from your lips" (NIV).

116 Strongs 3709, Phonetic Spelling is or-gay'

Orge is not something we want to foster or allow to fester, rather, as these passages suggest, we must run from this level of intensity for sin is close at hand. We know Jesus did not sin but here Jesus is infuriated and outraged. Have you seen someone outraged before? What does it look like? What does it sound like?

We can imagine Jesus' body, face and reactions would have conveyed the strong emotion yet Jesus stayed connected and remembered who He was and held onto what was important (Skill 12). Jesus continued interacting at a high level of energy, which is what we expect when Skill 15 is available. In this case Skill 15 was present and Jesus brought healing and life.[117] If we remember Cain who was very angry or incensed[118] because his brother Abel offered a sacrifice that was pleasing to God and Cain's sacrifice was not, Cain lacked Skill 15 and did not master or have dominion over his cold and calculating anger which led to killing his brother.[119]

In one case the presence of Skill 15 brought life and in the latter its absence led to death. Teachers, parents, policemen, prison guards, counselors and anyone who serves people on a regular basis knows full well what happens when individuals lack this crucial relational skill.

Skill 15 is a difficult skill to train because training must happen under ideal conditions at high levels of energy with observers to step in if trainees miss overwhelm cues. Skill 15 takes Skill 9, *Take a Breather*, to a new level because Skill 9 means we simply stop when we notice the first sign of overwhelm. Skill 15 keeps the interaction going at high energy levels with short pauses to avoid going over the top. The moments in our lives where people were missing Skill 15 while interacting with us are some of the more painful moments, so there is a delicate balance of practicing the skill while we stay in relationship where we can quiet as needed.

At *THRIVE Training* we have a series of exercises designed to train Skill 15 in manageable doses in each of the training tracks. In one style of exercise, attendees practice Skill 15 using a variety of emotions while telling verbal and nonverbal stories as they move closer to

117 I first heard about this teaching from Dr. Jim Wilder.
118 OT:2734 *Charah* meaning to glow, blaze up, zeal, jealousy, incensed
119 Genesis 4:4-8

their partners. These exercises have anywhere from four to six people who observe the exercise to ensure trainees do not overwhelm too intensely. Story-tellers must pause at the right times otherwise observers step in. Practice improves Skill 15 along with feedback and guidance from trainers and observers.

Each training track grows in complexity and attendees frequently express how meaningful these exercises have been. Practice in a safe environment where people are watching for overwhelm cues to ensure the exercises stay safe is redemptive and meaningful. In Track One attendees practice on the easier Skill 15 exercises, while in Track Two attendees are strengthening their ability to quiet interactively. By Track Three, the exercises have grown in complexity and intensity as attendees in Track Three focus on propagating the skill as they train members from the other tracks. When people graduate from the three tracks of *THRIVE Training*, they will have learned, strengthened and practiced spreading Skill 15 to others so they can now equip their communities.

Additional activities such as tickling, wrestling, chasing games, extreme adventures from camping and backpacking to survival training also utilize Skill 15. For younger children, interactive facial fear retraining and freeze games where children have to stop and freeze at certain times after doing a high-energy activity such as jumping jacks or running in place can also engage the intelligent branch of the nervous system that uses Skill 15.

Skill 15 - Action Step

When in the last several days have you observed or experienced someone in a one-sided "blasting" mode with another person? What were the results of this interaction for both people?' In other words, what was the relational toll that was paid for this non-relational moment? What happens in you when you have an intense interaction with another person?

Recent event in previous days:

Relational toll:

What happens in you when you have an intense interaction with another person?

Skill 15 - Next Step

Attend *THRIVE Training* with a bonded partner for the ideal training format to learn Skill 15. Bolster your skill practice with the *THRIVE Skill Guides*. Watch the *THRIVE Lectures* and participate in the *THRIVE-at-Home* online curriculum for greater understanding on Skill 15. Visit the YouTube channel: *Chris Coursey - THRIVE* to watch Chris and Jen use Skill 15 with their sons.

Conclusion

Our relationships suffer the painful consequences when people are unable to sustain interactions at high levels of energy without going over the top. Trust is diminished, and abuse and violence are not far behind. A lack of trust and intimacy between people arises whenever Skill 15 has dropped out. For this reason, chesed communities utilize Skill 15 to sustain closeness and protect one another's limits during interactions. People who use Skill 15 bring others together and foster the development of chesed communities. It is crucial within our pools of koinonia for people to have and use Skill 15 as they demonstrate to observers how to stay anchored during intensity without going too far. This becomes the "here is how we do conflict" standard.

Transformations must include Skill 15 to avoid passing on pain and trauma both relationally and generationally. It is not a far stretch to conclude anyone who wants to successfully reflect Christ to the world must develop Skill 15.

When I have Skill 15: I usually stay connected with people who are angry. I am good at helping people calm down when they are very upset. I let people rest when I interact with them. When I am very upset I continue to protect people from myself.

When Skill 15 is missing or underdeveloped: I avoid angry people. It feels overwhelming for me to interact with someone who is intensely upset. I usually "blow up" when people make me angry. People feel run over by me when I am upset.

Skill 15 Application Step - *Little Sister's Tempestuous Temper Tantrum*

Years ago I received an invitation from my cousin to watch her two elementary-aged children while she and her husband went on a cruise. While I did not consider myself a baby sitter, I was single at the time and working on a book so I had flexibility in my schedule. "How hard could watching children be?" I thought to myself. "I am a pastoral counselor and I train people in brain skills; this should be a piece of cake!" Little did I know.

I arrived for the adventure, and my cousin and her husband left early the next morning. On their way out the door, they woke up the children to say goodbye. Of course, having mommy and daddy leave was a big deal, so the children stayed awake hours before school started; this set the stage for a very long day.

After dinner the children began arguing and fighting, I knew the volcano was soon to erupt and it did. At one point older brother said *or did something to upset little sister which caused an outburst of unprecedented proportions. Little sister fell on the floor screaming, kicking and resisting all things logical. "You are tired; it's time for bed!" I said, hoping my words would somehow fix her distress. It only made things worse as she countered my response with, "*NO! I AM NOT GOING TO BED AND YOU CAN'T MAKE ME!*"*

Knowing little sister was tired, I carried her to bed and sat down next to her. She was still hitting, kicking and screaming. I was baffled what to do next and all creativity was gone. I then remembered my Kindergarten teacher, Mrs. Sheem, and how she would patiently sing a song when the class became too loud and disruptive. Mrs. Sheem would simply sing the chorus, "Quiet voices do I hear, Quiet voices do I hear" over and over again until the class calmed down. Amazingly this song always worked to settle the class down.

In my desperation I decided to try the song, hoping it would disarm the crisis. Starting at a high level of energy to match little sister's screaming, I sang, "Quiet voices do I hear, Quiet voices do I hear" over and over again. I then dropped my voice and lowered my energy levels moment by moment. I paused at the right times and in under two minutes I was whispering the song and little sister was whispering her temper tantrum. It was a most remarkable sight. Little sister was on the verge of sleep but every now and then, with her eyes closed, she would kick a leg and whisper, "I am not going to sleep!" Within seconds she had given up the fight and fell fast asleep. To this day I share the story with little sister who is now grown and in college.

Mrs. Sheem's song (and my example) worked because of Skill 15. Mrs. Sheem would start at a high level of energy to match the noise in the room, pause, then drop her energy and voice until the students calmed down. The brain's fast-track processor knows what to do when it has the training, and Skill 15 can be passed on generationally because it is used to bring peace and resolution. Singing is a practical way to keep the brain's hemispheres synchronized so that we stay connected during hard times. I used this same song and steps with my sons, and Skill 15 works beautifully to help us stay connected during intense emotions.

Chapter Eighteen

Brain Skill 16 - Recognize High and Low Energy Response:

Sympathetic and Parasympathetic - Some people are at their best with activity and others with solitude. Knowing our styles and needs brings out the best in all our interactions.

After taking a moment to ask God, "Why does this skill matter to You?" I found myself thinking,

> "There is no "one size fits all" when it comes to My people. I created each of you in My image with distinct qualities that reflect aspects of My character and nature. Some of My sheep like to play and run about while others sit quietly beside the still waters - both can hear the sound of My voice."

Not only are we wired to feel emotions, we can assign our emotions into two categories: high-energy and low-energy responses. Joy, anger and fear are energy-producing emotions that result from the "accelerator" or sympathetic branch of the autonomic nervous system. Sadness, disgust, shame and hopelessness reduce our energy levels. The energy-reducers are responses from the parasympathetic branch of the nervous system that act as the "brakes" to slow us down so we can quiet and rest. Tendencies to activate and engage or shut down often become "pursuit and withdrawal" or "anger and tears" instead of healthy, joy-based relationships that move in rhythm with each other. With practice, we can learn to regulate our emotions and match the energy levels of other people. Skill 16 helps us identify whether we are high-energy or low-energy responders so we can find what best suits the needs of our nervous system.

While the nervous system cycles between high and low energy states throughout the day, people tend to have a dominant response they gravitate toward. Some of us are high-energy responders who enjoy adrenaline-releasing activities, while others are low-energy responders who turn to quiet and "low-key" activities for our normal state. My friend Julie and I are good examples of this contrast. When I want to feel connected with God, for example, I find a nice quiet place free from noise and distractions so I can look out the window, pray and journal. (This is a challenge at times with two rambunctious sons!) My friend Julie prefers to go for a run up the mountains near her house while listening to loud worship music in her headphones. Julie becomes bored and distracted trying my method while I feel exhausted and overwhelmed trying hers. We are both unique, and there is no right or wrong style although some churches tend to think otherwise when it comes to worship music.

Let's look at more examples of Skill 16 with a sort of litmus test so that we can identify whether someone is a high-energy responder or a low-energy responder. When confronted with fear or "I'm not glad to be with you" shame, low-energy, parasympathetic responders are more likely to respond with self-deprecating attacks on themselves. In *Joy Starts Here*[120] we call this "possum behavior" as possums beat themselves up with, "I am such an idiot!" "I can't do anything right." "I am worthless!" Problems and feelings are about them, and low-energy responders often deny they matter or have any intrinsic value. Parasympathetic responders tend to feel like door mats and, to some degree, feel hopeless and helpless about life

120 E. James Wilder, et al. *Joy Starts Here: The Transformation Zone.* Shepherd's House, Inc. 2013.

and relationships. These responses may even define their personalities.

As parasympathetic, low-energy responders become possums who hide, sympathetic, high-energy responders develop "predator reactions" and attack. In their predatory moments, high-energy responders react to fear and shame with arousal and anger. They typically avoid these low-energy emotions, especially shame, by shaping the responses of other people through their anger; they also try to control and may even use punitive responses to get their way.[121] Blame, accusations and self justification are common. We may hear phrases such as, "Who do you think you are?" and "What's the matter with you?" We notice a knot in our stomach when we must work under or correct someone who runs their life, relationships and organization this way. It is common for critical responses to dictate how high-energy responders live and interact with family and coworkers. Noticing how people respond to healthy shame can tell you a lot about their ability to process the "not glad to be together" state.[122]

High-energy responders prefer hot emotions and avoid energy-draining emotions. Low-energy responders experience sadness as a more common emotion compared with anger or fear. Correcting unwanted patterns starts with Skill 16, which provides mutual understanding for each of our God-given differences. We extend grace through the delightful discovery that we are uniquely created. We remain mindful that people are wired for high-energy activities in the form of worship, exercise, music, play, extreme sports and hobbies while others seek low-energy activities. Low-energy responders gravitate to relaxing music, hot baths, quiet moments and environments low in stimulation. High-energy responders may become bored with what fuels low-energy responders. Likewise, low-energy responders become overwhelmed by some of what fuels high-energy people. There is no right or wrong style but trying to force others

121 Learn more in *Keeping Your Ministry Out of Court* by Dr. E. James Wilder and Dr. Ed M. Smith.

122 Healthy shame provides an opportunity to correct behavior while toxic shame is simply unhelpful and damaging to life and relationships. Learn more with JIMTalks Volumes 24 and 25.

to conform or change their styles proves exasperating. Who do you know who is a high-energy responder and a low-energy responder?

Leaders develop more joyful and efficient teams when they learn Skill 16 because they recognize individuals as high-energy or low-energy and then guide them toward roles and opportunities that best suit their preferences. Pastors may offer high-energy worship for sympathetic responders or low-energy worship for parasympathetic responders. Supervisors create a work environment that best suits the workforce and better meets the needs of their clients. Couples reach understanding when they recognize energy response styles and foster a home environment to best match those needs. When we fail to recognize Skill 16 we become resentful, even bitter, at other people for their differences and preferences. We may even hear people say, "If you were more like me we would get along so much better!"

Some people pursue prayer activities in an environment where the room is quiet, lights are dim, music, if any, is slow. Others prefer to jog, bike ride, exercise, dance and play to feel connected in prayer. Looking at these differences brings Skill 16 to the forefront of our minds and relationships. Skill 16 leads to acceptance and mutual satisfaction. With Skill 16 we identify these distinctions and respond with appreciation for what God has placed in each of His children.

How Skill 16 Is Normally Acquired, Practiced And Propagated

Families develop Skill 16 when they recognize different response styles in one another, and provide opportunities for children to play according to what works best for the child's nervous system. High-energy children are able to play, run, jump and ride their bicycles to "burn off energy" while low-energy children use books, puzzles, coloring books and lower energy activities.

Skill 16 is strengthened when teachers, counselors, coaches and pastors provide and alternate options for children to learn and play according to the response style that works best for them. Children will tend to gravitate to peers who share their response style but over time children develop the ability to "give and take" for the various activities they want to do that suits their nervous system - and they play with friends according to the response style of their friends. An example of this is, "I will play tag with you (high energy) but when we are done let's work on my new puzzle (low energy)." Skill 16 is best propagated with maturity (Skill 8) where people work toward mutual satisfaction in their relationships to interact with others in ways that make all parties feel satisfied, seen and stable. Activities are chosen based on what works for both styles. By discussing these options and making decisions that suits all parties, people begin to intuitively recognize these that differences are gifts to be respected, not faults worthy of shame or blame.

How Skill 16 Is Remedially Acquired, Practiced And Propagated

Let's examine how transforming fellowship/koinonia can restore the missing *Recognize High and Low Energy Responses* skill. With Skill 16 people have both high-energy responses and low-energy responses but we tend to have a dominant response that is either high or low energy. Let's look at some examples starting with Nehemiah.

Nehemiah was in great anguish for the state of his people. In spite of the risk to his own life, Nehemiah was sad in the presence of King Artaxerxes, the king he served in the capacity of a cupbearer. The king noticed Nehemiah's state and asked why his cup-bearer was so glum. Here is a pivotal moment for Nehemiah that spells his demise or allows him an opportunity to help his people. Thankfully the king responds favorably to Nehemiah and sends Nehemiah on an expedition to his people where he eventually rebuilds the wall around Jerusalem.[123]

While in Jerusalem, Nehemiah, Ezra and the Levites gather and teach the people God's Word. As the Israelites hear God's law for the first time they start weeping and grieving at how God's law has been broken and the painful ramifications of this neglect. At this point Nehemiah stops the people and reminds them the day was holy and sacred. It is the beginning of Sukkot, the Feast of Tabernacles, and this was to be a time of remembering, celebrating and rejoicing. Nehemiah instructs the people,

> "Go and enjoy choice food and sweet drinks, and send some to those who have nothing prepared. This day is sacred to our Lord.

123 Nehemiah 1

> Do not grieve, for the joy of the Lord is your strength." The Levites calmed all the people, saying, "Be still, for this is a sacred day. Do not grieve." Then all the people went away to eat and drink, to send portions of food and to celebrate with great joy, because they now understood the words that had been made known to them" (Nehemiah 8:10-12, NIV).

By their leaders guidance the people used Skill 16 to transition from mourning to rejoicing. This sounds easy but only a trained brain can synchronize energy levels and go from high-energy to low-energy back to high-energy. Without this habit in place we stay stuck in our emotional state. Do you know anyone who stays at a high level of energy or a low level of energy?

We see other examples in Scripture where people must use Skill 16 as they respond to ever-changing circumstances. In 2 Samuel 6 we read how David comes into town leaping, dancing and praising God with the Ark of the Covenant. Sounds of trumpets and shouts fill the air and David's wife, Michal, the daughter of Saul, watches the high-energy commotion at a distance from her window. Rather than engage in the festivities, join the party and praise God like David, Scripture tells us she "despised him in her heart" and does not join her husband. She remains misattuned and disconnected instead of rejoicing and celebrating. Here we see two different reactions that were neither matched nor shared. As the story unfolds we see it becomes a most painful and unsatisfying ordeal for Michal, who, if she had used Skill 16, she would have transitioned to join David in his celebration for a mutual mind state with high-energy rejoicing.

Not long after this in 2 Samuel 12 we read David is grieving the looming death of his newborn son with Bathsheba and he fasts, prays, pleads and lies on the ground hoping God will relent. He doesn't eat or move. This low-energy state, likely hopeless despair, consumes the king. Once he realizes his child is gone, David gets up, washes, puts on new clothes and worships God then eats a meal.[124] While this response confuses his servants we see where someone alternates energy states from low-energy back to high-energy. The Psalms are full of

124 2 Samuel 12:20

differing energy levels as a response to our worship and adoration of God as well. There are times we are instructed to be high-energy to clap, dance and rejoice before the Lord and other times we are to be low-energy and meditate on God's Word with rest.

> "Clap your hands, all you nations; shout to God with cries of joy" (Psalm 47:1, NIV).
>
> "Praise the Lord. Sing to the Lord a new song, his praise in the assembly of the saints. Let Israel rejoice in their Maker; let the people of Zion be glad in their King. Let them praise his name with dancing and make music to him with tambourine and harp" (Psalm 149:1-3, NIV).
>
> "Be still before the Lord and wait patiently for him; do not fret when men succeed in their ways, when they carry out their wicked schemes" (Psalm 37:7, NIV).
>
> "My eyes stay open through the watches of the night, that I may meditate on your promises" (Psalm 119:146, NIV).

With Skill 16 we can transition between "a time to weep and a time to laugh, a time to mourn and a time to dance" (Ecclesiastes 3:4, NIV). We use Skill 16 to engage Immanuel and one another for the ideal energy state that works best for our nervous system. Our communities must redemptively practice Skill 16 to move together rhythmically from differing emotional states and energy levels in unison. We meet others, particularly the youngest and weakest members, where they are emotionally at any given point and we attune with them. We begin to notice how this contingent communication feels. The times we fail to use Skill 16 become clearer, and we use these moments as teaching opportunities so everyone learns and grows.

We practice Skill 16 at *THRIVE Training* very purposefully and alternate from high-energy activities to low-energy activities. This flow provides a refreshing combination of joy and rest, but we take it even farther with practice noticing our own response styles and interacting with Immanuel during the style that best matches our needs.

Each day of training provides this opportunity with activities for all tracks so the skill is learned, practiced and strengthened by doing the exercises with other people. Then attention is drawn to how people feel and what they notice after trying activities that work best for their nervous system. After five days of intense practice, it is not too hard to return home and continue the practice and share what we discovered with our friends and family.

Skill 16 - Action Step

Stimulating the body's vagus nerve, the major component of the parasympathetic branch of the nervous system, releases the neurotransmitter acytlecholine which has a tranquilizing effect and relaxes us.[125] Activate this release by taking some deep breaths from your belly then notice how you feel.

Next, practice the *Shalom My Body* exercises to engage the vagal quieting response. View Dr. Jim Wilder demonstrating the exercises at the YouTube channel: *Chris Coursey - THRIVE.*

Last, answer the following questions.

Would you prefer a worship service high in energy with loud music or a low with soft music?

What activities do you turn to when you need to unwind and rest?

125 https://www.psychologytoday.com/blog/the-athletes-way/201607/vagus-nerve-stimulation-dramatically-reduces-inflammation

In your closest friends and family members who do you see as high energy responders? Who do you see as low energy responders?

High Energy	Low Energy

Find a friend or family member then tell them what you learned about Skill 16 and help them identify their response style.

Skill 16 - Next Step

Use the JOYQ online assessment to measure your skills including Skill 16 as well as attend *THRIVE Training* and use the *THRIVE Skill Guides* to improve your fast-track ability to identify response styles in yourself and your community.

Conclusion

At the surface Skill 16 does not appear to be a difficult skill to learn however much of the difficulty lies in our ability to use and apply it to our busy lives. Once we identify our response style we can adjust our prayer times, worship, study, work and exercise routines to match what best suits our individual and corporate design. When we notice possum or predatory responses in ourselves and others, we must embrace relational brain skills so we can change unwanted patterns to match the heart Jesus gave us.

Skill 16 is a natural part of the flow within chesed communities where a variety of fellowship activities meet the needs of all people whether they gravitate toward high or low energy activities. Relationships respect the limits of one another, and people with Skill 16 are the pockets of koinonia where limits are not only respected but people interact according to their "relational language" which can lead to deep transformations where people grow, heal and even encounter Immanuel for the first time.

When I have Skill 16: I am good at adapting to activities that best match the needs of other people. I understand people can have different responses that are unique to them. I am glad to accommodate the distinct preferences of other people.

When Skill 16 is missing or underdeveloped: I expect people to meet my needs. I believe everyone should be able to worship and hear God like I do. I find it difficult to accommodate the unique preferences of other people. I often become agitated when people do not have the same responses as me to situations and circumstances.

Skill 16 Application Step - *Lisa's Love of All Things Sports*

Lisa learned about Skill 16 and immediately her mind turned toward her family. Lisa recognized her preference for high-energy activities to keep the family busy and have fun. Lisa's husband Rob, on the other hand, preferred getting lost in books and watching television opposed to Lisa's desire for extreme sports and exercise. In the past, Lisa resented Rob for his "lack of interest" in her hobbies and activities, however, Skill 16 gave her a frame of reference for their relationship and some of the observable differences in their children. After sharing what she learned about Skill 16, Lisa and Rob found activities the family could do in order to meet the high-energy responders and the low-energy responders. This change felt much more satisfying and rewarding for the entire family.

Chapter Nineteen
Brain Skill 17 - Identify Attachment Styles

Our lives and reality need to be organized around secure love. Fears, hurts and emotional distance create insecure relational styles that will last for life unless we replace them.

After taking a moment to ask God, "Why does this skill matter to You?" I found myself thinking,

> "I created My children to approach Me with joyful anticipation of good things, particularly My delight over them with a loving, gentle response. One of the tragic consequences of sin and death is fear. My children become afraid and they hide and run away from Me. I am grieved to see the effects of Adam and Eve's downfall in this world, but My Son has come to give the gift of life, free from the plague of fear that binds My children to the evil one. Skill 17 is a gift to draw My children to Me and to one another in love."

When my wife Jen and I were early in our dating relationship we found ourselves doing a dance in how we related to each other. Jen was the pursuer who initiated date nights and frequently called to chat and check in. While I deeply enjoyed and looked forward to our time together, I felt a bit overwhelmed by her calls and requests to connect. Sometimes we would be driving home from our date night and she was already planning our next several date nights.

My beloved was searching for security by connecting while I was searching for security by running. If our relationship was compared with the sound of a car radio while driving down the road, I turned the volume down while Jen turned the volume up. My dismissiveness overwhelmed and made her more anxious while her intensity put me on the defensive. "What is wrong here?" I wondered. Neither of us felt very satisfied with this dance but she chased, I ran, and when she stopped chasing, I turned around and ran after her. Little did we know how much we needed Skill 17 to stop the teeter-totter effect in our relationship. Jen and I were operating from a foundation of fear that was in place long before we would ever take our first steps as infants. The issues we were having in our relationship are some of the most studied in childhood development and psychology.

From the moment we are born we require quick, predictable, consistent responses to our ever-changing needs. How well caregivers and family members respond to our moment-by-moment needs establishes a template for how we view ourselves and the world around us. These responses become the bedrock in the foundation of our emotional house. When our bonds are joyful, consistent and predictable, we develop a secure base, the strong foundation that holds up under the storms of life. We learn to regulate our emotions and engage the world with curiosity and creativity. When bonds are fear-based and unstable, we see the world through a distorted lens. A house built on this fragile foundation easily shakes with every breeze that blows our way. We become rigid and have difficulty regulating our emotions.

Skill 17 has to do with where we focus our attention, and the bonding center deep within the limbic system of the brain is where our reality is formed. This means the people we are bonded to tell us what is important, they mold and create our reality, and anything that happens at this level feels like it's simply part of who we are as a human being. People say things like, "It's how God created me" and "This is just who I am" to justify their attachment distortions and relational deformities. Deep down we know this is not who God created them to be. Skill 17 provides the impetus for joyful change.

We see ourselves through the lens of how we think others perceive us. Faces that light up to see us, Skill 1, are the nonverbal confirmation there is something innately valuable about us. Faces that do not light up to see us convey something is wrong or bad about us. Over time, this joy or absence of joy becomes internalized. For the developing brain, these patterns are influential on the development of our personality and identity. The bonding template impacts not only how we view ourselves and the world around us but also our interpretation and understanding of God. Do we feel that God lights up to see us, or do we feel that God is angry or even uncaring and disconnected? The answer to this question will shed light on the quality of our attachment template in the nonverbal right hemisphere.

Attachment Patterns

An earned, secure attachment where our needs are met in a timely fashion instills joy, peace, resiliency and flexibility into our character and these qualities are expressed relationally. We navigate hardships with confidence. In times of distress we remember who we are and hold onto what is important. We are able to express our deepest-held values while keeping our relationships intact. Who do you know that fails to express their values during moments of upset, strain or overwhelm? Odds are high it starts with you as every one of us has some work to do in this area.

We can have a secure or an insecure attachment style, and insecure attachment styles can be categorized into three distinct patterns. While we can have all three patterns show up in our relationships we will have one dominant pattern. The first is a dismissive attachment style[126], which is an underactive bonding pattern that leads to someone underestimating the importance of feelings and relationships. As I mentioned in my earlier example, this group turns down the volume of the car radio and usually thinks things are fine and upsets are "no big deal." Dismissives undervalue the importance of all things

126 Also known as an Avoidant attachment style. Learn more in *Joy Starts Here: The Transformation Zone* by Wilder, et. al.

relational and feel overwhelmed by other people's needs. When you go to them with a problem, they are likely to dismiss you and minimize your feelings. "You're overreacting!" "Get over it already!" "You are fine!" they say. Sadly, their life experience has taught them, "Why have needs when no one is going to meet my needs?"

By the time children reach the age of 12, their brain goes through an intricate rewiring process, a "house-cleaning" time that will make it harder for children to notice their own attachment signals, signs that tell them they want and need to attach to other people.[127] As they grow older, children become lost in their masks and coping mechanisms that cover their pain from lost connections. Addictions and compulsions develop from the failure to mutually and correctly attune relational rhythms of joy and peace. At this point, children get lost in non-relational activities such as computers, television, video games, pornography and more. A dismissive style is formed when mother or the primary caregiver is consistently distant and unavailable to respond to her child's needs. Over time the child concludes, "What is the point of having needs when my needs are not met?"

Second comes the distracted attachment style,[128] an overactive bonding pattern that leads to excessive intensity and anxiety over my own and other people's feelings. Here is the heightened, exaggerated response to emotions, hurts and needs. When distracted, people may constantly feel hurt or worry that other people are upset with them. They come across as "needy" to bystanders. In my experience with Jen, I can remember moments she would check in with me to be sure "we were ok" and in many cases she would inadvertently "make a mountain out of a mole hill" when there was a misunderstanding while I would completely dismiss what was important in the situation. My dismissive responses would usually include, "You are overreacting, calm down" while her distracted responses would say, "You are underreacting to me so wake up and pay attention!" I turned down the relational radio while Jen cranked it up. Distracted styles form when parents are inconsistently available and children never know

127 Learn more with the *THRIVE Lecture* series by Dr. E. James Wilder.

128 Also known as a Preoccupied attachment style. Learn more in *Joy Starts Here: The Transformation Zone* by Wilder, et. al.

what to expect. Because children never know what to expect they maintain a hyper-vigilant state to be on guard and constantly ready for any interaction with the parent. Additionally, parents insert their own desire for bonding onto the child and interact on their terms and in their timing. This interrupts the child's play. This intrusion looks innocent and is done with good intentions, but the interaction is more about the parent and less about the needs of the child.[129]

Last comes the disorganized pattern of connecting. Disorganized attachments are due to an unpredictability in the relationship. The child feels afraid to get too close to the parent because the parent is fearful or due to the parent's extreme, scary responses toward the child. The parent is both the source of terror and the source of love and affection.[130] This toxic pattern is the most difficult to correct. The child wants to connect but is afraid to get close. Just as we can imagine the consequences of pressing the accelerator and the brakes at the same time in our car, this is a similar reaction on the nervous system of the child. Disorganized responses have the highest percentage of a mental disorder later in life[131] and their signature is on more mental and post traumatic stress cases than the previous response styles. Disorganized styles hinder our ability to navigate life. Because of the extremes in connecting, children end up feeling depressed, angry and hopeless. We want to connect but we fear getting too close so we conclude "love hurts." For most of us, we notice our own disorganized responses when we need to talk with a difficult boss or a colleague who is known for angry outbursts. We feel our stomach turn in knots as we expect to be criticized and humiliated. Parents who are disorganized in their style of relating raise children who become disorganized.

Here is where Skill 17 comes in. Each of the insecure patterns are anchored in fear. A disciple of Jesus once said, "There is no fear in love. But perfect love drives out fear, because fear has to do with punishment. The one who fears is not made perfect in love" (1 John

129 Learn more about parental intrusions and attachment styles with Daniel Siegel, M.D. *The Developing Mind* and *Parenting From The Inside Out* by Siegel and Mary Hetzell, M.Ed.

130 E. James Wilder, *The Complete Guide To Living With Men.* Shepherd's House, Inc. 2004.

131 Siegel, Daniel, M.D. (2001) *The Developing Mind.* Guilford Press. Page 119.

4:18, NIV). Love is a better and much preferred motivation than fear. As we correct our fear patterns, we develop what is called an earned secure attachment where love and joy fuels and feeds our relationships. We function out of a secure base of operations. Not only do we disarm our fears, but we process the pain behind our insecure styles. This pain, the pain of loss, is known as attachment pain. While attachment pain is the hardest of the five pain levels to process in the brain's control center, we use Skill 17 to identify and Skill 18 to bring the solutions we need to disarm unwanted attachment patterns. We learn the Immanuel Lifestyle where we live with the awareness of God's interactive presence, and we invite Jesus to come and meet with us in the places our peace is absent. We start to build joyful bonds. People who respond to our needs with attunement and our weaknesses with tenderness help us grow. Attunement, validation, comfort and responsive timing to requests for connection help us feel seen, valued and satisfied.

Life and relationships are deeply rewarding when our attachments are secure and synchronized. With Skill 17 we begin to recognize the urges and fears that drive our thoughts, decisions and relationships. We examine the reasons for our deepest cravings that drive us to rely on BEEPS, which can be anything we use to artificially regulate our emotions and counterfeit relational joy. Skill 17 shines a flashlight on where we put our attention so we can adjust patterns of relating to the people we love. These are patterns that, in most cases, feel like the essence of who we are. We discover a treasure trove of hidden gems as we embrace the reality of who God created us to be, namely people who love, feel, rejoice, weep and celebrate as reflections of who God created us to be in relationship with the Good Shepherd and His people.

How Skill 17 Is Normally Acquired, Practiced And Propagated

Ideally we grew up in a home where our needs were met in a timely fashion with attentiveness, predictability and consistency. Joy and rest provided the relational landscape to build security. When this foundation is laid, we feel the world is a safe place and no matter what happens, everything will work out in the end. Secure bonds develop by caregivers who consistently meet our needs and repair when things go wrong. Good parents don't parent perfectly; they repair with children when they recognize mistakes and accept responsibility for the pain they cause. This builds trust and strengthens the bond.

In this way, we gravitate toward secure bonds as we grow older and people consider us confident, stable, and maybe even boring because we do not draw a lot of attention to ourselves. During interactions, people feel seen and respected by us, and we do not "scare easily" when others use fear as an attempt to motivate us. People enjoy our company because they find us a calming and "non-anxious" presence. Our example demonstrates what Skill 17 is all about and, additionally, we help people identify the fears that drive them. In this way, we not only build a secure attachment but we also help others identify their insecure styles as they notice the fears that drive their behavior and relationships.

We see this in Jesus' response to the wealthy ruler who asked what he needed to do in order to inherit eternal life. After suggesting he follow the commandments of God, Jesus points out the source of the man's fears when He asks the ruler to sell everything he has and give his belongings to the poor - then he can follow the Master.[132]

With a stable Skill 17 we remain a rock in that we are not easily moved when strain and stress strikes our life. We spread Skill 17 as we demonstrate what secure love looks like during interactions in our relationships and we help people identify their motivations. We repair when things go wrong, and we show others how to use basic skills that strengthen attachments and diminish the fears that dominate life and relationships.

How Skill 17 Is Remedially Acquired, Practiced And Propagated

Let's examine how transforming fellowship/koinonia can restore the missing *Identify Attachment Styles* skill. Imagine what life must have been like for our ancestors, Adam and Eve, who had everything at their disposal. They held dominion over the garden, had all the food they needed, and they enjoyed companionship with each other as well as intimacy with the Creator. Just picture the beauty of the trees, the flowers and the animals in this perfect state of peaceful tranquility!

132 Luke 18:18-23

Before the Fall of Mankind, God's children knew no shame or fear; joy was their motivation and reality. There were no fears for their safety, no worries about paying the bills and no threats of war or violence. Life was delightful, wonderful and blissful. Then the unimaginable happened and everything changed. God's children malfunctioned. At this point the pair started hiding, dodging, blaming and avoiding – all fear responses. We can say Adam and Eve enjoyed a secure bond with God until *their eyes were opened*[133] then they ran from the very One who was there to help them. We know this avoidance as an insecure fear bond and in many ways humanity has been running from God ever since. As only a good parent would, God pursues, provides and protects them in spite of the dire ramifications of their actions. While there were awful consequences in this story, God keeps the relationship bigger than the problem and the rest of Scripture tells that narrative.

In studies where toddlers have a disorganized attachment with a parent, the children will avoid the parent, hit the parent, curl into a ball, avoid eye contact, crawl backwards to the parent and, in some cases, crawl toward the parent while hitting their head on the floor.[134] We are not designed for fearful relationships. In Matthew 23 Jesus longs to embrace His people and, seeing the future devastation of Jerusalem that looms on the horizon in 40 years when General Titus lays siege to the city, says:

> "O Jerusalem, Jerusalem, you who kill the prophets and stone those sent to you, how often I have longed to gather your children together, as a hen gathers her chicks under her wings, but you were not willing…" (Matthew 23:37, NIV).

We can only imagine the grief Jesus must have felt speaking these words. As only a secure parent would, Jesus wants a relationship with His people. He pleads with them and it is exactly this desire for a lasting relationship that compels Jesus to the cross,

> "For God did not send his Son into the world to condemn the world, but to save the world through him" (John 3:17, NIV).

---

133 Genesis 3:7

134 Siegel, Daniel, M.D. (2001) *The Developing Mind.* Guilford Press. Page 74+.

In His everlasting love God continues to pursue, provide and protect us. These responses, including God's correction[135], are anchored in love. Speaking of love, 1 John 4 tells us,

> "There is no fear in love. But perfect love drives out fear, because fear has to do with punishment. The one who fears is not made perfect in love. We love because he first loved us" (18-19, NIV).

Perfect, mature, secure and complete love is free from fear.[136] According to 1 Corinthians 13, the love chapter, love is everything and love always wins. Remember Adam and Eve before the fall? They enjoyed perfect harmony and unbridled joy - free from fear. It is no accident God frequently reminds His people to "fear not" when He or His messengers show up on the scene. Let's face it, we are jumpy people, aren't we? Because of the fall of our ancestors, our natural inclination is to be afraid. Frequently God's solution to our fear is to remind us that He is with us. In Acts 18 God speaks to Paul one night in a vision about the work in Corinth, saying,

> "Do not be afraid; keep on speaking, do not be silent. For I am with you, and no one is going to attack and harm you, because I have many people in this city." So Paul stayed for a year and a half, teaching them the word of God" (Acts 18:9b-11, NIV).

Secure love casts out Paul's fear. God helps Paul stay motivated by love rather than fear. Fellowship must provide the opportunities and guidance for members to live joyfully in bonds of love while correcting bonds of fear. This starts by recognizing where fear runs amok in our relationships and guides our decisions. We ask, "Who among us justifies?" "Who placates?" "Who avoids conflicts?" Restoration of Skill 17 requires us to be open to our blind spots and invite Immanuel to heal the areas fear still dominates our reality.

Learning new skills happens best in secure relationships. While there are a number of books, resources and methods available to address insecure attachments, Skill 17 is a crucial skill woven into *THRIVE Training* from the beginning to the very end of the training. Attendees

---

135 Proverbs 3:12, Hebrews 12:6

136 Strongs 5046 *Teleios*, having reached its end, complete, perfect, full-grown

learn Skill 17 by identifying insecure styles of relating to people along with hindrances that keep fear in place. Attendees then practice building joy with Immanuel to increase emotional capacity and interact with Immanuel about those unhelpful hindrances that rob joy. *THRIVE Training* provides structured exercises to practice interacting with others in ways that build security, and this strengthens Skill 17. By Track Three, attendees are helping others identify their attachment styles, identifying the attachment styles of people in their community and using Skill 18 to address the pain that drives their insecure attachments and cravings. We propagate Skill 17 when we help others notice the difference between fear and love in their relationships and adjust their bonding template to be secure and stable in joy and peace.

Skill 17 - Action Step

Look at the attachment style table below then go through the summary to determine what you think your normal 'bonding base of operations' tends to be with other people. While you can have more than one pattern, you should notice a consistency in your dominant pattern. See if you can identify any fears or beliefs you have as it releates to your personal needs. Once you finish, share with someone what you are learning, and ask their opinion of your attachment style.

Attachment Style:	Child's Light	Parent's Light (Response)
Secure Child	+ (ON)	+ (ON)
	- (OFF)	- (OFF)
Dismissive Child	+ (ON) hidden	- (OFF)
	- (OFF)	- (OFF)
Distracted Child	+++ (ON)	-+-+-+(Inconsistent)
	- (OFF)	-+-+-+(Inconsistent)
Disorganized Child	+- (Fear)	(Anger/Fear)

Attachment Light Summary

I like Dr. Jim Wilder's use of an attachment light to understand the brain's attachment center and its moment by moment need to connect and rest.[137] The following information offers a glimpse into the ways adults respond to a child's attachment light for each attachment style. When the attachment light is "ON" we want to connect and interact; when it goes "OFF" we want to rest. The goal is always to match and attune with these signals in our relationships.

- Secure - my attachment light goes on and off as needed. The world is a safe place. I have little difficulty expressing my needs and wants to my partner. Sometimes people see me as boring because I create little drama in relationships.
- Dismissive - my attachment light is usually off (or hidden) so my spouse/friends pursue me. I like being by myself. I must protect myself from the world around me. I tend to feel bombarded by other people. My partner often wants me to be more intimate than I feel comfortable being. I find it difficult to depend on my partner.
- Distracted - my attachment light is usually on and I pursue my spouse/friends. I fear my needs will not be met, so I push hard to connect. I frequently feel I am not being heard or understood. When my partner is away, I'm afraid that he or she might become interested in someone else. I often worry my partner will stop loving me.[138]
- Disorganized - my attachment light is sporadic and I feel uncomfortable with too much connection. I want to connect but I fear being vulnerable and getting overwhelmed.

Skill 17 - Next Step

We can work on Skill 17 and transform our bonds to joy with *THRIVE Training* for bonded pairs and *Connexus* for communities. *Joy Rekindled* Marriage Retreats provides couples with hands-on exercises to correct faulty attachment patterns and start joy. Each of the three *THRIVE Skill Guides* continues the skill practice with 52-weeks of interactive exercises. Watch the *THRIVE Lectures* and participate in the *THRIVE-at-Home* online curriculum for greater understanding of the dynamics surrounding Skill 17.

---

137 Learn more with the *THRIVE Lecture* series by Dr. E. James Wilder.
138 Scientific American Mind, Jan/Feb 2011. *Get Attached.*

Conclusion

Skill 17, *Identify Attachment Styles*, changes the way we relate to both people and God. Our brain concludes we are "the sum of our experiences and relationships" as it uses the past to predict the future. However, there is more to the story. We are designed by the Creator for joyful relationships where people are glad to be together. We learn to attune with the needs of other people in mutually satisfying ways. Hurts and distortions that arise from our relationships do not have the final word on our identity and character. We can "update" and develop an earned secure attachment where fear is replaced with loving bonds of joy. This process sounds easy on paper, but in action it is no small task. It takes a chesed community with deep pockets of koinonia where transformations result because people engage the Good Shepherd, work on their relational skill repertoire and process the pain behind their insecure attachments.

Chesed communities utilize Skill 17 because they value relationships and emphasize a non-anxious approach to life and interactions. Secure relationships are the foundation of chesed communities. Pockets of koinonia are necessary to demonstrate what secure bonds look and feel like under good times and bad. Because a secure bond is a reflection of a stable and properly trained control center, transformations result when Skill 17 helps us identify and correct distortions. It is here that love guides our interactions and guards our relationships.

When I have Skill 17: I recognize the moments fear impacts my decisions and relationships. I highly value relationships. People frequently feel understood by me. Fear has little influence over my life, relationships and decisions. Sometimes I initiate with my friends and at other times my friends initiate with me.

When Skill 17 is missing or underdeveloped: I feel as though people are the source of my problems. I usually feel misunderstood and alone. I feel hopeless that my needs will be met. I almost always initiate with my friends. Or, I never initiate and my friends reach out to me. I do not recognize the moments fears and pain influence my decisions and relationships.

Skill 17 Application Step - *Simon's Self-Sufficiency*

During their dating years, Adrian found herself drawn to a lone wolf named Simon. Simon's independent spirit attracted Adrian and pulled her in like a magnet. Simon seemed comfortable in his own shoes and he liked the attention from Adrian. His charisma and attention made Adrian feel special. Within a short time they were married. To their friends, this was a match made in heaven. Little did Adrian and Simon know their relationship was about to implode.

Once the dust settled and the newness wore off, the qualities Adrian admired in Simon soon shifted to qualities she despised. Between work, the gym, friends and television, Simon checked out. Adrian felt hurt and abandoned by this disconnect. What happened to the man who swept her off her feet?

This disconnect reminded Adrian of her father's abandonment. The more she pressured Simon to change the more he withdrew. Soon both believed the other was the source of their pain and misery. If something didn't change their marriage was about to die and they knew it.

One of Simon's friends told him about a weekly class that was about to start where people would learn how to live in joy. Simon's first thought was, "What is joy?" then he wondered, "How do I get it?" While he wasn't sure what he was getting into, he was desperate for change. That evening Simon told Adrian about this class and asked if she would like to join him. She agreed.

Together they started the weekly Connexus classes and both were deeply impacted by the experience. While the journey was not easy, learning about joy, rest and attachment styles, Skill 17, has transformed their marriage. Simon has worked on staying relational and connecting with Adrian in joy and rest. Adrian discovered why her pushing backfires and how she overwhelms Simon. They see how their attachment styles and unprocessed pain from their families are hindering them from a mutually satisfying, joyful relationship. Both have more work to do, but Skill 17 has brought the language, training and understanding to ignite joyful change into their marriage. The future looks promising.

Chapter Twenty

Brain Skill 18 - Intervene Where the Brain is Stuck: Five Distinctive Levels of Brain Disharmony and Pain

Each of the five levels of brain processing react with a different kind of distress when it gets stuck. When we know the signs we will know the solutions.

After taking a moment to ask God, "Why does this skill matter to You?" I found myself thinking,

> "The Good Shepherd knows His sheep. When injured, the Shepherd attentively responds to mend a broken bone or comfort the frightened animal. Because the Shepherd knows what to do, His response instills security while His presence brings stability. Skill 18 equips My people to be ministers of peace during times of trial, upset, and injury."

There are five levels in the brain when we count the four in the right hemisphere control center and add the left hemisphere as the fifth. By knowing the characteristics of each, we know when one level is stuck and what kind of interventions will help. For instance, explanations help Level 5, but will not stop a Level 2 terror like the fear of heights. Skill 18 helps us apply the correct solutions to pain and problems so we know what is needed when.

Dumpster Diving

Early in our marriage I decided to make a short trip to the office for a few errands while Jen stayed home. Once I arrived at the office, I noticed some old boxes of papers that needed to be disposed, so I planned to toss the papers into the dumpster behind the building. It was then I realized much of the paperwork contained sensitive information, such as bank accounts and credit card numbers, so I decided to burn the papers in the dumpster. Seems like a good idea, right?

I noticed an empty corner in the dumpster, so I decided this space would make the perfect location for a small fire. Here, I could once and for all rid myself of these papers. I dropped some of the papers into the dumpster, lit a match, then walked back to the building to grab more files.

After a period of time, I returned to the dumpster with a new batch of papers when, much to my surprise, the dumpster was a magnificent blaze of glory, filled with shooting flames! Seeing the fiery inferno, I panicked and screamed, "Oh no! What have I done?" The entire dumpster was engulfed in flames. My small fire morphed into something very big and out of control. With woods and trees all around the dumpster, including a storage shed filled with gasoline only yards from the dumpster, I was concerned my fire would scorch down acres of land as well as the office building. I needed a solution - fast.

I searched for a water spigot behind the building. Much to my surprise, there was not a single outdoor faucet or hose. I ran around the building as fast as I could, searching for a spigot. Nothing. "Who builds a building without water spigots?" I wondered to myself. I then tried the next best option, and located a bucket. I ran to the nearest faucet, deep inside the office building. I quickly filled the bucket with water. Once filled, I ran to the dumpster, and tossed the water onto the fiery flames. My first few attempts seemed fruitless, but I continued for over two hours. At last, the flames subsided. I noticed cans of paint, paint thinner and even some dried wood that was hidden in the bottom of the dumpster. My small fire became a raging inferno once the flames reached these elements. Needless to say, I was covered in sweat and exhausted. I returned home with disheveled clothes, smelling like a campfire. I had a story to tell my wife, who was worried I had gotten lost. I decided to use a paper shredder the next time I disposed of old stacks of paper.

While a hose would have been more convenient, I was grateful for water as a solution to my problem. Without water, I would have been in serious trouble. We all know using gasoline to put out a fire is foolish and dangerous. Relationally, we turn sparks into forest fires when we use the wrong solution to resolve pain. We speak when we should listen, and we try to fix when we should attune and validate. Skill 18 provides the wisdom and expertise to effectively solve problems so we reach peace and keep relationships bigger than problems.

Skill 18 adds strategic solutions to our relational tool belt so we effectively stay connected, process pain and protect our relationships. When Skill 18 is missing, we rely on misguided responses to try and stay connected when things go wrong. This results with methods that only exacerbate distress. For example, it is all too common to rely on words and information to solve problems when only one of the five pain levels is resolved with more information. Can you think of a time someone tried to talk with you and give you more information and this "solution" left you feeling misunderstood and alone? Skill 18 opens the door for freedom and flexibility by using solutions that work as opposed to making a fire bigger than it needs to be.

I've heard Jim Wilder say there are two ways to kill a flower: stomp on the flower or starve the flower of essential nutrients like water and sunshine. The Life Model calls negative experiences A and B Traumas. A is for painful absences and B stands for bad things that should never happen. When unaddressed, unprocessed pain hinders us from reaching our full potential. Pain stops the growth process and keeps us from being the person God designed us to be. When something goes wrong in our development or our relationships, the results can be catastrophic. Intense pain arises when people are unable to enter in and join us in our hurts, struggles and trials. We see a classic case in the Bible with Job, who we mentioned earlier. Job lost everything.

After suffering tremendous loss to his family, possessions and health, Job's friends hear the tragic news and quickly gather in order to offer him sympathy and comfort. What good friends, right? Their pal is hurting and devastated. His health is really bad. The community has been talking about him. The friends approach Job.

Once they see Job, the friends barely recognize him. They sit with Job for seven days. As mentioned under Skill 13, seven is the number of days for mourning in Judaism. This time period, *Shiva*, means "seven." The friends sit in silence. After seven days, the friends share their theology that Job must have sinned because bad things happen to people who sin. They believe sin causes all suffering and surely Job did something wrong. After listening to them, Job responds to their lack of attunement and sark-filled responses with:

> "I have heard many things like these; miserable comforters are you all! Will your long-winded speeches never end? What ails you that you keep on arguing? I also could speak like you, if you were in my place; I could make fine speeches against you and shake my head at you. But my mouth would encourage you; comfort from my lips would bring you relief" (Job 16:2-5, NIV).

Job informs his friends that their accusations and explanations are not helping. In other words, they are using the wrong solution and if the tables were turned, Job would use a much better solution to bring comfort. Skill 18 tells us that someone in attachment pain, the pain of loss, requires more than words and information. They need to feel connected with someone else instead of feeling alone. Job's friends should have stayed silent. Without validation and comfort, giving more information when someone is hurting will be gasoline on a fire.

With this in mind, let's look at a brief overview of the five levels of the brain along with corresponding pain starting first with the easiest pain to resolve. The five actions at each level are *Articulate, Act, Attune, Assess* and *Attach.*[139] You can see the right hemisphere brain graph on the following page for the hierarchical brain region that corresponds with each level.

---

139 Four out of five actions are taken from *RARE Leadership* book with Dr. Warner and Dr. Wilder. Thank you Dr. Warner for your catchy acronyms and acrostics!

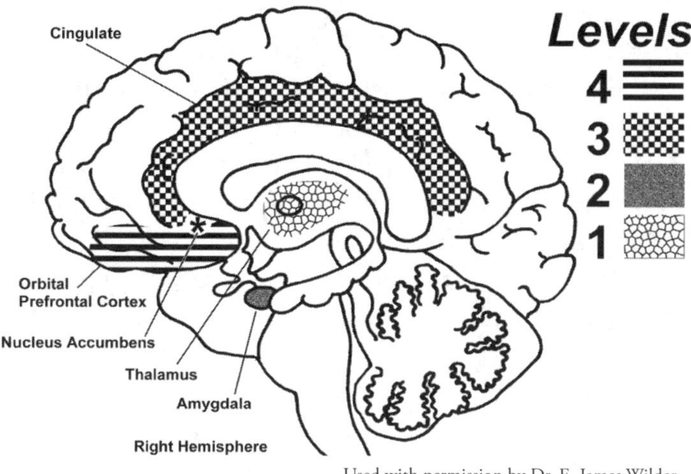

Used with permission by Dr. E. James Wilder.

Level 5 - Articulate

Level 5 is what happens when the left and the right hemispheres work together as one whole brain. The human brain has the remarkable ability to craft coherent narratives and create meaning from personal experiences. We call this Level 5 or four-plus (4+) as in telling four-plus stories, Skill 7, because it takes a working brain to formulate these narratives. When the four nonverbal levels in the right hemisphere control center synchronize and work together, the left hemisphere joins the fun. At this point the left hemisphere relies on emotional content from the right to pull together details from life and weave coherent stories that synchronize the brain and captivate our listeners. This means our feelings in the right and explanations in the left fit together so we craft coherent narratives.[140] Level 5 pain, therefore, is what we feel when we are in a situation where our mistakes or behaviors become the most important thing about us and our stories break down. This is the first sign that Level 5 brain processing has taken a hit: an internal conflict ensues as our explanations no longer fit with our feelings.

We notice a Level 5 breakdown when, for example, our explanations tell us God is good and He will take care of us and we encoun-

140 *How storytelling holds the key to a joy-filled lifestyle* blog by Chris M. Coursey at lifemodelworks.org.

ter a crisis where we feel God has forgotten us. This is a common pain seen in the Psalms when the Psalmist feels forgotten and alone.[141] Level 5 pain is an internal conflict where some piece of information is missing. This means it is time to update and fill in the gaps, but without accurate information we stay stuck in confusion and uncertainty. Every place and moment in our life where peace is missing becomes an opportunity for Immanuel to meet us with His interactive presence and loving comfort. For the brain, everything gets harder the lower we drop in the control center, and solutions require more resources.

Level 4 - Act

Level 4 is the right prefrontal cortex located in the front portion of the right hemisphere, just behind our right eye. Level 4 is one of the most complex areas of the human brain and also happens to be the section of the brain that doctors used to lobotomize in an attempt to alleviate schizophrenia, bipolar, manic depression and more neurological issues. Thankfully, we now have better solutions.

The Level 4 is the executive system of the brain that requires interpersonal training. This brain region is nonverbal and is known for its role in behavior and personality. It is the main hub for our personal identity, creativity, personal preferences as well as our ability to regulate emotions, predict negative outcomes and find the least damaging solutions.[142] While Level 4 is in charge of a number of essential functions, pain arises when we are in a situation that is very important but we do not know what to do. We lose a sense of who we are and, in spite of our best intentions, we are as relational as our ability to manage what we feel. This means we are as good as our brain is trained to suffer well and stay synchronized both inside and out. This may not sound very spiritual, but on this side of heaven God has given us a brain and a body with limitations.[143] The limitations

141 Psalm 13 for example.

142 Learn more about the role of Level 4 in *The Complete Guide To Living With Men* by Dr. E. James Wilder, *RARE Leadership* by Dr. Marcus Warner and Dr. E. James Wilder and the *THRIVE Lectures* with Dr. E. James Wilder.

143 If you question we have limitations, see how long you can hold your breath and let me know how that goes.

are on our end and we must learn how to properly use the brain and the body God has given us. Problems at Level 4 show up with rigidity and the inability to see from another person's perspective. Our attention becomes hijacked by something else.

Speaking of limitations, the disciples who walked and talked with Jesus had limitations that Jesus recognized when He said, "I have much more to say to you, more than you can now bear" (John 16:12, NIV). My translation of this passage is, "If you, the disciples, heard what I, Jesus, know right now, you would be unable to get out of bed tomorrow." Our Level 4 learns best from examples where people remember who they are under increasingly demanding situations. How well Level 4 is trained largely determines whether our character shines or sinks during hardship and strain. Jesus would offer many useful examples under demanding conditions as a gift for those who spent time with Him. This leads us to an important point. What if every follower of Jesus had the absolutely best trained Level 4 to remember who they were at all times and best reflect the One they serve?

When we are unable to calm our feelings and stay connected with people, our Level 4 begins to waver. We see a Level 4 meltdown in zealous Peter who at one point was convinced his friends could deny Jesus, but he would never do such a thing. As a mature guide would, Jesus understood Peter's capacity and limitations much more than Peter, so Jesus informs Peter he would in fact deny knowing Jesus not one but three times.[144] Fear got the best of Peter, as fear tends to get the best of us when our brain is not fully trained or when events are bigger than our ability to manage them. We can see by the intensity of Peter's remorseful response after denying Jesus that he deeply regretted his actions. We are told Peter "wept bitterly" as he walked away, which can also mean "to wail aloud violently."[145] Peter wasn't just pouting; he was devastated.

We lose a sense of ourselves when Level 4 is unprepared to navigate distress. We have no idea how to act much less understand what Jesus would do in a given situation. We require an example - "Jesus with skin on" as some would say. Because our Level 4 gives us a strong

---

144 Luke 22:34

145 Strong's 2799 klaio and 4090 pikros.

sense of who we are and what we are about (our identity) we effectively learn from observing other people and how they respond in similar situations. When faced with situations and circumstances that are new and unfamiliar, our Level 4 tries to find "files" from past experiences to rely on for the present. When there are no files to rely on, we experience a loss of focus and direction. We flounder, or we may be reactive and experience obvious signs of immaturity. This is easier to spot from the outside looking in, so it is apparent to the people around us more than it is to ourselves. Level 4 is always searching for a greater mind to show the way. If only we had someone who was always with us, who would never leave us.

Level 3 - Attune

The brain region for Level 3 is the cingulate cortex and there is a front (anterior) and a back (posterior), each with important jobs to do.[146] We refer to the Level 3 as the "mental banana" because when Jim Wilder, who grew up near the Andes Mountains of Columbia, observed a SPECT[147] scan of Level 3, it reminded him of a banana because of its shape in the brain.[148] Level 3 must learn how to return to joy from negative emotions. It also shares mental states and synchronizes energy levels so we know if it's time to rejoice or grieve or to engage at a high level of energy or tone it down with low energy responses. Level 3 is where we require attunement as we navigate negative emotions in order to feel understood and connected. As we share joy and rest states, we quickly get back to joy when things go wrong. These skills keep us connected and help us stay "on the same page" in mutually satisfying ways. Level 3 training doesn't mean we have to agree, but we stay relationally connected, keep relationships bigger than problems and quiet the negative emotions that surface during interactions. What would change if every relationship, marriage and organization in the world knew how to stay connected and return to joy from negative emotions?

146 Learn more about Level 3 in *The Complete Guide To Living With Men* by Dr. E. James Wilder and the *THRIVE Lectures* with Dr. E. James Wilder.

147 SPECT stands for Single-photon Emission Computed Tomography which shows activity in the brain.

148 And you thought neurotheologians didn't have a sense of humor.

On paper Level 3 tasks sound easy but learning these skills is another issue. Between 2 and 9 months Level 3 is copied and downloaded from mother's brain to baby's developing brain. What is learned in the next 2 years will determine our ability to stay connected and transition back to joy from negative feelings. Level 3 pain is what we experience when we feel stuck in our feelings and cannot calm down. This is where Skill 11 comes in, and without it we stay stuck in a negative emotion and do not return to joy. In an ideal world, we can return to a relational, joyful state from moderate upset in 90 seconds or less. Our Level 3 must learn to feel and quiet the six negative emotions while staying connected with the people we love. The "Big Six" emotions are fear, anger, disgust, hopeless despair, sadness and shame. We will look at what happens when these feelings combine in the next section on Skill 19.

Level 3 pain means we are stuck in our painful feelings and cannot escape what we feel. Unprocessed pain at Level 3 can consume our focus, drain our energy and disrupt our attention. There is a reason Elijah and Jonah wanted to die and prayed God would grant their wish while both Job and Jeremiah cursed the day they were born.[149] Staying stuck in strong feelings is exhausting and miserable. Have you ever felt so ashamed you couldn't face someone again or lost sleep because of worrying? This is Level 3 pain, and we are not designed to stay there for long. The solution is to share what I feel and calm down while return to joy from negative emotions. Anyone who knows how to do this will show me the way.

Level 2 - Assess

Our brain's survival circuit makes up Level 2 and this area of the brain is called the amygdala. While both sides of the brain have an amygdala, the amygdala on the right side is a key part of the emotional control center. The amygdala is the small but mighty area of our brain that can keep us alive or, when problems arise, make us wish we were dead. God has provided this survival circuit deep inside our brain to sustain and preserve our life from threats. When it works properly we do not touch hot stoves a second time and we avoid poisonous snakes on the walking trail.

149 1 Kings 19, Jonah 4 and Job 3, Jeremiah 20

Level 2 is the guard shack in our brain that tells us if we should flee from a threat, fight the threat, or freeze and play dead so the threat will go away. Level 2 is subcortical, which means it is deep in the brain below the cortex, so the nonverbal Level 2 is not open to discussion or dialogue. Level 2 does not ask our permission before responding. It has three opinions: everything is either good, bad or scary. The amygdala never forgets what it learns.[150]

Speaking of never forgetting what we learn, when I was a young child I unfortunately watched a popular movie about a killer shark that would attack unsuspecting swimmers and fishermen. These popular shark movies were intense and my young brain quickly developed a Level 2 opinion that sharks are scary and the ocean is bad because the ocean contains sharks. There is simply no changing my brain's opinion about sharks and while I enjoy snorkeling, water skiing and swimming, my immediate reaction to getting into the water is that a large, highly intelligent killer shark is going to sneak up and attack! My Level 2 can still remember the haunting music the movie used when the predator was lurking in for the kill. If a Hollywood movie could do this to my brain, imagine what real-life horrors around the globe can do to traumatize people. The younger we are, the more susceptible we are to painful Level 2 responses. Thankfully, we can quiet these responses because God has given our brain the means to update and override Level 2 fears as long as there is a fully functional and trained Level 4. Otherwise, we remain stuck at Level 2 reactions, which are rigid and intense. In my case, without the ability to override Level 2, I would avoid the ocean altogether and rigidly dwell within the confines of my comfort zone, and there would be no discussing it to change my mind.

We know Level 2 pain as the reaction we experience when we look down the window of a high building. Our stomach drops in response to the view. Pain at Level 2 shows up in different ways because this pain often comes in the form of intense, non-relational reactions. Pain at Level 2 can keep us in ongoing states of hypervigilance and lead to withdrawing. We become dominated by what we feel and we interpret the world around us using a distorted lens. Level 2 has a number of

150 Learn more from the *THRIVE Lectures* with Dr. E. James Wilder.

important responses to the opinions it develops. Our reality can be extremely fearful and our reactions intense when Level 2 pain is active. Cases of Post Traumatic Stress Disorder and a number of mental disorders arise from problems at this level of processing. Changing our thoughts, using our will-power and trying to make better choices are all futile attempts to disarm an overactive Level 2. What we need is someone with a high-capacity mind who can stay connected with us during intense emotions so we learn to quiet and calm ourselves.

Level 1 - Attach

Since we already looked at Level 1 with great detail in Skill 17, *Identify Attachment Styles*, let's focus on the resulting pain that ensues when our needs are not met in a timely, predictable manner. To the infant, having mommy's joyful, attuned gaze is simply life and ecstasy to the child. The infant feels "on top of the world" and thanks to the body's release of endorphins, this is the highest of highs. When mom or dad checks out and disconnects when it is time to connect, the resulting pain is attachment pain, the worst pain the brain knows. It is at this point baby feels abandoned as though she is going to die. Level 2 responds to this Level 1 disconnect with bad and scary opinions, where we become hyper-focused or painfully detached.

We recognize Level 1 pain when we feel heart-broken, rejected, lonely and abandoned. Everything hurts. We recognize Level 1 pain by strong, intense cravings that make us feel we are going to die if we do not get what we think is needed for relief. Have you ever felt homesick, empty, rejected, alone or abandoned? If so, you know what Level 1 pain feels like, and it is not fun. Few things are as insidious as Level 1 pain which, when unaddressed, quickly destroys relationships, marriages, families, communities and organizations. Level 1 pain is the hidden iceberg that sinks many relational ships. Addictions often result from this unprocessed pain.

Skill 18 becomes the relational life-preserver that keeps our relationships intact. Skill 18 provides the training to stay connected, repair ruptures, and reconcile disruptions in our relationships. Here we know just what to do when something goes wrong. The overview on the next page shows us each pain level with feelings and solutions.

Level of Pain	Feeling	Solution
Level 5 Articulate	*Confused*	*More Information*
Level 4 Act	*Inadequate*	*An Example*
Level 3 Attune	*Overwhelmed*	*Mirroring*
Level 2 Assess	*Disconnected*	*Quieting*
Level 1 Attach	*Alone*	*The One I Love*

How Skill 18 Is Normally Acquired, Practiced And Propagated

We develop Skill 18 because our families learned what brings peace during times of conflict and distress. Parents comfort and calm their baby, they feed and change diapers at just the right times, and they know when baby is tired and needs some rest. Parents use solutions to effectively meet the needs of their children.

As baby grows parents know when to explain, correct, listen, attune, quiet, validate, comfort and connect because their experience has instilled these responses to differing levels of pain. Simply, these skills were used by their parents, caregivers or community members, so they are passing on to their children the comfort they received. When this is our relational heritage we naturally share it within our relationships as we grow older. We use Skill 18 to interact with peers and we are "in tune" with the mind and reality of others in ways that bring shalom where everything fits together in just the right ways. In many cases we learn fragments of Skill 18 when we have good teachers, coaches, counselors and friends who are intuitive and emotionally intelligent. We spread Skill 18 during interactions with the people we are bonded with *as we use the skill.* Of all the skills, however, Skill 18 is one of the more demanding skills to learn and most of us can use remedial work.

How Skill 18 Is Remedially Acquired, Practiced And Propagated

Let's examine how transforming fellowship/koinonia can restore the missing *Intervene Where the Brain Is Stuck* skill. Skill 18 provides the clarity to identify where people are stuck and quickly recognize what they need for peaceful resolution. Jesus knew how to get to the source of a problem when He encountered someone. He was also very good at giving people the gift of shalom, peace.

As mentioned under Level 4, Peter was remarkably devastated after denying Jesus. We can only imagine the shame, guilt, remorse and regret he must have felt. Scripture alludes to an initial separation where Peter is not with the other disciples when the women encounter one of the angels at the empty tomb, which makes us think he must have been estranged to some degree from the rest of the group.[151] Peter must have been feeling great attachment pain (Level 1 pain) with Jesus along with all of Jesus' close followers. In this context we find Jesus interacting with Peter after the resurrection.[152] Let's look at this interaction using the lens of Skill 18.[153]

After staying up all night trying to catch some fish, Peter and six of the disciples had nothing to show for their efforts. The men must have felt exhausted and exasperated, maybe defeated. We can imagine the sun starting to rise with a colorful sky as the backdrop when they hear a voice. Someone on the shore calls out to the weary men, "Friends, haven't you any fish?" After responding with a "No" the stranger then says,

> "Throw your net on the right side of the boat and you will find some. When they did, they were unable to haul the net in because of the large number of fish" (John 21:6, NIV).

This scene is all too familiar. John quickly recognizes the identity of the stranger on the beach and says, "It is the Lord!" Peter, in his zealous style, quickly jumps into the water and swims to shore. We can imagine his heart and thoughts racing as he approaches Jesus.

The Master feeds the cold, wet, tired, hungry men some breakfast. This isn't the first time Jesus fed a bunch of hungry people who had hurts and needs.[154] Peter's mind must have been buzzing with thoughts and questions to ask Jesus as he consumes his food. Likely one of the first questions was, "Are we ok?"

151 At the empty tomb the angel tells the women to "tell the disciples and Peter" which suggests he was not with the other disciples after his denial. Dr. Elizabeth Mitchell, https://answersingenesis.org/jesus-christ/resurrection/the-sequence-of-christs-post-resurrection-appearances/.

152 This is not the first time Peter interacts with Jesus since the resurrection.

153 John 21

154 Matthew 8 and 14, Mark 6 and 8, Luke 9, John 6

Peter's big emotions must have been swirling. The joyful exhilaration of being together must have been tamed by the sting of guilt that still made him grimace. What was going to happen; would Peter be chided for his betrayal or worse, cast out from the group?

With what we can only guess was compassion in His eyes and warmth in His voice, Jesus turns to Peter.

> "Simon son of John, do you truly love me more than these?" "Yes, Lord," he said, "you know that I love you." Jesus said, "Feed my lambs." Again Jesus said, "Simon son of John, do you truly love me?" He answered, "Yes, Lord, you know that I love you." Jesus said, "Take care of my sheep." The third time he said to him, "Simon son of John, do you love me?" Peter was hurt because Jesus asked him the third time, "Do you love me?" He said, "Lord, you know all things; you know that I love you." Jesus said, "Feed my sheep" (John 21:15b-17, NIV).

Jesus grabs Peter's attention and pursues Peter. With three questions Jesus negates the three denials. Jesus conveys to Peter – "I am not done with you" and that Peter will live and die for the King. Peter's mistake no longer defines him. Jesus keeps the relationship bigger than the problem. The Master restores Peter and Peter would go on to do great things for the rest of his life including, as Jesus said and Church tradition holds, laying down his life for the King of Kings.

With Skill 18 we keep relationships bigger than pain while we meet people where they are and respond with solutions for pain at each of the five levels in the brain's emotional control center. Our communities will do this when members have Skill 18 and, without realizing what they are doing, see someone in pain and respond with useful solutions that have personally helped them in the past. These trained brains simply do what has been done to them. We know the skill is missing when people attempt to be helpful but their approach leaves people feeling more alone and more misunderstood. We can initiate conversations around this topic and begin to improve our ability to be *quick to listen, slow to speak and slow to become angry*[155]

155 James 1:19, NIV

when it comes to conversations and interactions. Our redemptive stories provide the fodder to learn, strengthen and share Skill 18. In what areas of your life have you seen God heal and restore you? Share your story!

Skill 18 requires some careful steps to effectively train members in chesed communities. We want to have a strategy in place that includes three basic elements. First, we build emotional capacity with joy and rest, Skills 1 and 2. Second, we practice returning to joy from negative emotions using Skill 11 and third, we develop a solid foundation of Skill 13 where we learn the Immanuel Lifestyle. This is the interactive relationship with Jesus where we seek peace anytime we lose it. We practice these elements because learning solutions for pain involves moments from our life where we *experienced pain* at each of the five levels of brain synchronization. We don't want to purposefully activate pain memories unless the conditions are right to explore solutions that lead to peace and joy. Without these ingredients, we become triggered in our pain which, without solutions, is downright messy and harmful. Recovery that focuses on pain while neglecting joy and emotional capacity is incomplete. Searching for pain leaves people stuck in their unprocessed pain.[156]

During *THRIVE Training* we carefully lay out a plan to train attendees in Skill 18 that starts early in Track One and works its way to each training day in Track Three, where attendees practice a pain level starting with the easiest down to the hardest level of pain the brain knows. Attendees learn the solutions by experiencing the solutions in their own life and, with a variety of exercises, begin to introduce Skill 18 to Tracks One and Two through careful interactions that include stories and Immanuel interactions. In this way, Skill 18 is propagated as soon as Track Three members have learned and strengthened the skill with success. Attendees are now ready to return home and start spreading Skill 18 through their stories, examples and prayerful interactions with others.

---

156 Learn more in *Joy Starts Here: The Transformation Zone* by E. James Wilder, Ed Khouri, Chris Coursey and Shelia Sutton. Shepherd's House, Inc. 2013 as well as Dr. Karl Lehman's resources on emotional healing and capacity at kclehman.com.

Skill 18 - Action Step

Answer the following questions then share with a friend what you are learning about Skill 18.

How would you summarize your go-to response when you feel upset?

More specifically, what do you do for the different types of pain you encounter at each level of brain synchronization?

Level One pain - When I feel alone I:

Level Two pain - When I feel disconnected I:

Level Three pain - When I feel overwhelmed and stuck in a negative emotion I:

Level Four pain - When I feel lost and inadequate I:

Level Five Pain - When I feel confused I:

What is your go-to response when a friend or family member is in distress? In other words, how do you respond when someone you know is upset?

While you are learning an introduction to the levels of pain, what do you find most frustrating when you are hurting and someone tries to help?

Skill 18 - Next Step

Skill 18 is a mastery level skill that must be learned with practice over time; however, we can start today by building our capacity and improving our ability to interact with Immanuel.

Build your capacity with a plethora of resources mentioned in this book, starting with *Joyful Journey: Listening to Immanuel* book and *Connexus* curriculum for communities. Learn more by watching the *THRIVE Lectures* and participating in the *THRIVE-at-Home* online curriculum. Read up on the theory with resources by Dr. Karl Lehman, particularly his work on pain-processing-pathway at www.kclehman.com.

Attend *THRIVE Training* for the ideal steps to effectively learn and use Skill 18 along with the *THRIVE Skill Guides*.

Conclusion

Before raising His friend back to life, Jesus attuned and wept when He saw Mary and her community grieving over the loss of Lazarus.[157] Skill 18 allows us to sustain joy in our relationships because we know what to do when things go wrong. We learn solutions for the five levels of pain the brain knows. We avoid unnecessary trouble and we minimize relational casualties because our responses match the circumstances and the needs we encounter.

We see an example of Skill 18 when Paul is writing to the church in Corinth. He says:

> *Praise be to the God and Father of our Lord Jesus Christ, the Father of compassion and the God of all comfort, who comforts us in all our troubles, so that we can comfort those in any trouble with the comfort we ourselves receive from God. For just as we share abundantly in the sufferings of Christ, so also our comfort abounds through Christ.*[158]

Because Paul and his companions received comfort from God they were able to offer this gift to others. In this way with God, our families, and our communities, Skill 18 is learned and passed on. We share what we have received. This transaction happens in chesed communities that are rich in koinonia where relationships provide the skills to grow, heal and thrive. Transformations come from Skill 18, although most people do not understand exactly why transformations happened only that they took place under certain conditions that were meaningful. When conditions are right, people resolve and process the different levels of pain. Skill 18 sheds light on what these conditions are and how to participate with God in creating them so that pain does not have the final word.

When I have Skill 18: I feel confident helping someone in pain. When I see someone hurting I am glad I can help in some capacity.

When Skill 18 is missing or underdeveloped: I avoid upset people. I feel lost when I encounter someone who is struggling or hurting.

157 John 11:33-35

158 2 Corinthians 1:3-5

Skill 18 Application Step - *Mary's Misguided Solutions*

Mary sat with her friend Susan who was feeling intense sadness over some difficult family relationships. Mary wanted to help Susan, so she gave her friend advice and encouragement for her situation. Mary believed that her strategies, if followed, would help Susan better navigate her painful family dynamics.

Much to Mary's surprise, as she offered input, Susan's distress intensified. Rather than helping her friend, Mary was inadvertently adding gasoline onto the fire. At one point Susan turned to Mary and asked, "Can you please stop talking and sit with me? I need you to be here with me so I don't feel alone." Mary was stunned by Susan's request. "Doesn't she want my help?" Mary wondered to herself.

Respecting her friend's request, Mary sat silently and honored Susan's needs. Susan shared her grief and after a short time, Susan settled down and looked more peaceful. Susan expressed how much better she was feeling and she thanked Mary for being with her and made a comment how much it helped her that Mary was able to stay present during her upset. Once calm, Susan asked to hear Mary's encouragement and advice for her family.

This interaction surprised Mary, but she learned a valuable lesson that day about Skill 18. Her calm demeanor and care for her friend was more important than any advice when big, negative emotions were present. This was the start of joyful growth and, after learning Skill 18 at THRIVE Training, Mary and Susan gained valuable training to better understand and navigate pain levels in themselves, each other and their communities.

Chapter Twenty-One

Brain Skill 19 - Recover from Complex Emotions: Handle Combinations of the Big Six Emotions

Complex injuries from life leave us hurting many ways at once. We recover when we combine our brain skills and use them in harmony.

After taking a moment to ask God, "Why does this skill matter to You?" I found myself thinking,

> "Carrying burdens weigh My children down. When My children are lost in their emotions they become weary and discouraged. Come to Me, all you who are weary and heavy-laden, for I will give you rest.[159] Skill 19 is a gift I want all My children to have so that they can rest in relationship with Me and with one another."

When I was younger my friends invited me to join them for a day of snow skiing. There was just one problem: my friends were experienced snow skiers while I was not. However, since I grew up water skiing, I resolved this minor discrepancy by concluding that snow skiing must surely be similar to water skiing. After all, snow is simply

159 Matthew 11:28

frozen water, isn't it? While this was not bulletproof logic, I justified going with my friends for the fun day at the slopes by saying, "How hard can it be?"

We arrived and everyone quickly put on their gear while I rented boots, skis and poles. I should have known there was a problem when I had trouble staying upright and moving at the same time with my skis attached to my feet, but I persevered as my group made it to the first hill. I was excited for the adventure, and I watched as everyone began coasting down the slope with style and grace. Trying to follow suit, I leaned forward as I glanced over at a sign that read Black Diamond. I wondered what that funny sign was doing there. Little did I know it was a warning to people like me that this slope is an advanced hill for qualified skiers who have experience under their belt.

As soon as I started moving down the steep hill, I discovered I could neither steer or stop. I panicked. My speed increased. With no other options available, I used my voice to warn unsuspecting people caught in my path. I yelled, "Move!" "Look Out!" "Heads Up!" "Behind You!" The sheep scattered. People moved fast once they heard my loud voice and observed a flailing, out of control person zooming their way. My momentum increased even more. I looked up to see obstacles ahead of me. I noticed there was a line of people waiting for the ski lift at the bottom of the hill - with a very big fence behind them. I knew this ordeal was not going to end well.

The next thing I knew, two snowmobilers with flashing lights pulled up next to me. These were ski patrollers and they yelled, "Fall down!" "Fall down!" I responded with, "I can't! I'm going too fast!" Looking more determined than ever, they yelled, "Fall down, NOW!" Their tone told me staying upright was no longer an option. Since I was going so fast, I was convinced their suggestion was a bad idea, but I had no other choice. I leaned to the right, and with my left ski raised high in the air, I fell to the ground. Gravity worked its course as my body tumbled and rolled down the hill. Everything was a blur. Once stopped, I noticed a cloud of snow filled the air while my skis and poles were nowhere to be seen. As I tried to restore my equilibrium, one of the ski patrollers pulled up and commanded me, "Get off of this mountain and go straight to the Bunny Hill. I don't want to see you here again!" I couldn't agree more with his plan. Feeling battered and bruised, I slowly limped toward the ski lift and made my way to the Bunny Hill.

Once I arrived at the Bunny Hill, I began to practice some very basic, simple skills with the help of a ski instructor. First, I learned to stop and then I learned to turn. Then I practiced stopping and turning while looking around instead of peering down at my feet. These basic skills needed to become reflexes in order for me to ski successfully. The combination of learned skills only comes with practice, particularly practice with someone who knows what they are doing. By the end of the day, I gained enough confidence and expertise to try some beginner hills. To this day, I can safely navigate a Black Diamond slope because of much time, effort, practice and interaction with better skiers. The same is true for relational brain skills, particularly advanced skills like Skills 15, 18 and 19, which we can consider the "Black Diamond" skills.

Skill 19 requires basic skills such as Skill 1, *Share Joy;* Skill 2, *Simple Quiet;* and Skill 11, *Return to Joy from the Big Six Feelings*. Much like my ski experience, when we try to jump in and learn Skill 19 without a foundation in place, it will not go well. For this reason, *THRIVE Training* starts with Track One on *Joy and Rest* which builds capacity. Next, attendees move to Track Two to learn *Return to Joy* skills. Then people are trained and ready for the advanced training, Track Three on *Applied Strategy,* where we learn solutions to identify and resolve the five levels of pain the brain knows (Skill 18). *THRIVE: True Identity* is a great place to start for individuals who want to jumpstart their joy skills. Attendees can participate in *THRIVE: True Identity* anytime in the training sequence. Each training track introduces training methods to both learn and spread the skills so attendees can train family and friends in their communities. Doing this takes some expertise along with a commitment of time, energy and practice.

Once we build joy and feel comfortable quieting ourselves, along with having moderate return to joy skills, we are ready to start training Skill 19. When any of the *Big Six* emotions combine and merge into what we know as a complex emotion, these feelings are harder to manage. Shame and anger combine to form humiliation, while fear and hopeless despair (with any other feeling) form dread. These combination feelings can be very draining, and difficult to quiet, because they use both branches of the nervous system we discussed under Skill 16, *Recognize High and Low Energy Levels*. When the accelerator and the brakes are pressed at the same time, the engine experiences strain. You may recall anger is a high-energy emotion while shame is a low-energy emotion. Anger makes us want to stop something while shame causes us to withdraw and want to hide. Our nervous system requires greater training and deeper capacity to stay relationally connected with people when we are feeling a complex emotion.

We learn Skill 19 in a similar way we learn Skill 11. We practice using four-plus, return to joy stories with trained brains who show us how to stay relationally connected and calm big feelings. All of us can remember times in life when our heart raced with fear but we felt hopelessly stuck at the same time. Because we can only manage the emotions our brain has learned to feel, returning to joy from dread is no small task. On the one hand, we want to make a threat disappear, but we lack the time and resources to throw at the problem. We feel small while circumstances and emotions are big. One can imagine the Israelites felt some dread when cornered between the Red Sea and an approaching army who wanted to decimate them. Returning to joy does not simply mean removing the problem; rather, *we stay relationally connected with one another while we quiet our big feelings in the midst of the problem.*

Thankfully, we can learn how to better manage and quiet our emotions. We practice with the koinonia "pooled resources" where trained brains join us in our emotions and show us how to quiet what we feel as we stay relational with ourselves, God, and the people around us. Staying connected with Immanuel in joy states or in negative emotions is fundamental to living an Immanuel Lifestyle. If we do not have the training to guide us during these moments of distress, our control center will be unable to manage big emotions, and we revert to non-relational responses. We may use left-brain analytical strategies to try and talk our way out of it, but we end up feeling alone and "checking out" of our upset in some way. This nonrelational response is a good sign our brain is no longer able to effectively process the experience. We would do well to remember this when we see someone else melting down like my airport friend mentioned in the Introduction. When pain is unprocessed, we avoid similar people or situations that remind us of these moments. We have no shortage of opportunities to practice a complex emotion.

Skill 19 keeps us grounded, relational and level-headed when emotional turbulence invades our life and relationships. With Skill 19 we quickly return to relational joy when feeling big feelings. Who do you know who stays relational when feeling big feelings?

How Skill 19 Is Normally Acquired, Practiced And Propagated

We learn how to return to joy from the six basic emotions starting after the first year of life (Skill 11), then we are ready for combinations of these emotions. Mom, dad, caregivers, family and community show us how to manage complex emotions because they already have Skill 19. They know just what to do, so they stay connected and keep the attention on us during our big feelings. They help us quiet what we feel. Our "trained brains" validate, comfort and soothe us when we are feeling our swirling emotions. This is a harder workout for our nervous system so fatigue, unprocessed pain, attachment pain (Skill 17, 18) and hunger can increase difficulty; however, our brain learns big feelings will not kill us. We will have countless opportunities to practice Skill 19 during interactions where the "Big Six" combine.

The neurological pathways becomes strengthened with every practice returning to joy, so our work is not in vain. Once learned and strengthened, we begin to show others how to return to joy from complex emotions because we now know just what to do. We propagate Skill 19 when we join others in their distress to help them quiet and regulate what they feel and when we tell return to joy stories about times we were stuck and returned to joy.

How Skill 19 Is Remedially Acquired, Practiced And Propagated

Let's examine how transforming fellowship/koinonia can restore the missing *Recover from Complex Emotions* skill. Complex emotions are very difficult to navigate because, well, they are complex! Imagine bench-pressing one-hundred pounds then someone adds another hundred pounds to the barbell. The additional weight becomes much more demanding. The same is true for our emotions. When two or more feelings combine it requires more resources to manage, quiet and return to joy.

We see examples in Scripture where people are overcome by intense emotions. Fearing for his well-being, Abraham stretched the truth and misrepresented his wife as his sister - twice.[160] Moses invited God to kill him[161], Job and Jeremiah cursed the day they were born[162], Jonah and Elijah begged God to die[163], David pretended to be insane[164], a young follower of Jesus fled in his birthday suit[165], Peter denied Jesus three times[166], Judas hung himself[167] and Roman guards were frozen with fear.[168] These are just a few examples in the Bible where real people experienced real emotions. All of us can relate to feeling overwhelmed by our own emotions.

When our brain has learned Skill 19 it knows what to do when big feelings arise. We learn Skill 19 in our communities when we first recognize areas of weakness then we identify the resources in our midst, these are the people who have Skill 19 to varying degrees. We invite these trained brains to tell us return to joy stories from complex emotions. We use real-time opportunities to share negative emotions and demonstrate what it looks like to return to joy by weeping and rejoicing together[169] and by using the VCR method of interaction: Validate, Comfort and Repattern.[170] This means we share emotions

---

160 Genesis 12:13 and 20:2. In Genesis 20:12 he says, "And yet indeed she is my sister; she is the daughter of my father, but not the daughter of my mother; and she became my wife" (NIV). Abraham did marry his sister but she was a half-sister, the daughter of his father, but not the daughter of his mother.

161 Numbers 11:13-15

162 Job 3:1-14, Jeremiah 20:14-18

163 Jonah 4:8, 1 Kings 19:1-14

164 1 Samuel 21:13

165 Mark 14:51

166 Matthew 26:69-74

167 Matthew 27:5

168 Matthew 28:4

169 Romans 12:15

170 *RARE Leadership,* Dr. Marcus Warner and Dr. E. James Wilder, Moody Publishers, 2015.

and validate the person saying, "I see you are really upset. This must feel overwhelming for you." Then we comfort, "I am glad I can be here with you. What do you need when you feel this way? Can I pray for you or bring you something to drink?" Validation and comfort help us feel seen and understood so our brain updates to recognize we are no longer alone. This process also helps us process pain.

Speaking of no longer being alone, Psalm 23 is a beautiful picture of the VCR method where David acknowledges God as his Shepherd who meets his every need, joins him in the scary places and brings him comfort so that he does not have to be afraid.

> "The Lord is my shepherd, I shall not be in want. He makes me lie down in green pastures, he leads me beside quiet waters, he restores my soul. He guides me in paths of righteousness for his name's sake. Even though I walk through the valley of the shadow of death, I will fear no evil, for you are with me; your rod and your staff, they comfort me. You prepare a table before me in the presence of my enemies. You anoint my head with oil; my cup overflows. Surely goodness and love will follow me all the days of my life, and I will dwell in the house of the Lord forever" (NIV).

As chesed communities pool resources together people become aware of their missing skills. This helps us actively work toward restoration. Let's take a look at what needs to be in place for Skill 19 to grow.

Before learning Skill 19, we must build joy (Skill 1), learn to quiet (Skill 2), tell four-plus stories (Skill 7) and return to joy (Skill 11). In this way, we have a solid foundation to build our relational house, particularly returning to joy from humiliation and dread.

THRIVE Training focuses on the above skills in Tracks One and Two, then by the end of Track Two into Three, Skill 19 is practiced by hearing and telling return to joy stories from humiliation and dread. We use the four-plus story elements, we name the emotions, and we review our stories to ensure all the story ingredients were present. While it takes practice and we use a variety of exercises, Track Three members spread Skill 19 by their stories that are personal, genuine and precise. All of us can spread the skill once we are effectively able to return to joy, and outside of *THRIVE Training* we spread Skill 19 with our stories but also by sharing distress with others so they can quiet and return to joy. Many crisis, conflicts and painful encounters can be avoided and resolved when Skill 19 is available to keep people connected.

Skill 19 - Action Step

How well do you stay relational when your emotions collide? Write out your thoughts below and share your answers with a friend. Ask your friend to share observations on your ability to use Skill 19 and see if you can find Skill 19 koinonia guides in your community to tell you return to joy stories about times they felt humiliation and dread and how they recovered to peace and joy.

When I feel humiliated (shame plus anger) here is how I currently respond. (Include how I would like to respond)

When I feel dread (fear/hopeless despair or any big six combinations) here is how I currently respond. (Include how you would like to respond.)

Skill 19 - Next Step

Attend Track One of *THRIVE Training* to build your joy and improve your quieting skills then experience Tracks Two and Three to practice Skill 19. *Mastering Returning to Joy* and *Mastering Applied Strategy skill* guides will give additional practice as well. Watch the *THRIVE Lectures* for the theory and participate in the *THRIVE-at-Home* online curriculum for the application of Skill 19 and all of the nineteen skills.

Conclusion

Skill 19 is connected with Skill 11, *Return to Joy*, and a foundational ingredient in our chesed communities with koinonia pockets of pooled resources. Here people know what to do when they feel big feelings that are stacked on each other, and the strong embrace opportunities to help the weak with tender responses, chesed, and comfort so they can quiet distressing emotions such as humiliation and dread. When Skill 19 is missing we will see broken relationships, violence, rejection, abandonment and a slew of problems. There is more momentum when any of the six emotions combine, particularly high and low energy emotions, so the skill mastery at this level is significant.

Transformations include Skill 19 because processing Level 3 pain is returning to joy through shared mutual-mind states where people are glad to be with one another during upset. We rejoice with those who rejoice and mourn with those who mourn.[171] With interactive practice, we become efficient rejoicers and mourners, and, more like Jesus. Skill 19 leads to transformations because we are able to process pain and focus on being the people God designed us to be.

When I have Skill 19: People say I am good at comforting them when they struggle with big feelings. I know what to do when I or someone else feels dread and humiliation.

When Skill 19 is missing or underdeveloped: I avoid big emotions. When I or someone else feels dread or humiliation it makes me want to get away or lash out at others.

171 Romans 12:15

Skill 19 Application Step - *Jose Returns to Joy*

Jose was a successful ministry leader who was highly respected for his teaching and writings. Drawing people to Jesus was a high value for Jose who prayerfully tried to not only "talk the talk" but "walk the walk" with his family, community and ministry.

During a question and answer time at a seminar one evening, a woman in the audience raised her hand. Jose called on her, she stood up then bluntly reprimanded him by saying how wrong it was for ministries like Jose's to use scripture to bring people in, then fail to present Jesus to them. She closed with, "You should be ashamed of yourself; I will be praying for you." The room fell silent. Jose was stunned by the woman's words and her piercing demeanor. Jose felt misunderstood. His face flushed with shame. Jose also felt angry with the woman for her caustic response. While Jose recognized the signature of the sark, he was feeling humiliated in front of the audience.

Jose took a deep breath and quieted himself then thanked the woman for sharing her concerns. Jose invited the woman to stay afterwards so they could discuss this in more detail and clarify her beliefs. After several more questions, Jose dismissed the audience and the woman approached. With concern and curiosity, Jose invited her to share the source of her disgruntled feelings and asked what she needed from him to resolve this issue because he felt like she had misunderstood his approach. During the several minutes of interaction, mixed with moments of quieting, Jose stayed connected. He attuned with her feelings, validated her upset, and alleviated the woman's fears. In a matter of time, the woman apologized for her behavior. Jose asked if he could pray with her and she agreed. The interaction ended smoothly in a state of joy. If not for Skill 19, Jose would have justified and defended himself, stayed stuck in his humiliation, and probably shamed her back as a response. Skill 19 kept the relationship bigger than a problem.

Chapter Twenty-Two
Conclusion

The loss of relational skills along with the painful shortage of mature guides continues to whittle away at the relevance and credibility of the Western church. If we are to restore credibility where credibility is missing we must stay tender to our own and one another's weaknesses. We must learn to keep relationships bigger than problems and embrace transformation by acquiring and propagating relational brain skills. These ingredients, along with the development of an interactive Immanuel lifestyle, will foster the seeds of growth which spread by the winds of joyful relationships into the fabric of our communities. This brings us to Father Ubald.

Father Ubald is a survivor of the Rwandan genocide where 800,000 people were massacred including his family members and his parishioners, but he is also a man of faith who has dedicated his life to restoring victims and perpetrators of the genocide through forgiveness. One of his conclusions for ministry is this: "We need to teach people how to love." Ubald's life and work exemplify his mission[1] and, in many ways, this book is a step in the direction of restoring basic relational skills that allow us to both love God and love one another as God loves us.

By now I hope it has become clearer why we need to acquire, practice and grow the motivation to pass on the nineteen gentle protector skills in a chesed community of pooled resources (koinonia) where we are transformed into people who reflect the Good Shepherd. Developing Christ-like character does not happen overnight through will-power or good intentions. However, God designed each of us for relationships where we are glad to be with one another. We embrace a new way of life that is anchored in a chesed community where we interact with Immanuel and develop the necessary skills to express this life through relationships. Here lies the fertile soil to grow, learn to suffer well, and spread God's joy.

The skills mentioned in this introductory book help us stay connected and express the best of ourselves under ever-changing conditions. There is no greater time than right now for followers of Jesus to live with consistency and a joyful disposition in their lives and relationships. Anytime we lose our peace we must return to Immanuel's shalom. In this way we discover how to live with the active awareness of the God who is always with us.

My hope for you after reading this book is that you pursue training and discover opportunities to practice joyful skills in the context of your relationships. My prayer is for the legacy you leave to be established on your character and the quality of your relationships as well as your accomplishments. All of us, weak or strong, have the God-given opportunity to deepen our reserves of joy and share this Immanuel life with our thirsty communities. May God richly bless and guide you. May His face shine upon you!

---

1 https://frubald.com/

Appendix A
The Nineteen Skills

Gentle Protector Skills For Relationships

Skill 1: Share Joy. Mutual amplification of joy through nonverbal facial expressions and voice tone that convey, "We are glad to be together." This capacity allows us to bond and grow strong brains as well.

Technical description: Right-hemisphere-to-right-hemisphere communication of our most desired positive emotional state.

Skill 2: Soothe Myself, Simple Quiet. Quieting (shalom) after both joyful and upsetting emotions is the strongest predictor of life-long mental health. Lowering my own energy level so I can rest as I need to makes me feel stable. This self-soothing capacity is the strongest predictor of good mental health for the lifetime.

Technical description: Release-on-demand of serotonin by the vegetative branch of parasympathetic nervous system to quiet both positive and distressing emotional states.

Skill 3: Form Bonds For Two: Synchronize Attachments. We can share a mutual state of mind that brings us closer and lets us move independently as well. We are both satisfied. The essence of a secure bond is the ability to synchronize our attachment centers so that we can move closer or farther apart at moments that satisfy us both. Synchronized attachment centers provide the basis for smooth transfer of brain skills and learned characteristics.

Technical description: Two-way bonds involve simultaneous activation of the attachment centers (Level 1) between two people. This activation helps create a state of mutual mind at the cingulate cortex level (Level 3) that can only be maintained by direct facial contact with one other person at a time.

Skill 4: Create Appreciation. High levels of the emotional state of appreciation closely match the healthy balanced state of the brain and nervous system. Creating a strong feeling of appreciation in yourself or others relieves unpleasant states and stress. Appreciation is very similar to the let down reflex that produces milk flow when nursing and the warm contented feeling that follows for mother and child.

Skill 5: Form Family Bonds: Bonds For Three. Family bonds allow us to feel joy when people we love have a good relationship with each other. We experience what they feel and understand how they see our relationships through our three-way bonds. Joy bonds between two adults form a couple style bond, so community joy building requires bonds for three or more.

Technical description: The prefrontal cortex (Level 4) contains our capacity to maintain three points of view simultaneously.

Skill 6: Identify Heart Values From Suffering: The Main Pain and Characteristic of Hearts. Caring deeply can mean hurting deeply. Everyone has issues that particularly hurt or bother him or her and are the way he/she is likely to get hurt. Looking at these lifelong issues helps identify the core values for each person's unique identity. We hurt more the more deeply we care. Because of how much pain our deepest values have caused, most people see these characteristics as liabilities not treasures.

Skill 7: Tell Synchronized Stories: Four-plus Storytelling. When our brain is well trained, our capacity is high and we are not triggered by the past, our whole brain works together. A simple test as well as a means to train the brain is telling stories in a way that requires all the brain to work together.

Technical description: The four levels of the right-hemispheric control center work together and allow the bonus (+) of having our words in the left hemisphere match our experience. When emotional and spiritual blockage is resolved our whole brain works in a synchronized way. By selecting stories we can test and train our brains to handle specific aspects of life and relationships.

Skill 8: Identify Maturity Levels. We need to know our ideal maturity level so we know if our development is impaired. Knowing our general (baseline) maturity level tells us what the next developmental tasks will be. Knowing our immediate maturity level from moment to moment lets us know if we have been triggered into reactivity by something that just happened or have encountered a "hole" in our development that needs remedial attention. Watching when maturity levels slip also tells us when emotional capacity has been drained in us or others.

Skill 9: Take A Breather: Timing When To Disengage. Sustained closeness and trust requires us to stop and rest before people become overwhelmed or when they are tired. These short pauses to quiet and recharge take only seconds. Those who read the nonverbal cues and let others rest are rewarded with trust and love.

Technical description: All the brain-developing and relationship-building moments that create understanding and produce mutual-mind states require paired minds to stop a moment (pause) when the first of the two gets tired, nears overwhelm or is too intensely aroused.

Skill 10: Tell Nonverbal Stories. When we want to strengthen relationships, resolve conflicts, or bridge generations and cultures we get much farther with the nonverbal parts of our stories than with words.

Technical description: This workout for the nonverbal control center in the right hemisphere develops all the timing and expressive skills used to develop good emotional and relational capacity.

Skill 11: Return To Joy From The Big Six Feelings. Although we live most of our lives in joy and peace we need to learn how to stay in relationship and quiet our distress when things go wrong. When we take good care of our relationships even when we are upset, the upset does not last long or drive people away. We quickly resolve our "not glad to be together" moments.

Technical description: The brain is wired to feel six unpleasant emotions. Fear, anger, sadness, disgust, shame and hopeless despair are each signals of something specific going wrong. We need to learn how to quiet each of these different circuits separately while maintaining our relationships. Training under these six emotional conditions covers the full range of our emotional distress.

Skill 12: Act Like Myself In The Big Six Feelings. Part of maintaining our relationships when we are upset is learning to act like the same person we were when we had joy to be together. A lack of training or bad examples causes us to damage or withdraw from the relationships we value when we get angry, afraid, sad, disgusted, ashamed or hopeless.

Skill 13: See What God Sees, Heartsight. Hope and direction come from seeing situations, ourselves and others the way they were meant to be instead of only seeing what went wrong. This spiritual vision guides our training and restoration. Even forgiveness flows from seeing people's purpose as more important than their malfunctions and makes us a restorative community instead of an accusing one. Through our hearts we see the spiritual vision God sees.

Skill 14: Stop The Sark. False "Godsight" may seem true to us at the moment, but leads to blame, accusation, condemnation, gossip, resentment, legalism, self-justification and self-righteousness. This Greek word (also rendered sarx) refers to seeing life from our personal view of who people are and how things should be. This conviction that I know or can determine the right thing to do or be is the opposite of heartsight in Skill Thirteen. When we use the sark, people become what they have done (the sum of their mistakes) or what we want them to become for us.

Skill 15: Quiet Interactively. Facial cues, particularly of fear, help us to know when we are pushing others too hard. Sometimes we need and want to maintain a high-energy state without "going over the top," like knowing when to stop tickling so it stays fun. Fast recognition and response to facial cues means optimum interactions and energy.

Technical description: Using the ventromedial cortex (Level 4) together with the intelligent branch of the parasympathetic nervous system allows us to control the upper end of arousal states. Instead of taking us all the way to quiet/peace, this type of quieting allows us to operate at high levels of energy and quiet just enough to avoid going into overwhelm. This system controls aggressive, sexual and predatory urges so we can avoid harmful behaviors.

Skill 16: Recognize High And Low Energy Response: Sympathetic And Parasympathetic. Many characteristic responses to emotions and relationships are strongly shaped by our tendency toward high or low energy reactions. Recognizing who tends to respond with high energy (adrenalin based emotions) and who would rather withdraw helps us match minds with others and bring a more helpful variety to our own response tendencies.

Skill 17: Identify Attachment Styles. How well we synchronize our attachments (Skill 3) early in life leaves the most enduring pattern in our personality. These patterns change the way we experience reality. At one end we may give almost no importance to our feelings or relationships and at the other we may feel hurt almost constantly and think of nothing but feelings and people. We may also become afraid of the very people we need. All these factors distort our reality but feel real to us at the time. Knowing how to spot these distortions helps us compensate.

Skill 18: Intervene Where The Brain Is Stuck: Five Distinctive Levels Of Brain Disharmony And Pain. By recognizing the characteristic pain at each of the brain's five levels we can pinpoint the trouble and find a solution if someone gets stuck. The type of pain gives us a good idea of the kind of solution we will need when someone is not "keeping it together," is "falling apart," or is "stuck" as we commonly call these losses of synchronization.

Technical description: There are five levels in the brain when we count the four in the right hemisphere control center and add the left hemisphere as the fifth. By knowing the characteristics of each we know when one level gets stuck and what kind of interventions will help. For instance, explanations help Level 5 but will not stop a Level 2 terror like the fear of heights.

Skill 19: Recover From Complex Emotions: Handle Combinations Of The Big Six Emotions. Once we can return to joy and act like ourselves with the six big negative feelings taken one at a time, we can begin to learn how to return to joy and act like ourselves when the six are combined in various combinations. Shame and anger combine to form humiliation. Fear and hopelessness (with almost any other feeling as well) form dread. These combination feelings can be very draining and difficult to quiet.

About Life Model Works

Life Model Works is a nonprofit organization whose vision is to bring people into a thriving relationship with God, self, and others. Jim Wilder is founder and chief theoretician of Life Model Works.

This book has introduced you to the Life Model. Life Model Works has a myriad of additional resources to train you and in those you lead and influence. All of these additional opportunities can be found at www.lifemodeworks.org. A combined personal and community assessment is available at www.joystartshere.com.

The ideal fast track training is THRIVE, www.lifemodelworks.org/thrivetraining.

Each spring Life Model Works invites all who are intrigued by our message to enjoy fellowship with like-minded leaders and compare notes on helping people develop a thriving relationship with God, self, and others. This Annual Gathering is also our annual opportunity to present our most recent applications of the Life Model. Look for it at www.lifemodelworks.org/events or subscribe to our newsletter to be notified of our next Annual Gathering, www.lifemodelworks.org/signup.

Life Model Works also offers regular webinars and a series of regional events, www.lifemodelworks.org/events.

Many of our books can be used as group studies, and our Connexus DVD series is designed to spread fast-track skills in your church or community, www.lifemodelworks.org/connexus.

The theory behind these fast-track skills is available in the THRIVE Lecture Series (search www.lifemodelworks.org/shop) and by listening to JIMTalks available by searching iTunes and other music download services for Dr. Jim Wilder or on disc from www.lifemodelworks.org.

If you would like someone from Life Model Works to speak at your church, group, or in your community please contact us at info@lifemodelworks.org. If you would like to include fast-track skills inside a book or program you are developing, please reach us at info@lifemodelworks.org.